FLORIDA STATE
UNIVERSITY LIBRARIES

MAY 16 1994

TALLAHASSEE, FLORIDA

Early Observations of Marquesan Culture

Early Observations of Marquesan Culture, 1595–1813

Edwin N. Ferdon

The University of Arizona Press
Tucson and London

The University of Arizona Press
Copyright © 1993
Arizona Board of Regents
All Rights Reserved

⊗ The book is printed on acid-free, archival-quality paper.
Manufactured in the United States of America

98 97 96 95 94 93   6 5 4 3 2 1

Library of Congress Cataloging-in-Publication Data
Ferdon, Edwin N., 1913–
    Early observations of Marquesan culture, 1595–1813 / Edwin N. Ferdon.
      p. cm.
    Includes bibliographical references and index.
    ISBN 0-8165-1391-0 (alk. paper)
    1. Ethnology—Marquesas Islands   2. Marquesans—Social life and customs.   3. Marquesas Islands—Discovery and exploration.
4. Marquesas Islands—Description and travel.   5. Marquesas Islands—Social life and customs.   I. Title.
GN671.M3F47   1993   93-13575
996.3'1—dc20   CIP

British Library Cataloguing-in-Publication Data
A catalogue record for this book is available from the British Library.

To Thor and Yvonne Heyerdahl
 Who introduced me to Polynesia

Contents

	List of Illustrations	ix
	Preface	xi
1	The Islands	1
2	The Marquesans and Their Dwellings	9
	Tattoos 12	
	Dress and Ornament 15	
	Settlements and Dwellings 20	
3	Social Organization and Government	26
	The Commoner Class 26	
	The Tabooed Class 27	
	Marquesan Social Ranking 29	
	The Governing Chiefly Class 31	
4	Religion	37
	The Superior Gods 37	
	The Parochial Gods 38	
	Priests 41	
	Me'ae 46	
	Spirits and Sorcery 49	
5	Daily Life and Diversions	52
	Division of Labor 53	
	Tools and Domestic Crafts 53	
	Meals and Their Preparation 57	
	Diversions 61	
	The Koina 65	

6	**From Birth to Death**	70
	The Youthful Years 72	
	Marriage and Divorce 76	
	Illness and Medical Practices 79	
	Death and Burial 81	
7	**The Quest for Food**	86
	Domesticated Crops 86	
	Animal Husbandry 93	
	Fishing 95	
	Drought and Famine 98	
8	**Transportation and Trade**	101
	Canoes and Voyaging 101	
	Trade 109	
9	**Warfare**	112
	Weapons 113	
	The Nature of Wars 115	
	Fortifications 122	
	Signs of Peace 123	
10	**In Retrospect**	125
	Marquesan Roots 125	
	Potential Marquesan Source of Useful American Plants 131	
	Glossary	139
	Notes to the Chapters	143
	Bibliography	171
	Index	179

Illustrations

Map of the Marquesas Islands	3
A partially tattooed Marquesan with head shaved except for two hornlike tufts of hair	11
A fully tattooed upper-class Marquesan	13
A Tahuata chief wearing ear ornaments	19
Typical early Marquesan dwellings	24
Outrigger canoes at Vaitahu, Tahuata island	104
Mouina, a Nukuhiva chief warrior	114

SOURCES OF ILLUSTRATIONS
(by page or plate number)

Plates XVII, XXXIII. Cook, James. 1777. *A Voyage Toward the South Pole and Round the World. Performed in His Majesty's Ships the Resolution and Adventure, in the Years 1772, 1773, 1774, and 1775.* London: W. Strahan and T. Cadell. Reproduced by permission of Special Collections, University of Arizona Library.

117, 119, 126. Langsdorff, G. H. von. 1813. *Voyages and Travels in Various Parts of the World During the Years 1803, 1804, 1805, 1806, and 1807* . . . . London: Henry Colburn. Reproduced by permission of the Bernice P. Bishop Museum, Honolulu.

II:26. Porter, David. 1815. *Journal of a Cruise Made to the Pacific Ocean by Captain David Porter in the Frigate Essex, in the Years 1812, 1813, and 1814.* Philadelphia: Bradford and Inskeep. Reproduced by permission of the Bernice P. Bishop Museum, Honolulu.

Preface

The importance of the Marquesas as the locality of one of the early founding populations arriving in eastern Polynesia and a prehistoric source of cultural dispersals to other islands is made clear by the excavations of Yosihiko H. Sinoto. However, the nature of the society that left its preservable remains in, and on, the soil of the Marquesas can only be theorized. The end product of its prehistoric evolution was first revealed to Europeans near the close of the sixteenth century. It was not to be seen again until near the close of the eighteenth century, when Europeans began to explore the archipelago. Some came only to renew their supplies, others to increase their knowledge of these lands, and a very few to live precariously amid a warring society whose gods required human sacrifices so that all might go well.

In contrast with Tahiti, Hawaii, and to a lesser extent Tonga, most of the early ethnohistoric data for the Marquesas do not derive from the direct observations of a variety of voyagers and naturalists. Quite the contrary: they were largely dependent upon the recorded observations of two men, William Pascoe Crook and Edward Robarts. The former, a missionary, lived among the Marquesans for a year and a half; the latter, for seven years. A brief history of the sources for this synthesis will clarify the situation.

Pedro Fernandez de Quiros's report of Alvaro de Mendaña's discovery of the islands in 1595 included brief notes on the people of the Marquesan island of Tahuata. However, he was too concerned with recording personnel problems and the brutality of the Spanish soldiers to elaborate on the ethnographic scene even though he spent seven days on the island. Captain James Cook, and his father–and–

son team of naturalists, John R. and George Forster, were the next to arrive on Tahuata, in 1774. Although they were more attuned to the recording of such observations, their stay on the island was a mere five days. In April 1791, Joseph Ingraham, on the American trading ship *Hope*, spent two days cruising through the achipelago. Although he made new discoveries, he did not land and wrote only a line or two about the people he had seen. In June of the same year, Étienne Marchand arrived in the Marquesas on the French trading vessel *Solide*, and spent the better part of his eleven-day stay visiting Tahuata. He and his officers appear to have made a valiant effort to record what was observed during their visit. Their chronicle stands in strong contrast to the miserable record left by the American trader Josiah Roberts. Although he spent from November 11, 1792, to February 24, 1793, on Tahuata while his men built an additional vessel for his operation, his total observations consisted of only a few pages of commentary.

This dismal record of early ethnographic observations abruptly changed when Captain James Wilson's missionary ship, *Duff*, arrived at Tahuata on June 5, 1797. When he departed on June 28, he left on the island a Tahitian boy named Harroweia, a Swede named Peter, and the young missionary William Pascoe Crook. The latter set himself to learn all that he could of island life, probably because it had quickly become clear that any effort to convert the "heathens" was a lost cause. In January 1799, he gratefully accepted an invitation to board the ship *Butterworth*, which returned him to England in April of that year. There his experiences and observations were recorded by the Reverend Samuel Greatheed. The resulting manuscript is now in the Mitchell Library, Australia, and although plans for its publication were reported as early as 1974, it is readily available only in the form of typescript copies produced by the late George M. Sheahan, Jr. A reproduction of one of these copies was supplied to me by the historian Robert Langdon so that I might complete this study.

Only a month before Crook's departure for England, the whaling ship *New Euphrates* had put in at Tahuata, where one of its crew, Edward Robarts, took the opportunity to desert. He rose to chiefly status through adoption, and years later, after leaving the islands on the English privateer *Lucy*, in February 1806, he wrote of his life and experiences with the Marquesans. Although at times it aggrandizes himself and his relationships with the islanders, Robarts's published journal, carefully edited and annotated by Greg Dening, is, like Crook's manuscript, a veritable mine of ethnographic data.

While the observations and experiences recorded by these two men are remarkable for their content, they failed to include some aspects of Marquesan culture of which they were cognizant. Nevertheless, they unwittingly supplied history with at least some of this information prior to producing their own accounts. For instance, although Edmund Fanning visited the islands for only about three days in May 1798, he not only recorded his own observations but chronicled much of what he had learned through questioning Crook during the time the latter served as his translator and guide. A similar situation obtained with Robarts when the Russian expedition under A. J. von Krusenstern arrived in the Marquesas in May 1804. Krusenstern was impressed with Robarts, his high standing among the people, and his apparent knowledge of Marquesan life. He thus came to use him as his primary source for describing Marquesan culture. Some of this information, such as natives having resorted to cannibalism during periods of drought, never appeared in Robarts's later account.

During Krusenstern's twelve days in the islands, a young Frenchman who gave his name as Jean Baptiste Cabri, offered his services to the Russians. He became the source of Marquesan information for the expedition's naturalist, G. H. von Langsdorff. Cabri appears to have been the French boy, whom Crook reported as being named Jean Joseph, left on Tahuata by a Captain Gardner of the whaling ship *London* in 1799. Cabri had married a girl of relatively low rank and was accordingly shown little respect by the islanders. While some of the information Cabri gave to Langsdorff matches that reported by Robarts to Krusenstern, Langsdorff noted differences in other subject matter. This may have been a matter of ignorance on the part of Cabri, or perhaps reflected the understanding of those in the lower ranks of Marquesan society.

With the departure of Robarts there appear to have been no further recorded observations of Marquesan life until 1813, when David Porter arrived in the American naval vessel *Essex*. This is not to say that other ships had not visited the islands during this interim. How many had passed that way must remain an open question. Porter was greeted upon his arrival by an American, John Maury, and an Englishman named Wilson. The latter had been in the islands for some years, spoke Marquesan fluently, and thus served Porter as an interpreter.

Maury, with a small party of others, had been left on Nukuhiva by the *Philadelphia Packet* for the purpose of trading for sandalwood to be loaded on board upon the return of the vessel. In a sense, his presence was a foreshadowing of things to come: missionaries, whalers in abundance, and the annexation of the islands by the French in 1842.

To a degree, Porter chronicled the beginning of the end of Marquesas culture as Crook, Robarts, and the others had found it. He spent seven weeks at Nukuhiva, during which his war against the Taipi was a portent of other modifying forces yet to come. It thus seems appropriate that his observations of the Marquesans in 1813 are the terminating point for this synthesis of early efforts by Europeans to describe what they saw as Marquesan culture only slightly modified by foreign contacts.

As Greg Dening has discussed in his reflective study *Islands and Beaches*, each of these chroniclers brought his own broad cultural heritage and personal idiosyncratic background that colored his view and understanding of what he saw of a culture vastly different from his own. Each recorded what he thought worthy of documenting, and each saw differing aspects of Marquesan life, according to time and situation. Thus, since the observations of any one of them represented but a single swath of varying width on the broader field of Marquesan culture, there is need for a synthesis of all such observations within our designated time frame if we are to gain any insight into Marquesan culture prior to its modification by major acculturative forces. While some anthropologists may gainsay the value of such observations with all their potential for error and bias, they nonetheless represent a far better reflection of early Marquesan culture than later studies dependent upon traditions, myths, and time-modified oral accounts of what the past was thought to have been. One need only refer to Nicholas Thomas's more focused study, *Marquesas Societies*, to see a superb example of what can be accomplished by using early historic observations.

In completing a work of this nature it is always a pleasure to acknowledge and express my appreciation to those who have aided me in my endeavors. Had it not been for Robert Langdon and his gift to me of a reproduction of one of George Sheahan's typescripts of Crook's Marquesan account, this work might never have been brought to fruition. To say that I am most grateful for this thoughtful act is to understate my feelings. Having not worked in the Marquesas since 1956 and wanting to refresh my geographical knowledge of those islands, I was again given a most pleasant surprise: a request that I travel on the modern sailing ship *Wind Song* as a guest lecturer on one of its 1990 cruises from Tahiti to the Marquesas; I had been recommended by my friend Dr. Yosihiko H. Sinoto. I am indeed beholden to Dr. Sinoto and to the splendid crew and staff of that fine vessel. In regard to my search for up-to-date maps of the islands, I must express my appreciation for the efforts made on my behalf by Ross Togashi of the map department of the University of Hawaii at Manoa. As with my two previous books on Polynesia, my dear friend and colleague, Dr. Jane H. Underwood of the Department of Anthropology of the University of Arizona, gallantly and critically scrutinized each chapter of this manuscript. Her comments and suggestions, as well as those of my most patient and supportive wife, Vearl, have added immeasurably to this work. To all I offer my sincere thanks.

Early Observations of Marquesan Culture

CHAPTER I

The Islands

"Bold," "rugged," and "enticingly forbidding" are words that best describe the majority of the islands of the Marquesas. Nowhere among the tropical high islands of Polynesia did nature conspire so resolutely to make human occupation difficult as it did in this archipelago. Volcanic in origin, the twelve islands forming a northwest-southeast line rest atop a midplate swell of the ocean floor, though the hot spot, or plume, that produced them either is no longer present or has not yet been found.[1] Located well within the tropics, roughly between 8° and 10°30' south latitude and 138°30' and 141° west longitude, the Marquesas are usually regarded as composed of two groups. Those forming the northwestern (leeward) group are Uapou, Uahuka, Nukuhiva, Motuiti, Eiao, Hatutu, and Motuone; those of the southeastern (windward) group are Fatuhiva, Mohotani, Tahuata, Hivaoa, and Fatuhuku.

In spite of their tropical location there is a complete absence of coral reefs and their accompanying lagoons, thus precluding access to a ready and ample source of easily captured sea life. In addition, the absence of reefs and lagoons prevented the formation of coastal plains with their normally high agricultural potential. Instead, direct wave action and faulting created cliff-bound coasts, some cliffs reaching heights of 300 meters and more. A rising of the ocean, or a sinking of the landmasses, as well as wave erosion, has created embayments, usually found at the mouths of valleys or where the rims of ancient craters have been partially worn away, as at Taiohae on Nukuhiva and Atuona on Hivaoa.

On the higher islands, wind and rain have formed a distinctly rugged landscape. In the wetter zones, there are erosional amphitheaters. Draining inward, some have combined their many rivulets to form a single stream that, in cutting its way to the sea, has created steep, even, cliff-walled valleys. In other localities, youthful valleys, V-shaped in cross section, empty directly into the ocean. Lateral erosion has created knifelike ridges separating many adjacent drainage basins. However, on the low, drier islands, as well as on the arid western (leeward) slopes of Nukuhiva and Hivaoa, the land between valleys consists of broad, sloping surfaces (planezes). Only on these two islands are there plateau remnants, that of Tovii on Nukuhiva being at an elevation of 800 meters, while those of Hivaoa are some 300 meters lower.[2] Except for these and a few narrow, flat valley floors usually found near the mouths of larger streams, island terrain may be said to range from rounded hills near lower coastal zones to steeply inclined, or even vertical, valley walls and narrow ridges. In addition, there are occasional spectacular pinnacles and domes of volcanic origin.

As if rugged island terrain were not a sufficient challenge to Marquesans and their horticultural pursuits, the islands' weather patterns contribute their share of problems. Although records at Atuona, Hivaoa, reveal an average annual temperature of 26°C (78.8°F), with a difference between the warmest and the coolest months of less than 2°C, marked variations in amount and periods of maximum precipitation were, and still are, characteristics of these islands. Climatic records for Taiohae, Nukuhiva, and Atuona, Hivaoa, reveal that rainfall in some months has exceeded the long-range average precipitation for those months by from four to seven times. On the other hand, it is important to note that in terms of agricultural endangerment, there have also been times when a single year's total rainfall was only about half of the long-range average annual precipitation of 1,110 mm for Taiohae and 1,215 mm for Atuona.[3]

While there are no adequate rainfall records for the eighteenth and nineteenth centuries, early accounts indicate that the extremes of rainfall recorded in the twentieth century are generally similar to those in the earlier period. Both Crook and Robarts recounted how normally minor stream flows of the larger valleys had been turned into raging torrents that washed out trees and carried them downstream during periods of heavy rain.[4] At the opposite extreme they also noted extended droughts during which the loss of crops resulted in famine.[5]

In addition to the variation in precipitation, there were occasional

The Islands 3

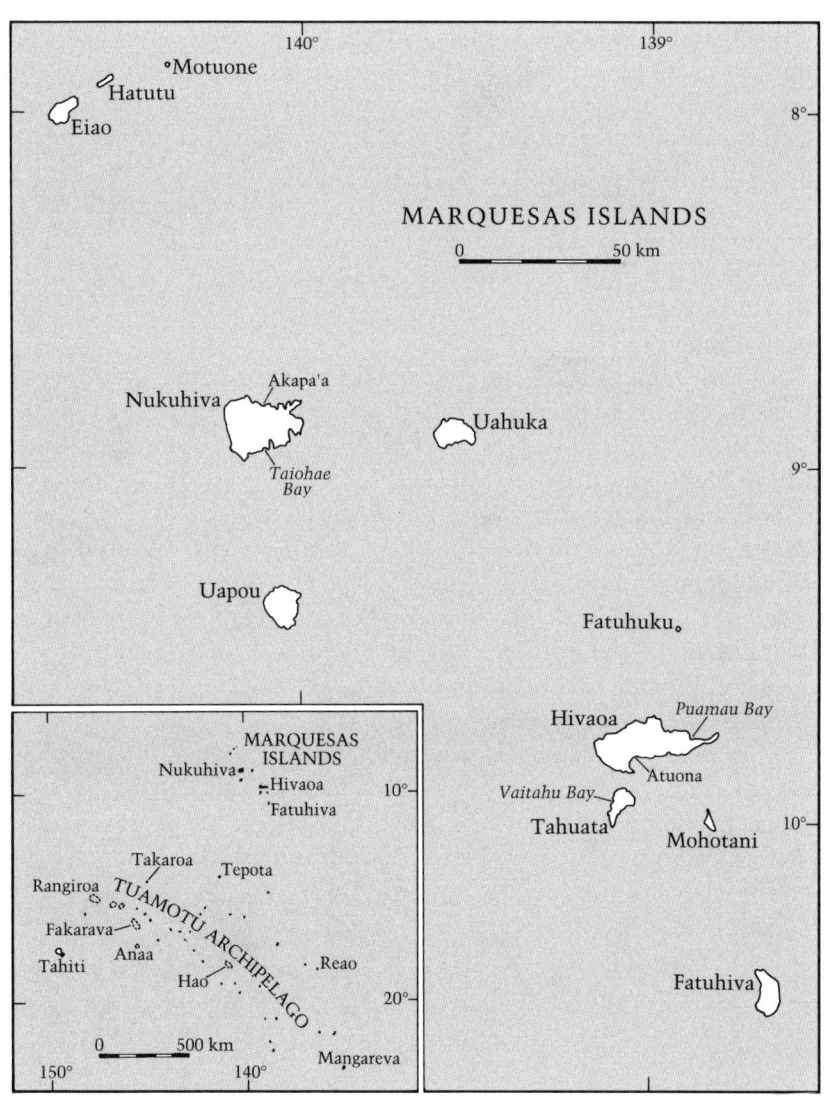

Map of the Marquesas Islands.

changes in the seasonal rainfall pattern. For instance, although Taiohae and Atuona normally have a rainy season lasting from March to August, with a distinct peak in June, and a dry season extending from October through December, this pattern occasionally changed. Infrequently a distinct second peak of rainfall exceeding 100 mm, sometimes even surpassing 200 mm, would occur in November or December, months whose average precipitation measured below 50 mm at Taiohae and 80 mm at Atuona. In addition, infrequently precipitation during the normal rainy season was reduced and the June rainfall peak disappeared.[6]

All this, including the absence of reef-building coral, would seem to be linked to the phenomenon known as the Southern Oscillation with its El Niño and La Niña events. Although the dominant winds in the Marquesas are the easterlies, we know from the accounts of Crook and Robarts that these winds slackened in November and December, the southern hemisphere summer. This allowed brief annual incursions of narrow bands of rain-bringing westerlies during what was normally the dry season. At the time of these intrusions Marquesans of the northern islands sailed with these winds to Hivaoa and Tahuata in the southeastern group, counting on a renewal of the easterlies to bring them home again.[7]

Considering the above, if such minor, brief incursions of westerlies could occur on an annual basis, it seems reasonable to expect that when a full El Niño event took place, it would be felt at the islands. With its warm, eastward ocean surface drift appearing in the southern hemisphere summer, it could readily account for the infrequent occurrences of increased rainfall on the islands during the normal dry season. That this may well be the case is indicated by the high increase in precipitation at Atuona, from an average of 115 mm to 216 mm for the month of January 1942, when a strong El Niño event occurred on the South American coast. Another strong El Niño event on the continental coast in 1957 seems to have been reflected at Taiohae in a December increase in rainfall from an average of 56 mm to 280 mm and, at Atuona, from an average of 78 mm to 297 mm.[8] In addition, there can be little question that the 1982–83 major El Niño event along the South American coast was felt at Atuona.[9] In 1982 the December precipitation at Atuona was 360 mm, nearly four times the average for that month (91 mm), and the January figure was no less than 883 mm, well over seven times the average figure for that month (115 mm).

Since El Niño events appear to result in increased precipitation in the Marquesas, it is expectable that the reverse effect should accompany a La Niña event with its strong westward ocean surface drift of cold water.[10] The cooler air accompanying this drift could be expected to be warmed when striking the lower elevations of the islands, resulting in arid conditions in those locales. This situation could thus account for the occasional disappearance of the normal June rain peak, as mentioned earlier. Such conditions, if occurring in consecutive years, would result in the devastating droughts reported by Robarts. They might also have discouraged the growth of reef-building corals around the islands.

Although El Niño and La Niña have only recently been recognized, their infrequent occurrences in much earlier years, even before the human occupation of the islands, seems a reasonable assumption. As will be noted later in Chapter 7, "The Quest for Food," droughts, seemingly resulting from La Niña events, were a strong force in inducing human migrations away from the archipelago in search of better land. Thus, nature-induced events may have been a factor in the Marquesas' becoming a source of human dispersals to other islands in the eastern Pacific.

As is usual on equatorial high islands in the Pacific, changes in the character and density of vegetation with increasing elevation reflect a concomitant increase in precipitation. This is most notable on windward slopes, where the effects of mountains and high ridges on the easterly trade winds is most clearly felt. It is thus the higher islands of Nukuhiva (el. 1,227 m), Uapou (el. 1,232 m), and Uahuka (el. 855 m) of the northwestern group, and Hivaoa (el. 1,276 m), Tahuata (el. 1,000 m), and Fatuhiva (el. 1,109 m) of the southeastern group, where high levels of precipitation are encountered on the loftier heights. Here the effect of orographically induced rainfall has resulted in sufficient precipitation at elevations above about 750 meters to maintain the growth of a dense, humid rain forest in what has been aptly termed the cloud zone.[11] It is probably in this zone that porous deposits of ancient volcanic ejecta have served as conduits to the many freshwater springs at lower elevations that were reported by Crook and Robarts.[12]

Below the humid cloud zone, a gradual lessening of rainfall with decreasing elevation is reflected in a change in flora. However, on the leeward side of these islands this change is more abrupt due to rain shadow effect. What now appears to be nearly barren land at the lowest levels does not necessarily reflect extreme arid conditions. It is thought once to have been more forested, the destruction of trees and brush being the result of the historic introduction of grazing animals. As for the smaller and lower Marquesan islands of Eiao, Hatutu, Fatuhuku, Mohotani, Motuone, and Motuiti, their inability to generate much, if any, orographic rainfall has left them dependent upon the vagaries of convectional showers from drifting clouds. As a result their vegetation is rather xerophytic.[13]

It was on this seemingly formidable island landscape that the first Marquesans made their landfall, though on which island and when are not precisely known. Nor do we know how many later migrants added their gene pool and their culture to this founding population. As it stands, archaeological work by Yosihiko Sinoto has revealed the presence of people on this archipelago as early as A.D. 300. However, since Tonga and Samoa, in western Polynesia, were occupied by pottery-making people as early as 1200 B.C. and 1000 B.C., respectively, it is possible that this date may not represent the initial settlement period for the Marquesas.[14] Regardless of the actual date, the known cultural content of the people living on the islands in A.D. 300 was indeed simple. They appear to have depended primarily upon fishing. There is no clear evidence that they practiced agriculture except, perhaps, for the growing of coconuts. Neither pigs nor chickens were present, and dogs, though present, seem to have been scarce. Besides simple tools of shell and stone, these people either brought pottery with them or manufactured it locally. However, its usefulness must have diminished with time, and it finally disappeared. During the period 600–1300, pigs appeared, as did shell peelers, vegetable scrapers, and a specialized stone food pounder, suggesting that additional migrants had arrived, bringing food crops as well as pigs.[15]

Since there are no coastal plains, it was a foregone conclusion that with the introduction of agriculture, adequate soil and water, as rainfall or stream flow, could be found only in the valleys of the moist and more elevated islands. With population increase and, quite probably, additions to the inventory of food crops via the arrival of further migrants, increased valley use occurred. In time, this resulted in forcing an overflow of inhabitants into unoccupied drainage basins, as well as onto the better-watered plateau remnants. Certainly by the close of what has been called the Expansion Stage, 1300–1600,[16] all agriculturally viable land on the better-watered large islands had been occupied. Steep-walled valleys separated by rugged ridges had by then enhanced the development of political enclaves with their own leaders. Land, with the crops that grew on it, was primal. Its continued fertility required religious manifestations in the form of specialized architecture and ceremonialism, and its protection mandated a prepared fighting force.

William Pascoe Crook's record of the number of warriors claimed to be available on each island during his stay in the Marquesas in 1797 offers an idea of the distribution and size of the population in the archipelago. In the northwestern group, Nukuhiva claimed to have 10,000 fighting men; Uapou, 1,200; and Uahuka, 800.[17] While Crook seems to have known little or nothing of the smaller islands of this group, in 1791 Étienne Marchand found Motuiti to be a bird sanctuary, and made no mention of sighting any evidence of human inhabitants on either Eiao or Hatutu.[18] However, in 1798 Edmund Fanning reported seeing a number of "smokes" on the latter island, which he named Nexsen.[19] They were probably the fires of temporary occupants, since Porter noted in 1813 that both Hatutu and its near neighbor, Eiao, were visited annually to collect the tail feathers of tropic birds.[20] Motuone, a low, sandy waste, seems never to have been visited.

In the southeastern island group Crook stated that Hivaoa was believed to have 10,000 warriors; Tahuata, some 1,200; and Fatuhiva, 5,000.[21] Neither Fatuhuku nor Mohotani had permanent inhabitants. However, Crook did observe that the latter was frequently visited for the purposes of fishing and gathering various unidentified odiferous plants.[22] Fatuhuku must also have been visited on occasion, since A. M. Adamson reported the discovery of ancient steps cut into the low cliffs on the northwest side of the island.[23]

In only one instance did Crook suggest a formula for computing the population of an island based upon the number of its fighting men. This was for Uahuka, in which he stated that given its 800 warriors, it probably had a total population, including children, of 3,000 individuals.[24] In other words, each fighting man represented 3.75 individuals in the population. For whatever value that figure might have, applying it to the fighting forces for all the islands results in a total population numbering 90,750, of which by far the greatest number, 60,750, lived on the southeastern group of islands.

Crook further noted certain cultural differences between the northwestern and southeastern island groups at the time of his visit. One of these involved language.[25] Here one must leave to specialists the problem of whether these differences were sufficient to justify recognition of separate languages or merely represented variations of a single tongue. Such differences may well have evolved as a result of geographic isolation coupled with intrusions over time of small migrant populations. These could have added some of their own linguistic elements to the existing basic language, thus exacerbating the difference. However that might have been, the other cultural differences between the two groups noted by Crook appear to have been nothing more than differences of degree or emphasis within a similar cultural context.[26] In only one respect was there a clear difference: certain unspecified vegetables, along with the "cashu," presumably the American tree *Anacardium occidentale* L., grew only on Nukuhiva.[27] Except for these minor differences, the cultures of the two groups appear to have been essentially similar and are here treated as such.

CHAPTER 2

The Marquesans and Their Dwellings

Men of the Marquesas impressed their early European visitors by their height. Various estimates indicate that they ranged from about five and one-half to six feet, with some exceeding the latter figure by a few inches. While the women were described by some as being, on the whole, relatively short,[1] G. H. von Langsdorff observed that those of the lower class, at least those who had come aboard his ship, were "little, puny creatures" with oversized stomachs, while women of the higher classes were taller and had fine figures.[2]

Although many of the Marquesan men were so heavily tattooed that their natural skin color could not be determined, others were less decorated. Among the latter, skin color was variously stated to be brown, copper, or tawny, and a few were described as having a very fair complexion. There may have been far more in this latter category, at least on Fatuhiva, since Pedro Fernandez de Quiros described the numerous natives who greeted the Spaniards on that island as being almost white. As for women who did not artificially lighten their skin, a technique that will be described elsewhere, their complexion was described as being of a brownish cast. In all probability the upper-class women, who lightened their skin and made every effort to stay out of the sun, accounted for several mentions of exceptionally fair women.[3] Nonetheless, naturally fair complexion must have existed to some extent, since David Porter described young girls as being no darker than American brunettes,[4] and Captain James Cook noted that youths and children were as fair as some Europeans.[5] Perhaps at this point it should be noted that William P. Crook mentioned the presence of a few men and women who, from his description of them as having white skin and hair and being "moon-eyed," almost certainly were albinos.[6]

Just as skin color varied among Marquesans, so did the form and color of their hair. Though it is generally described as black, some had locks classified as brown or auburn,[7] and Quiros mentioned one young woman on Fatuhiva with strikingly red hair.[8] There are also reports of a few Marquesans having sandy or flaxen hair.[9] However, this light color may have been chemically induced by applying the sap of the *papa* plant (*Rhynchosia minima* (L.) DC.,[10] which, though normally used by Marquesans to lighten skin color, was also claimed by Crook to lighten any color of hair except black.[11] It is therefore possible that flaxen hair was the result of treating brown or auburn hair with this liquid.

Whatever the color, most observers described Marquesan hair as being either straight or curly.[12] However, A. J. von Krusenstern stated that the hair of the lower class was woolly and coarse, though not quite so much as that of African blacks.[13] This is probably what the French were referring to when they mentioned the presence of frizzled hair in the Marquesas.[14] A common hairstyle among the men was to shave most of the head except for one long lock on either side. Each of these was tied in a knot and occasionally wrapped in white bark cloth, the end result appearing like a pair of horns.[15] While this style was present on Tahuata, other men on that island either cut their hair short or, as was the case on Fatuhiva, allowed it to grow long and hang loose.[16] Some women cut their hair short, while others left it long and occasionally tied it in a knot on the top of the head.[17] According to Edmund Fanning, the two styles reflected social ranking, with women of the upper classes having the longer tresses.[18]

While the above hairstyles seem to have represented the norm, there were those among the Marquesans who wore distinctive hair treatments. Some were reported to have had one side of their head shaved, but to have left the hair long on the opposite side, while others shaved various parts of their head to form patterns. Still others, including women, shaved all the hair from their head.[19] No explanation for these deviations from the norm was ever forthcoming. A similar practice occurred in Tonga, where it was limited to men in the lower ranks of society, though it was copied somewhat later by some women of those islands.[20] In Tahiti this same practice represented a symbolic display of mourning for a deceased relative.[21]

Beards were quite common on Tahuata. Some were full, but a

Physical Characteristics 11

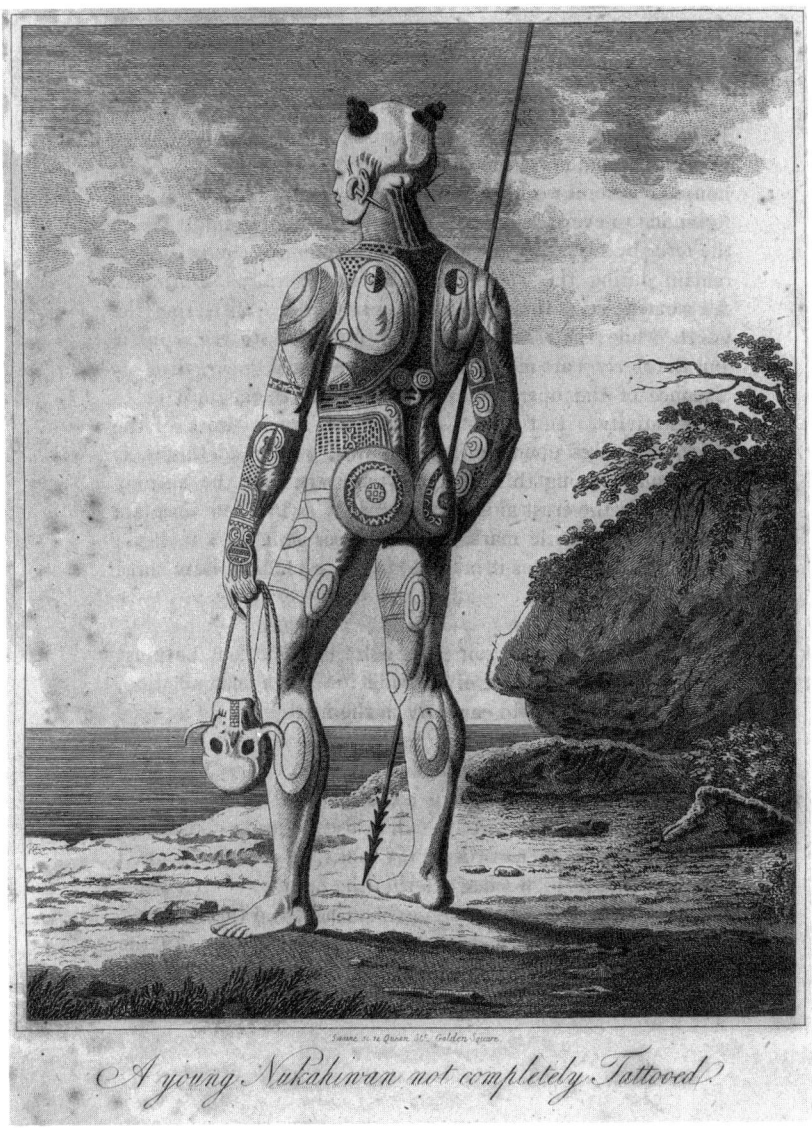

A partially tattooed Marquesan with head shaved except for two hornlike tufts of hair. The trophy skull is seemingly decorated with inlay. Engraving by Swaine. Courtesy of Bishop Museum, Honolulu.

frequent style consisted of shaving or plucking the hairs of the chin but allowing the whiskers on either side to grow to their natural length. Each of these was either parted into strands, which were then braided, or left natural and decorated with fish or human teeth, bits of bone, or shell.[22] It must have been this bifurcated style that John Marra saw on Tahuata in 1774, when he wrote that beards were shorn in a peculiar fashion and tied beneath the chin.[23] Also found on Tahuata was a beard style that consisted of shaving the sides of one's face and letting the chin whiskers grow to their full length.[24] There also were some on both Tahuata and Nukuhiva who plucked out all their facial hair,[25] and others on the latter island who left a small tuft of hair, like a goatee, on the chin.[26]

Obviously, hair on the head and face, regardless of the style, was acceptable to the Marquesan sense of propriety. However, body hair below that level was regarded as distasteful and was removed by using a pair of shells as tweezers or employing a firebrand for singeing. Shaving of the head and beard was accomplished through the use of a shark's tooth mounted on a reed handle.[27] According to Edward Robarts, a degree of ceremonialism was involved when a man shaved another man's head. They both removed their *hami*, or loincloth, and proceeded to the *me'ae* of the man to be shaved; all removed hair was placed beneath a stone.[28] This latter act was probably a precaution against the use of such cuttings by a sorcerer (see Chapter 4). While it was thought best to remove body hair growing below the neck, those of the upper class thought differently about fingernails, which were allowed to grow long,[29] a custom also recorded for Tahitians of the late eighteenth century.[30]

TATTOOS

For Marquesans, especially males, the human body served as the perfect medium for artistic expression that took the form of intricate, and for the women delicate, tattoos that, once applied, could not be erased. As was done for many artworks in Europe at the same time, the Marquesan tattooer was commissioned to create the desired complex of designs pursuant to Marquesan concepts of appropriate art forms. While women refrained from massive tattoo displays, the ideal for a male seems to have been full tattoo coverage of the body from head to foot.[31] The multiplicity of designs involved circles, spirals, bars, checkered squares, and fine cross-hatching, as well as

Tattoos 13

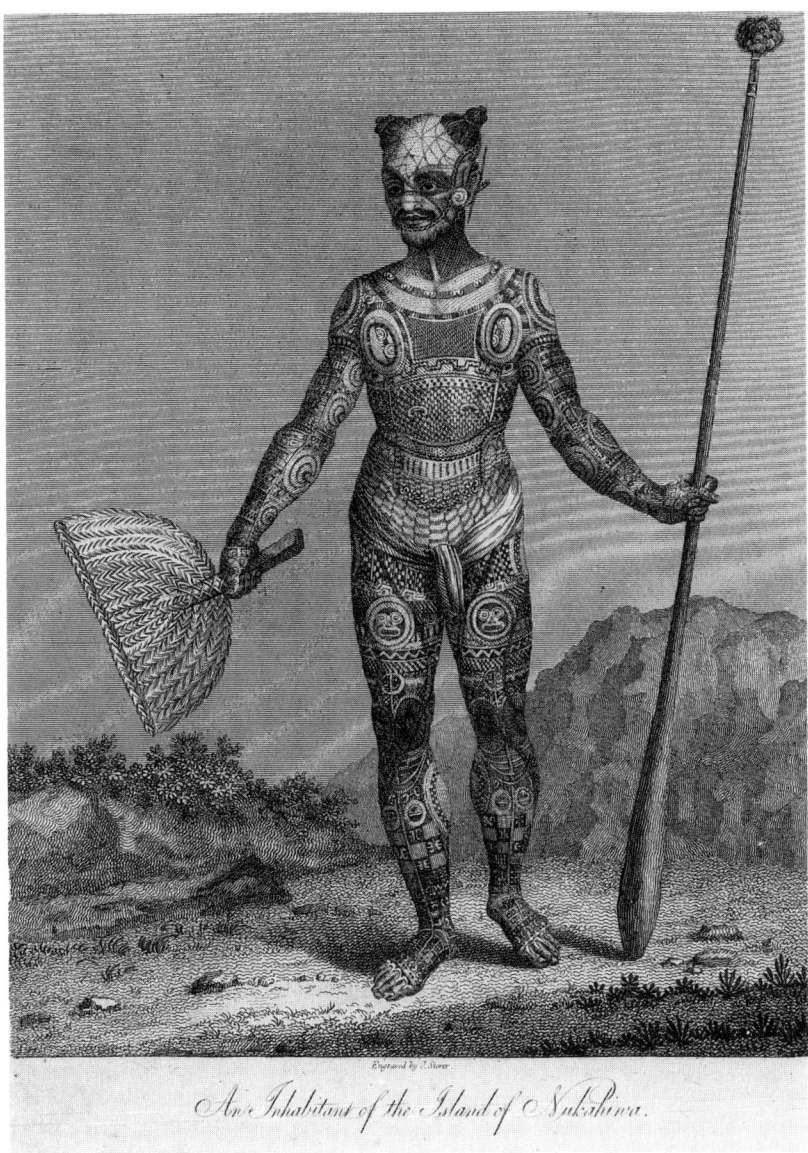

A fully tattooed upper-class Marquesan wearing tufted hairdo and holding the longer type of fighting club and a woven fan. Engraving by J. Storer. Courtesy of Bishop Museum, Honolulu.

figures of fish, lizards, and the like. Usually these were laid out in symmetrical arrangements to create superb works of art.³² Since tattooers were paid (the best ones in pigs), and full tattoo coverage of a male took years to complete, only the higher ranks of the wealthy could afford such extended works of art. Thus, a gross estimate of the social ranking of a man could be made on the basis of his apparent age and the amount of tattooing on his body.³³ However, there were more precise techniques to estimate social ranking.

For the knowledgeable Marquesan, particular designs were quite precise in signifying the position and relationship of a tattooed male. Thus, men belonging to what Crook referred to as the *mattatoetoe* class, which consisted of high-ranking wealthy families, were distinguished by having their eyes encircled by tattoo punctures. The nature of the design around the eyes, and even the eyelids, indicated to which division within the male taboo class the person belonged.³⁴ Since such indicators could not be erased, these latter designs would suggest either that there was no mobility within the taboo class subdivisions, or that the insignia was not tattooed until the individual had attained the particular grade desired or available to him. There were also males who, in times of famine, attached their loyalties to a particular person, usually a chief, who agreed to feed them from his personal store of food. Such members of a chief's group were given a distinguishing tattooed design. All males carrying that insignia were henceforth bound to aid each other during periods of individual destitution. However, having joined one loyalty group did not bar one from joining another, so a man might carry several group insignias.³⁵ Thus, Porter was close to being correct when he claimed that every tattooed line gave its bearer certain privileges at feasts or *koina*. Porter also maintained that every tribe he had encountered on Nukuhiva could be identified by its tattoo patterning.³⁶

In contrast to the extensive tattooing of the males, women who preferred such decoration restricted the art to delicate, lightly applied designs of a limited nature. These might appear on the small of the back, behind the ears, or on the lobes of ears. Shoulders, legs, and even elbows were not immune. A transverse line across, or even inside, the lips was noted, as were little star shapes on the arms or a design around the wrist, giving the appearance of a bracelet. Some had the backs of their hands delicately tattooed from the fingertips to the wrist, which, with a few parallel lines up the arms, gave the appearance of gloves. However, only high-ranking women were allowed to have their feet tattooed in a manner said to resemble half boots.[37] Perhaps because of the pain associated with such tattooing, women bearing such decorations were greatly esteemed.[38] Occasionally a wealthy husband might honor his wife with a feast of pig on the occasion of her being tattooed.[39]

Based upon the written record, it would appear that all tattooing was carried out by male *tuhuna*, or specialists, and those training to become masters of the art.[40] However, considering the restrictions toward women evidenced by the taboo class of males (see Chapter 3), and the almost certain membership of male tattooers in that class, it seems possible that women were tattooed by female specialists. However that might have been, the instruments of the tattoo artists were limited. They consisted of a comb, a tapping hammer, and a mixture of water and carbon soot derived from the burning of candlenuts.[41] The combs were of different types and shapes, depending upon the design to be executed. Some were small pieces of tortoiseshell with sharp teeth formed along one edge, while others were made from the wing bones of the tropic bird in which similar teeth had been formed; each comb was secured to the end of a stick seven or eight inches long. The hammer was a suitable stick of wood.[42]

Before beginning a tattoo, the specialist sketched the design in black on the client's skin. Then, choosing the appropriate comb, he covered its teeth with the soot mixture and applied the darkened points to the design, driving them through the skin by tapping the handle of the comb with the hammer.[43] An alternative technique described by Langsdorff had the teeth driven into the skin and the black mixture rubbed into the punctures.[44] Since the punctures usually caused immediate suppuration, it seems possible that Langsdorff misunderstood the process; penetration of the blacking would have been minimal at best with such a technique. For males desiring numerous designs on their bodies, the extended tattooing was a long, drawn-out ordeal. Since time was needed for the punctures to heal properly, the first year was devoted to developing only the principal figures. Additions to these basic units were added little by little, often over a period of thirty years and more.[45]

DRESS AND ORNAMENT

The normal dress of Marquesans was simple. The numerous references to men's garments makes it clear that they customarily wore only the *hami*, or loincloth. These were made of the prepared bark of the *hiapo* (*Ficus prolixa* Forst.) or *ute* (*Broussonetia papyrifira* (L.) Vent.). The best of the latter were white and made from the bark of young trees beaten into a fine texture; others, made from older bark, were much coarser.[46] Only occasionally did a man wear a *kahu*, or bark cloth robe.[47] The dress of Marquesan women was equally casual and limited. Their basic garment was a *ka'eu*, a short skirt of bark cloth reaching from the waist to the knees and fastened together between the thighs, thus creating a female version of the loincloth.[48] This skirt could not be touched by men and, like a man's hami, could not be used by another person or hung up with other things. When removed, both types of garments were laid on the ground or hung on a stick in a corner of a room.[49]

While men only occasionally wore the kahu, it was a common item of dress for women, at least for those of the higher ranks. Such robes of ute were the size of a small sheet and were wrapped around the body, the two upper corners being customarily knotted together over one shoulder. Such a garment extended from the shoulders to, or below, the knees;[50] some were pure white and others were yellow.[51] Such robes were primarily worn outdoors and usually removed when indoors,[52] a custom strengthening Langsdorff's claim that their prime purpose was to prevent sunburn.[53]

In addition to these simple garments there was a headpiece, or turban, made of the finest white ute and worn by both men and women. The simplest manner of wearing it was to wrap it completely around and over the head. However, women designed somewhat more interesting styles of wrapping.[54] As with the hami and the ka'eu, there were taboos pertaining to both the headpiece and the kahu. Neither should ever be walked upon, nor could anyone sit or lie upon a kahu.[55] Beyond this, the freedom of wearing the turban was, as in Tahiti, unencumbered by the rank-restricted taboos associated with similar headgear in Tonga.[56]

Although the plainness of dress allowed the intricacies of tattoo artistry to stand out more impressively, there were other means to add a bit of interest to one's overall finery. The simplest was the covering of one's body with coconut oil, which might be scented with sandalwood or given a yellow color derived from tumeric.[57] Women also found that pure coconut oil added a pleasing gloss to their hair.[58] Such oil was obtained by scraping a large quantity of meat from mature coconuts and placing it on banana leaves set in the sun. After four or five days, a quantity of oil was expressed from fresh coconuts and added to the older scrapings, after which the mixture was allowed to stand for an additional two or three days. The resulting oil was stored in bamboo containers.[59] Although grating mature coconut meat and allowing time for the oil to exude was practiced in both Tahiti and Tonga,[60] the addition of freshly pressed coconut "cream" to the older gratings seems to have been unique to the Marquesas. It is possible that Langsdorff, who recorded this process, may have been given two distinct techniques of extracting the oil and mistakenly combined them into one operation. However, considering the numerous taboos pertaining to the sexes, his observation that coconut oil prepared by a wife could not be used by her husband, nor could she use that prepared by her spouse, was probably correct.[61]

Adding to the finery of attire were a variety of ornaments, a few of which clearly indicated the high status of the wearer. Chief among these was a crescent-shaped gorget made from pieces of breadfruit wood held together with the resin from the same tree. Glued to its outer surface were innumerable rows of red seeds identified by such early naturalists as John R. and George Forster, Anders Sparrman, and G. H. von Langsdorff as being of the plant *Abrus precatorius* L.[62] I make a point of this only because many years later the botanist Forest Brown claimed that the seeds of this plant had been introduced into the Marquesas by Catholic missionaries for use in rosaries.[63] If so, it would have had to have been the priests on the Mendaña expedition of 1595. Regardless, this gorget appears to have been worn by men of importance. George Forster noted that only leaders wore this ornament, and Sparrman presumed these leaders to be chiefs.[64] However, a few years later Krusenstern wrote that this gorget was the particular mark of a priest.[65] Whether he meant an inspirational priest or a *tuhuna ota ogo* priest was not indicated.

An additional ornament of great value and an indication of its wearer's being of superior rank or wealth was the tooth of a sperm whale hung from the neck as a pendant.[66] For the lower and poorer classes who could not afford the real item, a simulated whale tooth made from thick shell or bone was worn or, lacking that, a flat piece of shell ground down into the outline of a whale tooth sufficed.[67] Whale teeth and their simulated counterparts have a long history as ornaments in the Marquesas. They have been found archaeologically from the earliest known prehistoric phases right up to historic times.[68] Natural whale tooth ornaments had a wide distribution in

Polynesia,[69] but by the late eighteenth century they were not recorded in either Tahiti or Tonga.[70]

One other pendant that must have had special significance was sufficiently rare that it was mentioned only by Krusenstern. It was a ball, probably of wood, said to be the size of an apple and, like the crescent gorget, covered with red seeds.[71] Its peculiar shape and size are remarkably similar to the *tahonga* wooden ball pendant of the Easter Island natives, though the latter ornament lacked the red seeds.[72] Besides these specialized neck ornaments there were various necklaces of a more generalized nature. One or more boar's teeth strung on a coconut fiber cord were common, as were necklaces of shells and porpoise teeth. Polished bits of coral, bone, or shell worked into various shapes also served as neck pieces.[73] Elements of plant life also served to decorate the neck. The fragrant "keys" of pandanus fruit were strung into necklaces,[74] as were the leaves of aromatic shrubs, including those of the spicy *pimata, Cheirodendron marquesense* F. Brown.[75]

Although pierced ear lobes were common among men and women, the holes being no larger than about one-eighth of an inch, they were only occasionally used to affix ornaments to the ear.[76] Nonetheless, bits of tortoise or coconut shell cut into angular shapes and decorated with a few porpoise teeth were mentioned by Crook as ear ornaments, as were pearl shells mounted on a reed, or single flowers with their stems stuck through the ear lobe opening.[77] Large, flat, ovoid ear ornaments worn by men must have been reserved for special occasions. These stood out from the sides of the head, just in front of the ears, like modified miniature wings. Some were made of thin cross sections cut from sperm whale teeth, others were of white mussel shells, and still others were formed from breadfruit or the lighter hibiscus wood painted white with clay or lime.[78] On the back of each oval, and fastened perpendicularly to its flat surface, was a boar's tooth with a hole drilled through its free end. This tooth was passed through the hole in the ear lobe and was held in place by a wooden peg passed through the hole in the tooth.[79]

Special occasions also called for elaborate headdresses. Some were fillets of cock feathers of different colors, others were of feathers of the green dove, but probably the most valued were those decorated with the long tail feathers of the tropic bird.[80] There were also headbands decorated with plain or dyed strings twisted into patterns.[81] However, for technical artistry the most interesting headbands, said

A Tahuata chief wearing ear ornaments and a headdress decorated with a medallion of shell fretwork. Drawing by William Hodges. Courtesy of Special Collections, University of Arizona, Tucson.

to have been worn by chiefs,[82] bore diadems of overlaid shell and tortoise fretwork. Fastened to woven coconut fiber bands were disks of plain white shell about five inches in diameter, overlaid by a thin tortoiseshell disk cut in patterns that allowed the underlying shell to appear in the open areas of the design.[83] The most elaborate of those described consisted of a white shell disk overlaid by fretworked tortoiseshell of somewhat smaller diameter that, in turn, was covered by a still smaller shell disk with cutout designs, over which was yet a smaller perforated shell. While some of the diadem bands were plain, other were decorated with feather plumes.[84]

While feathers and shell, wood, tortoise, and ivory could be used to create intriguing personal ornaments, strands of human hair formed part of the attire of some males. Though these served a decorative function, the fact that great value was placed upon such ornaments suggests that they had a significance far beyond mere finery. Apparently depending upon individual preference, skeins of hair might be fastened around several parts of the body: from the wrists and arms to the waist, legs, knees, and even the ankles.[85] A coconut fiber belt to which human hair was fastened in bunches occasionally was worn around the loincloth,[86] and a favorite ornament was said to be a bunch of hair from a man's wife that her husband fastened on the back of his body.[87] However, the most highly prized headdress was one composed of small locks of gray beard from old men that had been further whitened by the sap of the papa plant.[88] Since hair could be used as a material for sorcery against an individual and, as already noted, a man's hair cuttings were secreted in his me'ae, the source of this decorative hair remains unknown. It seems possible that such material came from sacrificial victims or slaughtered enemies. If the latter were the case, the wearing of these valued decorations may have marked the wearer as a warrior.

SETTLEMENTS AND DWELLINGS

Langsdorff succinctly summed up the factors controlling human settlement in the Marquesas when he wrote, "The boundaries of their habitations are fixed by rivers and mountains."[89] In an archipelago lacking coastal plains and where the larger inhabitable islands featured rugged terrain deeply cut by steep-walled valleys and cliff-encircled basins, it was only the watered valleys and basins that Marquesans found acceptable for effective settlement.[90] Indeed, there were broad planezes, plateaulike expanses, between valleys on the lee side of Nukuhiva and Hivaoa, but they held little potential for settlement owing to their lack of sufficient rainfall.[91] However, there were a few small plateaus in the high, wet interiors of both of these islands where scattered houses were found.[92] That their full potential seems not to have been exploited may, in some cases, have been due to poor soil conditions or the fact that the Marquesans' favored staple, breadfruit, would not grow well in that environment. However, warfare was also responsible. Robarts describes having walked over a high plateau in Hivaoa that had once had a thriving population but was totally abandoned because of the constant use of these uplands as battlegrounds for warring tribes.[93] As it was, the settlement pattern was dispersed: irregularly linear where following a valley floor and its adjacent slopes, and more fanwise in basins and the great erosional amphitheaters at the heads of the larger valleys. Here and there, where a chief maintained a residential complex, including a *tohua*, or dance court, with its surrounding guest houses, there was a sufficiently large assemblage of buildings to cause several of the early European visitors to erroneously refer to them as villages.[94]

Wherever possible, dwellings were built alongside or near a stream channel,[95] while others were perched on high hills and even cliff ledges.[96] Most, but not all, were built on individual stone masonry platforms.[97] Those on flat land were the same height on all sides, but those on sloping ground were made level by building the walls facing downslope higher, thus creating a miniature terrace.[98] The surface of the finer platforms was paved with dressed and fitted stone masonry, which, in some cases, extended several feet in front of the building.[99] In one chief's dwelling this extension included four wide steps of a similar masonry that ran the length of the platform. In addition, it was protected from the weather by a twelve-foot-wide roof extending from the house and supported by posts and beams. The steps served as a stairway to the platform and also functioned as seating benches.[100]

The design of the characteristic Marquesan house was unique in Polynesia, although its customary rectangular floor plan was not. While a few dwellings were square, the majority were rectangular and ranged in width from about six to ten or twelve feet and in length from ten to twenty-five feet.[101] However, Crook claimed that some dwellings had a length of one hundred feet, and Fanning estimated one chief's house as having a width of twenty feet and a length of eighty feet.[102]

The typical Marquesan house was essentially a building with a single slope roof whose greatest height was almost directly above the rear wall. From this high point it slanted downward to the top of the front wall, which was from three to five feet high. The rear of the dwelling was formed by a wall that extended from the roof ridge to the ground or the surface of the stone platform. Its descent was not quite vertical, since it extended outward at a slight angle, thus functioning as a combined rear roof and wall. To paraphrase Fanning, the building somewhat resembled a one-story gable-roofed house that had been separated from its rear half by cutting along the length of the gable ridge and covering the exposed surface with a wall extending from the gable ridge to the ground.[103]

The framing of the front of the house was formed by setting into the ground or platform a three-to-five-foot-tall cylindrical wood column at each of the two front corners of the house and connecting their tops by a beam extending the full length of the dwelling. Where length was great, additional supporting posts were added.[104] This front framing was matched near the rear line of the building by two ten-to-fourteen-foot-high split log posts, set slightly in front of each rear corner of the dwelling and similarly connected by a long beam forming the ridge, or gable, of the house. As with the front roof beam, when additional support was needed, other uprights were inserted. Extending at right angles from this rear ridge beam were rafters of *fau* (*Hibiscus tiliaceus* L.) or bamboo spaced about one inch apart. Those forming the front of the roof sloped down to the beam at the front of the house, and those in the back extended all the way to the ground at a very steep angle. Across these rafters were lashed horizontal bamboo poles over which was fastened an overlapping thick layer of leaf thatch.

The long leaves of the coconut palm were made into thatching by splitting the full length of the rib, bringing the leaflets from each side together, and weaving them into a narrow mat. These were then fastened horizontally across the roof in double overlapping layers. This was the least common form of thatching, the large leaves of the breadfruit tree being more frequently employed. Here it is interesting to note that apparently due to the vital importance of breadfruit in the diet of the Marquesans, the green leaves of that tree were never plucked for thatching. Only those that had fallen to the ground were gathered for the purpose of roof covering.[105] A hole was made in the stem of each leaf, and groups of them were strung tightly together on a slender piece of *tutu* wood (*Colubrina asiatica* (L.) Brongn.) ten to twelve feet long and laid in overlapping ranges along the roof. The best and longest-lasting thatch was that of the leaves of the fan palm, *Pritchardia pacifica* (Seem and Wendl). The centers of the leaves were bound close together on a long split piece of fau wood and laid on the roof in a manner similar to that for breadfruit.

Although many houses used only breadfruit thatching, the better homes had fan palm leaves on the front roof, which took the brunt of any rain, and left the nearly vertical rear roof covered with breadfruit leaves. According to the Forsters, whose observations were limited to Tahuata, the lower class or poor thatched their homes with either breadfruit leaves or those of the *rata* (*Metrosideros collina* (Forst.) Gray, var. *toviana* F. Brown).[106]

The front and side walls of these houses were constructed of closely set vertical poles of bamboo, those in front extending to the forward cross beam and those enclosing the sides rising to the edge of the sloping roof to the height of eight feet.[107] Since the greatest elevation of the roof was at least ten feet, this construction left a ventilation opening at the peak of the roof at both sides of the house. On the inside of these uprights were lashed closely spaced horizontal bamboo poles that, in some instances, were covered with coconut leaves and dried fern.[108] In the center of the front wall was a rectangular doorway, sometimes with a sliding door.[109] In the finer homes the front beams might be decorated by wrapping them with black and yellow cords of braided coconut fiber. Others might be covered with white bark cloth and then bound with sennit to form decorative patterns.[110] However, there is no mention in the early literature of the carved posts mentioned years later by Ralph Linton.[111] Such decorative features probably came into use with the later access to metal tools.

In its simplest form, the interior of a Marquesan home was divided lengthwise into a rear sleeping area and a front sitting or working space. The former was furnished with two parallel coconut logs running the length of the building and four or five feet apart. The rear log, about one or two feet from the rear wall, functioned as a neck rest, and the opposing one was to rest one's legs on while sleeping.[112] The area between these beams was filled with soft grass over which to spread sleeping mats—if the residents owned such mats.[113] The space in front of the sleeping area was the bare stone of the platform, which, in some houses, was covered with mats.[114] Some of the dwellings of the upper class were partitioned into units that might consist of nothing more than small, closed-off spaces for the storage of valued items.[115] On the other hand, there was the more complex parti-

Typical early Marquesan dwellings on stone masonry platforms, Nukuhiva island. Engraving by Letitia and Elizabeth Byrne. Courtesy of Bishop Museum, Honolulu.

tioning that Fanning described in the house of the high chief of Taiohae. In this case, the interior of the building was divided crosswise by thick mats to form four equal segments, and the two end units were further divided into equal-sized smaller lodging compartments. Another chiefly establishment similarly divided into lodging quarters was mentioned by Robarts.[116]

Since restrictions forbade various individuals from walking over or under objects, which would have tabooed them from further use, household tools and other equipment were kept safe by hanging them on the interior walls of a dwelling.[117] There seems to have been at least one restriction concerned with a house. Langsdorff wrote that to keep a dwelling dry, no one was allowed to wash within a house, nor could water be dropped on the mats or stone flooring.[118]

Close by a dwelling, and occasionally in it, were one or more food storage pits, used primarily for breadfruit.[119] All cooking was done outdoors,[120] and close to many of the homes were stone-paved platforms that served as working and eating areas.[121] In the case of one high chief, such a platform was surmounted by a special eating house that, from Krusenstern's description, was open to both sexes, thus suggesting that all such areas were quite distinct from the taboo houses that were forbidden to women.[122]

According to Crook, all men of the general taboo class, whether rich or poor, maintained a separate taboo house, forbidden to women, where the men ate their meals.[123] While the household dwelling was built with the aid of both sexes, the tabooed platform and house were built by men alone and located a little distance from the family residence.[124] For lack of data to the contrary, it seems probable that the more permanent taboo houses were of the same design as the family dwelling. When a family was distant from their home, as when fishing, a temporary taboo shelter was built for the husband to have his meals.[125] Since there was ranking within the taboo class, seemingly based upon wealth and social position, taboo houses of the higher-ranking men were taboo not only to women but also to men of the lower taboo ranks.[126] All such structures served as the proper site for certain religious rites of the taboo class, and as repositories for items that were tabooed because of their special use or had accidentally become tabooed and thus could no longer be used.[127]

The complement of dwelling, work area, and taboo house, along with the adjacent fenced horticultural areas, made up the living complex of the Marquesan landed gentry.[128] Those who were less fortunate lived in homes on the property of such landowners, whom they served in various capacities. For the higher ranks who could afford it, such tenants might include fishermen.[129] However, not all fishermen had such security, for Robarts recounts having spent a night in a cave that was home to several families of fisher folk.[130] There were also families of means who enjoyed "country" homes in various parts of a valley. These were designed to be easily taken apart and moved to another location.[131] And at the height of the breadfruit harvest, workers customarily built what must have been little temporary conical dwellings, if that is what Robarts meant when he described them as "wigwams."[132]

CHAPTER 3

Social Organization and Government

"The classes into which these islanders are distinguished . . . are numerous, burdensome, and indispensable," wrote William Pascoe Crook after spending a year among the Marquesans.[1] He then noted that these innumerable divisions could be subsumed under one or the other of two major classes: commoner or tabooed. Those of the commoner class included both men and women, while membership in the tabooed class was limited to males. Whether this latter group should be categorized as a class is open to question, but for lack of more detailed information, the designation "tabooed class" will be used in referring to this restricted order. However, it should be noted that at least some male commoners were said to be allowed admission into this group by submitting to various ceremonies or for having killed an enemy.[2] This raises the possibility, if not probability, that this so-called class was a socioreligious men's society possessing special houses, tabooed to women, whose functions were basically akin to the men's houses of eastern Melanesia.[3]

THE COMMONER CLASS

Members of the commoner class included those individuals who, by social strictures, were forbidden access to the special houses of the tabooed class as well as others who, by choice, preferred to remain commoners. Those restricted to the commoner class included all women, regardless of their wealth or rank, their male servants and, with occasional exceptions,[4] their *pekio* mates. Also restricted to this class were members of the *ka'ioi* male entertainers whose varying landholdings and social rankings were, like those of women, of no consideration in their assignment to this category. In addition to those who had no choice in their classification were men who preferred the freedom of eating and associating with women, which was permitted among those of the commoner class, and thus chose to be members of that class.[5] Included among these were some chiefs,[6] as well as members of the landed gentry, or principal people, known as the mattatoetoe, who may not have had any chiefly affiliations but were distinguished from others by being tattooed entirely around their eyes.[7] There were also those whom Crook described as being below the "privileged classes," by which he probably meant the landless tenants, servants, and the like, who were not included in the tabooed class because they lacked knowledge of and interest in the gods and religious rites, and were more concerned with witches and ghosts.[8]

THE TABOOED CLASS

Crook was not consistent in his statements concerning male membership in the tabooed class. At one point he stated that all males, with the exception of ka'ioi, belonged to the general tabooed class.[9] Yet, as already noted, he clearly acknowledged that there were other males who chose not to be of this class. Regardless of this inconsistency, it seems likely that, with the probable exception of the landless lower ranks, a large number of Marquesan men belonged to this class, which appears to have been a stratified socioreligious group.

Common to the tabooed class of all of the islands were the three ranks of religious personnel. These were the *tau'a* and tuhuna ota ogo, some of whom were also chiefs, and the latter's assistants, known as the *u'u*,[10] all of whose duties are described in Chapter 4. Since the tau'a, as inspirational priests, had direct contact with deity, they were said by Edward Robarts to outrank *haka'iki*, or high chiefs, at least in the eyes of many Marquesans.[11] Next in rank were the tuhuna ota ogo, or ritual priests, and their assistants, the u'u, who must have been just below them. Although not present among the tabooed class on Tahuata, on Nukuhiva there was a rank superior to the priests known as the *matta puovo*, consisting mostly of old men. Since many chiefs were said to keep their tabooed houses, or "altars," as Robarts called them, supplied with food for their petty chiefs and

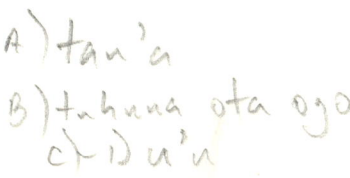

warriors,[12] these three social classes must have been included in the tabooed class. Beyond these were others whom Crook identified simply as of the general tabooed class.[13]

Being of the tabooed class was tantamount to having been invested with a degree of sanctity, depending upon one's rank within the class. Such a state of sanctity was not altogether indelible, since for certain occasions it could be temporarily nullified.[14] However, any object belonging to a commoner that had been handled by a tabooed man, regardless of rank, or had passed over his hand, became tabooed and could no longer be used. Furthermore, a tabooed man's food, clothing, and other objects were held sacred and could not be touched by commoners. Men of this class did not eat with women but took their meals at their special tabooed houses, which women were forbidden to enter.[15] Men of the common class who had proven themselves in war, or had shown some other exceptional ability, might be allowed to enter the house and share a meal. It was in these houses that tabooed men assembled prior to making a trip or going to war. It was here, too, that during certain religious observances they fasted or placed themselves in a state during which time they could have no intercourse with women. As sanctified edifices these buildings also served as repositories for sacred tabooed objects or common artifacts that, by accident, had become tabooed and could no longer be touched by others. As men's clubhouses, they also served as a site for feasting or a place where tabooed men could spend time making weapons, drums, or delicate ornaments.[16]

The tabooed class's penchant for restrictions was also found within the ranks of the class itself. Thus, the ranked levels of the tabooed class religious personnel—the tau'a, tuhuna ota ogo, and u'u—could eat together or eat the food of persons of lower rank. However, those of lesser rank were forbidden to eat the food of these priestly men.[17] In the case of the highest-ranking matta puovo of Nukuhiva, no other tabooed class members could eat food prepared for them or that had been in their tabooed houses.[18]

The number and nature of other ranks within the tabooed class were never made clear, but social mixing between ranks seems to have had limitations. For example, Crook wrote of how men would rise in the morning and go to a tabooed house to drink kava with men of their own rank.[19] And tabooed houses belonging to persons of "superior class" or rank could not be entered by men of what Crook called the general tabooed class.[20] That several ranks existed was made clear by Crook when he explained that each was distinguished by special tattooed designs around the eyes and even on the eyelids.[21] That individuals bore the tattooed design of their rank would seem to suggest that there was no upward mobility within the tabooed class. However, it is possible that the patterns representing the lowest ranks were sufficiently simple and open to allow added patterns as one rose through the ranks, though this seems a bit far-fetched.

MARQUESAN SOCIAL RANKING

How the rankings of the commoner and tabooed classes were integrated into a recognizable overall societal hierarchy is well nigh impossible to contemplate. Little wonder that Crook found the statuses of various Marquesan societal entities numerous and burdensome. While later nineteenth-century accounts and studies offer some enlightenment on Marquesan social ordering, they must, perforce, describe a society modified by the continued intrusion of foreign goods and influences. For that reason, and because this study has set its temporal limitations, which terminate with the year 1813, it seems best, despite the limited data, to stay within this frame of reference.

The most feared, and therefore the most respected, social controls in Marquesan society were the religiously prescribed taboos that, if broken, were believed to bring down the wrath of the gods on the miscreant. Since such taboos were promulgated by the tau'a priests of the principal me'ae of each tribe,[22] it seems probable that Robarts was correct when he wrote that in the eyes of the Marquesans such priests outranked the haka'iki, or high chief, of a tribe.[23] If this were the case, it would seem to follow that those tau'a who were believed to be gods incarnate must have ranked still higher. However, there appear to have been other tau'a, including women inspirational priests, not directly connected with the me'ae whose position must have been somewhat lower than the others. Be that as it may, since at least one chief was stated to have been a tau'a, and the haka'iki Keatonue was also a tuhuna ota ogo ritual priest,[24] it would seem that the ranking of at least the higher order of chiefs was equivalent to these two classes of priests. However, as will be noted later, their power, unlike the respect for their ranking, varied considerably.

Immediately below the high chief, certainly in terms of tribal influence, was the *toa*, or chief warrior;[25] the ranking of others having chiefly status seems to have varied. Although warriors of lesser rank than toa might assemble for rites and other preparations for battle, there is no clear indication in the early literature that they represented a distinct social class. Like tuhuna specialists, they may have been drawn from various social ranks.

Beneath the general rank of chief but not necessarily lower in terms of wealth and prestige, were the large landholders known as the mattatoetoe,[26] and below them were smaller landholders. At least Crook infers that such small landholders of lesser rank existed, since he claimed that there was no distinction of civil rank except that which arose from ownership of property.[27] In this regard it should be noted that both men and women owned property.[28] As for the array of tuhuna specialists—barbers, tattooers, ornament makers, and the like—it is probable that the perceived importance of their particular trade and their personal ability conjoined to establish their degree of respect but not necessarily their social rank. For example, Crook explained how the third wife of high chief Teinae of Tahuata became too friendly with a tuhuna ornament maker, for which she was nearly strangled by her husband. However, Teinae did nothing to the tuhuna because he was regarded as too respectable to be reprimanded.[29] There was also the situation of the brother of high chief Keatonue's mother, who, besides being a priest, was a highly competent ornament maker. However, he was never hired as a tuhuna specialist because of his high social rank.[30] This, in itself, suggests that all tuhuna serving as hired specialists had social ranks below that of chiefs or priests but above that of tenants and servants.

At the bottom of the social scale were the landless. Here, too, a further division is discernible. There were those who had lost their land through quarrels or fighting, and who had come to live on the lands of wealthier Marquesans. There they were employed to tend the crops on the plantations and seem to have served as fighting men for their employer in any altercation he or she might have with some other party.[31] The remaining landless class was made up of servants and fishermen. The fishermen's families lived in caves and bartered their fish for other supplies,[32] whereas the servants lived on the land of their employer, who housed and fed them. They were not slaves, however, since they were free to leave their employer even if he was a chief.[33] Nonetheless, during their employment they were open to the potential, at worst, of being killed for stealing fruit or allowing an employer's child in their care to be hurt. They appear to have been regarded as disposable adjuncts of Marquesan society, since they could be killed by higher-ranking men for no reason at all.[34]

THE GOVERNING CHIEFLY CLASS

Most of the population of the Marquesas was made up of various independent tribes, no island except Uapou being governed by a single paramount chief.[35] However, a considerable portion of Uahuka was said to be owned by one individual and thus may have approached a governmental situation similar to Uapou, especially since no particular tribes were mentioned for that island.[36] As for the other islands, Crook listed four tribes living on Tahuata and noted that before his arrival there had been a fifth tribe that had been totally destroyed through warfare. On neighboring Hivaoa, he recorded ten tribes, and eight living on Nukuhiva. Although he never visited Fatuhiva, he understood that several independent tribes existed there.[37]

How many of these tribes were the result of the arrival of independent populations by way of prehistoric migrations or accidental voyaging, and how many were the result of the breaking apart of a few original founding groups, is not readily determined. Crook surmised that all the tribes of Hivaoa had originated from what was then the small Teu tribe because when all were spoken of collectively, they were referred to as Teu.[38] However, he may not have meant to include the Tafate on the north coast of that island. Not only did that tribe not indulge in tattooing their bodies but they were said to be unable to speak the Marquesan language fluently,[39] which suggests that they might have been either relatively recent newcomers to the archipelago or an isolated enclave of very early migrants. Nonetheless, splitting of groups into separate tribes had certainly taken place. Crook noted that on Nukuhiva the Tekau, Bevvatane, and Puheehho came from one original group and were known collectively as the Tipe.[40] Although some of these tribes may have been subdivided into districts under a lesser chief,[41] each tribe as a whole was presided over, in secular matters, by its own high chief, or haka'iki, and in religiously prescribed matters by its tribal tau'a priests.

While the socioreligious expoundings of the tau'a of each tribal me'ae had the force of god-given mandates, thus giving such priests a strong, authoritative position within a tribe, this was not necessarily the case with tribal chiefs. There appears to be no evidence in the early literature that chiefly families were seen as having been related to particular gods, which would have given them a divine power of authority. In terms of the supernatural, the only thing such families had, which was shared by the landed aristocracy, was protection by their invisible spirits against anyone who might physically strike them in a manner thought to be insulting. Such an insult was believed to excite the rage of such spirits against the offender.[42]

Without divine sanctions, Marquesans of chiefly status were not seen as being naturally endowed with authority over those of lower rank. Nor did their presence in everyday social activities require awed deference or acts of obeisance by those of lesser status.[43] Given European attitudes of the day toward nobility, this apparent lack of deference to chiefs was interpreted by some as representing absence of authority, a view made still more convincing by a lack of special dress embellishment.[44] However, it was noted that chiefs and priests were the most extensively tattooed.[45] Since Krusenstern was apparently not given a full-dress reception upon his arrival in the Marquesas, he concluded that neither the "nobility" nor even the "king" had formal attire for receiving dignitaries.[46] In this he was mistaken, for both Captain Cook and Fanning had previously been received by chiefs arrayed in headdresses, gorgets, and the like.[47]

As for the apparent absence of acts of obeisance, while not commonly employed in daily life, they were performed on occasions of heightened formality, or when great deference was to be shown to an individual. While greeting between friends of either sex might include a simple touching of noses,[48] acts of obeisance were more flamboyant. In simplest form they consisted of prostrating oneself facedown on the ground,[49] while more elaborate observances included prostrating oneself before the honored person and then placing the foot or leg of that individual on one's head or shoulder.[50] This latter act, as well as touching noses as a form of greeting, was strongly reminiscent of basically similar acts performed for similar reasons in Tonga.[51] So was another act of humility reported by David Porter, which consisted of the wife of Keatonue kissing Porter's hand and then placing it upon her head.[52]

While authority was not inherent in the position of chief, the ranks within the chiefly families were known and respected.[53] Both John R. Forster and Porter saw tribal chiefs as exerting power in the manner of a benevolent father attending to the welfare of his children, a form of noblesse oblige, as it were.[54] Nonetheless, it was more than mere respect for rank that gave chiefs varying degrees of authority. Rank within a chiefly family was important for prestige, but wealth in land and the dispensing of the products of that land were also very important. As Robarts pointed out, when a chief was mild and generous with his subjects, he gained the love and esteem of his people. However, should he be difficult and selfish, his people might revolt and even drive him and his family off their inherited land.[55] The importance of land in relation to the perceived authority of a chief was reflected in Crook's assessment of Duteitei, high chief of the Ahheutinne tribe of Tahuata. He was perceived as having little authority among his people, some of whom owned more land than he did.[56] Thus, Crook noted that property and authority were not inseparable, nor were they proportionate.[57] The only clear conclusion that Krusenstern could reach in this regard was that wealth in land was certainly an important factor, in that a chief was thus able to provide for a large number of people.[58] Urey Lisiansky succinctly summarized the position of most chiefs: they had great privileges, owned large domains, and were held in high respect by their people.[59]

Land and chiefly status normally descended from the reigning chief to his eldest son. At least that was so in the cases for which we have early data: the Tahuata chief, Teinae, and Keatonue, high chief of Taiohae.[60] However, exceptions did occur. There was the case of Moana, former chief of all the basin of Taiohae, except the valleys of Havau and Pakiu, whose eldest son was, according to Crook, of weak mind and was passed over in favor of his sister, Butahaie. Butahaie was married to Temotei'i, eldest son of Puakakahu, chief of the Havau and Pakiu. While Temotei'i, being an eldest son, was in line to inherit his father's property and title, it appears that Butahaie, while inheriting her father's property and authority, could not, as a woman, inherit the title of chief; according to Crook, her husband was to receive that inheritance. However, all of this came to naught because her husband was lost at sea before Moana and his father died, the actual authority apparently not being passed down until the death of the two male parents. In the end, however, the eldest son of Temotei'i and Butahaie, named Keatonue, received both the inheritances, thus making him the high chief of all of Taiohae.[61] Nonetheless, it would appear that Butahaie's inherited authority from her chiefly father, Moana, continued even though her son was now haka'iki. Her residence was the scene of daily meetings of the family. It also served as the place of assembly for consultations of the superior ranks during times of public concern or crisis.[62] According to Robarts, the opinions expressed by Butahaie were tantamount to law, and her decision was required before war could be undertaken.[63]

On the basis of the above account of Temotei'i failing to receive his inheritance of chiefly authority before his death because his father and father-in-law were still alive, it would appear that such inheritance obtained only upon the death of the male parent. However, when Edmund Fanning and Crook landed at Taiohae, they were met by a formal retinue, including chief Keatonue, and taken to meet the young "king" of Taiohae, who appeared to be about fourteen years of age. At that family assembly there seemed little doubt that this firstborn son of Keatonue was recognized as the new chief.[64] With Crook as informant and translator for Fanning, it appears significant that the latter consistently referred to Keatonue as the "regent." This suggests that there had been a transfer of title from father to son, but not the authority of that position.

This arrangement was basically similar to the transfer of title from father to son in Tahiti, where the father remained regent until his son was old enough and had passed through certain rituals that transferred the full authority of the chieftainship to him.[65] However, it is not clear when the oldest son of a Marquesan high chief assumed the full rights and authority normally vested in that position. It would seem that this may not have occurred until the death or incapacitation of the father. For example, Crook noted that the Aki-toka tribe at Aakapa on the north coast of Nukuhiva had two chiefs. One, middle-aged, had lost the use of his legs and was not expected to live very long; the other, much younger, was said to be his relative.[66] This suggests that the latter was already taking over some of the chiefly authority and was thus seen as a chief in his own right.

Where no health problem existed, as in the case of Temotei'i, no relinquishing of authority to the heir apparent took place. This was equally true of Keatonue, who was still active as high chief of Taiohae in 1813, when Porter found him to be an infirm old man about seventy years of age.[67] By then his eldest son must have been approaching thirty years of age, yet there was no indication in Porter's account that he shared any authority with his father. The only thing that Porter noted was that at times he would lead the procession of bearers bringing food supplies to Porter, a position usually taken by his father.[68]

While giving the firstborn son of a chief the title of his father was similar to the Tahitian hereditary arrangement of that period, the withholding of power until the death of the father was similar to the situation in Tonga. There, however, the title of chief was also withheld from the heir apparent until the death of the father.[69] Thus, taken in toto, the Marquesan system of chiefly inheritance would appear to have been a merging of specific aspects of two different traditions of inheritance.

The unquestioned authority of a tribal chief extended only to his personal lands and the tenants working those lands. There is no indication in the early literature that he had the power, short of war, to dispossess others of their property. Crook made this clear when he wrote that no haka'iki had any right over the property of others,[70] and Robarts noted that a chief could not force tribute from anyone other than those living on his land.[71] His tenants were expected to give him, on request, up to one-quarter of what they produced, though in bad years this portion was reduced according to circumstances.[72] At the same time, this did not keep others of the tribe from acquiescing to requests from their chief, should they see fit to do so. In one case reported by Crook, a European vessel brought quantities of tempting goods for exchange. The local chief wanted the lot, and it was agreed that he would collect sixty hogs from his tribe for the exchange. However, tribal members preferred to trade their own hogs for some of the goods, so the chief was given only twenty of the sixty pigs he had requested. As Crook pointed out, the chief had never before failed to collect as many hogs as he desired for public feasts.[73] It would appear that in this case he was seen as being overly greedy in not considering the desires of his subjects, who therefore responded negatively.

Unlike the inspirational priests, or tau'a, whose authority was god-given, and hence obeyed, the power of chiefs beyond their own estates depended upon their perceived relationship to tribal members. It was also apparent that the support of the extended family was needed; Keatonue's entourage of lesser chiefly assistants consisted largely of relatives.[74] Mildness of manner and a liberality toward the poor could result in their willingness to support and conform to a chief's wishes, as when the major breadfruit season required numerous hands to pick and store the fruit in his *ma* pits.[75] As for gaining support of the higher ranks, Robarts pointed out how chiefs who generously supplied their taboo houses with an abundance of food for the use of petty chiefs and warriors gained respect and supporters.[76] Thus, for Marquesan chiefs, high rank accompanied by continued acts of noblesse oblige toward tribal members resulted in authority through appreciation and respect. Without that accompaniment there was only the respect of rank and little else.

CHAPTER 4

Religion

Early observers of Marquesan religious life were so intrigued with the practice of human sacrifice, occasionally accompanied by cannibalism, as well as numerous deity-prescribed taboos, that they recorded little else. By so doing, they left only a minimal and frustrating record of religious beliefs and activities. Gods there were aplenty, but information about their nature, their power, and the geographical extent of their acceptance within the archipelago is sadly limited, as are descriptions of religious ceremonies other than those of human sacrifices. All of this should not be too surprising, for the only prime sources, either directly or indirectly, are William Pascoe Crook and Edward Robarts, especially the former.

THE SUPERIOR GODS

Before leaving Crook on the island of Tahuata, James Wilson of the *Duff* gave him a list of questions to be answered concerning what he had already learned of Marquesan culture during the short time he had been on land. In answering the question on religion, Crook noted that the islanders had a multitude of gods, and listed the names of eight, none of whom was greater than the other.[1] Not one of these names can be identified with the more important deities known for other island cultures in Polynesia, such as Tane, Oro, Tangaroa, or the culture hero, Maui. Quite probably Crook's names were those of deceased ancestral gods. However, he later noted that there were different orders of gods, some dwelling in the sky and others in the sea, and yet others involved with the natural elements.[2] Be that as it may, somewhat later both Robarts and David Porter alluded to a belief among the Marquesans in the presence of a supreme being. Regrettably, neither man recorded the name, if any, of this higher god.³ However, Crook gave us a hint of who it might have been.

Conventionalized human figures in wood, associated with important me'ae, or religious precincts, were reported as early as 1595 and continued to be mentioned occasionally throughout our time period.⁴ By 1813 similar figures in stone were reported by Porter, suggesting a relatively late date for the larger classic figures carved in that medium.⁵ Nonetheless, their identity, other than being personifications of deity, was never hinted at, let alone revealed, in the early literature.

Within this context of humanized god figures, the seemingly enigmatic appearance of a nonhumanoid representation of a deity suggests the possible presence in the Marquesas of at least one major traditional god of Tahiti. In a brief reference to a religious ceremony, Crook described a "clothed god" that, at one point in the services, was raised on high. As this was done, the assembly arose and, standing, voiced a recitation in unison, after which the "god" was carefully lowered again. What is significant here is Crook's description of the deified object. It was, in his terms, a "log" wrapped in bark cloth to which several conch shells had been attached.⁶ This wrapped cylindrical conformation brings to mind the Tahitian material personification of one of their important deities, the god Oro. Like the "clothed god," the symbol for Oro was basically cylindrical and had no human features. It was associated with human sacrifices and, like the Marquesan god symbol, was exhibited on particular religious occasions.⁷

Equally intriguing, in terms of attempting to identify the more important Polynesian deities in the Marquesan pantheon, is a tradition noted by Crook. He reported that the natives believed the islands of their archipelago had been raised by the exertions of an *atua*, or god, beneath them.⁸ Such a concept immediately brings to mind the Tongan belief that the god Maui lay beneath the Tongan islands and that sporadic earthquakes were caused by his stirring.⁹ It might also be recalled that it was this same Maui who, Tahitian tradition claimed, dragged the Society Islands into their present locations.¹⁰

THE PAROCHIAL GODS

According to Crook, all spirits of the departed became atua. However, like those accepted as living gods, notably inspirational priests, there was a ranking as to their eminence and, presumably, their power. In the case of chiefs, only those who had been illustrious when living, and who left behind them relatives with wealth, were periodically honored, some with sacrifices.[11] For example, on Nukuhiva a high chief, Moana, once ruled over all the valleys of Taiohae, except those of Havau and Pakiu, which were under the domination of the chief Puakakahu. Upon the death of these two men, Moana became revered as the principal deity of all of the island of Nukuhiva. Puakakahu, though recognized as a god of the island, was given ceremonies of worship that were said to be inferior to those of Moana.[12] As for the less prominent atua, who must have been innumerable, since the souls of all the dead became gods, nothing is clear. However, every family was said to have its own individual me'ae, or religious ceremonial structure,[13] so it would seem likely that gods from families of lower social status may have received at least a degree of family worship from time to time. The spirits of departed tau'a were believed to have entered the highest ranks of the gods.[14] This is understandable, since during their lifetime the gods had spoken through them.

Beyond the invisible ancestral gods, the Marquesans recognized certain individual males as living gods. Like other deities, they appear to have been ranked according to their presumed powers.[15] What little information is available on this subject suggests that such deities were largely, if not wholly, limited to living tau'a. A. J. von Krusenstern, however, claimed that the living children and grandchildren of Keatonue, high chief of Taiohae, were looked upon as gods.[16] This, by extension, would have had to include the chief as well.

While these members of the chiefly class were accorded a godlike respect, there seems little evidence that they were thought to have the power of deity. As it stands, G. H. von Langsdorff probably came closest to the truth of the matter. His understanding was that people of distinction were protected by spirits who would rage against anyone who struck or otherwise physically insulted them.[17] The spirits were probably those of chiefly ancestors long departed. However, it was quite a different matter with tau'a who were believed to be living gods.

Only a few of the inspirational priests of the Marquesas seem to have been regarded as gods. Some had inherited this presumed power.[18] This was the case with the tau'a Tamapuameine, who lived on the island of Tahuata. There it was believed that he had power over the seasons and elements, and thus controlled the fertility of breadfruit. Being essentially a god of agriculture, he was invoked throughout the island. Within the confines of his tabooed me'ae, the bodies of scalped human sacrifices hung as witness to his needs.[19] Crook seems to have had reason to suspect that a similar living god of agriculture existed on Nukuhiva.[20] Given the importance of breadfruit, it would seem possible that such a living god figure may have been present on each populated island. While deity status was inherited along some family lines, there were other living tau'a gods who, for reasons unknown, did not or could not pass on their powers to their offspring.[21] These may have been regarded as less important, as was the case of the living god Touweiatua, who was considered less than equal to the agricultural deity Tamapuameine.[22]

While gods of the status of Oro and Maui, or their equivalents, could conceivably have been recognized and venerated throughout the Marquesas, this does not seem to have been the case with the parochial living and invisible gods. A few of this class of deity did hold divine power over an entire island, such as the spirit god of Moana of Taiohae, but the majority appear to have had more geographically limited areas of recognition. Quite likely these reflected tribal responses to the assumed godly power of individual society members, past and present.

Although parochial gods seem to have been important elements in the everyday life of the people, none seem to have been recognized and supplicated on all of the populated islands of the archipelago. This is not to say that their parochial rank and prestige were not recognized by visitors from neighboring islands. Rather, I would suggest that they were respected for what they were: local religious entities of importance. As such, they probably required a visitor's respect within their restricted area of potency.

Before leaving the subject of deities, it is worth noting Marquesan traditions of having been visited by other gods. Since the term *atua* was also used to identify foreign visitors, including Europeans,[23] such gods seem not to have been viewed in the same light as the Marquesan deities. While the elaboration of these traditions through years of oral recounting can make them appear spurious on occasion, their origin may have derived from the actual arrival of foreign vessels. That some of the atua were said to have introduced certain domesticates may illustrate the piecemeal manner in which the food complex of more than one island was created.

Crook was told that the ancestors of his Marquesan informants had been visited by atua from some of the forty-one islands enumerated in their songs.[24] While these visitors seem not to have brought any domesticates with them, this was not the case with similar accounts given to Porter in 1813. He was told that many generations ago coconuts had been brought to the Marquesas from an island named Ootoopoo by a god named Tao.[25] Given the nature of the crop, and the claimed location of the island to the windward of Fatuhiva, an atoll in the Tuamotus seems a reasonable possibility. He was also informed that some twenty generations ago a god by the name of Haii had visited all of the islands and brought hogs and fowl.[26] Since pig bones have been found in Phase II (600–1300) archaeological deposits in the Marquesas,[27] either the generation of the tradition was grossly in error, or Haii's arrival represented an additional introduction, perhaps in the historic period.

PRIESTS

Just as the will and prophetic knowledge of Marquesan gods was needed on occasion, so it was necessary to appease them through offerings and rituals, so that prayers might be answered and potential wrath avoided. The first of these necessities was accomplished through inspirational priests known as tau'a, while the rituals of ceremony and offerings were fulfilled by a separate class of priests referred to by Crook as the tuhuna ota ogo, some years later referred to as the *tuhuna o'ono*.[28]

Few in number, and including both males and females, tau'a were said to have obtained their power through inheritance.[29] They were capable of communicating with the gods, and their bodies served as the medium through which the gods could make known their desires or dictate their prophecies.[30] They were also believed to have the power of sorcery.[31] Aiding in their endeavors were individuals known as *moa*, though their capacity was never noted beyond the fact that they were known to participate in dances at koina festivities.[32] While tau'a were distinguished by wearing a crescent-shaped gorget of wood decorated with rows of red seeds,[33] moa wore special caps of hiapo and necklaces of boar tusks or, occasionally, pig ribs.[34] As already noted, there were a few tau'a whose abilities, at least in the eyes of the local populace, placed them in the class of living gods.

Since they had such a close relationship with gods, tau'a, as well as their possessions, could not be touched by others. Nor did anyone dare to speak contemptuously of them. To do so was deemed tantamount to insulting the gods who spoke through a tau'a, and was certain to bring death, or at least a curse, upon the offender.[35] This closeness to deity allowed an inspirational priest to offer spiritual aid and advice on personal secular matters. But such help came at a price. A new house could be protected from evil spirits through a tau'a ritual. This included feasting the priest, after which he was allowed to retire, thus being the first to sleep in the new dwelling.[36] Well-to-do families might employ a tau'a, usually a woman, to conduct incantations to facilitate a forthcoming birth.[37]

While inspirational priests did not participate in practical medicine, they could be called upon to alleviate illnesses thought to have been caused by atua. One technique was for the tau'a to pass his or her hands across the chest of the patient three times, thus drawing out the evil spirit causing the problem. In other cases the tau'a would ask the offending atua why he was making the patient ill. The explanation, spoken through the priest in a language only he understood, was then interpreted for the patient by the tau'a. Usually this amounted to the patient having broken some taboo, such as having picked a fruit from a tabooed tree. To appease the spirit, the tau'a would suggest an offering of a certain number of pigs, the number depending upon the wealth of the patient. The offering was then taken by the priest to his own me'ae, where it was eaten to ensure the patient's return to health.[38]

Such personal tau'a services were of small significance compared with the priests' role in affecting tribal life and activities. Their ability to consort with the invisible gods of their tribe gave them an influence over the multitude exceeding that of a haka'iki. The powerful tau'a lived close by their own tribal me'ae, or as Robarts put it, the "grand" me'ae, which was the principal center of religious life and ceremony.[39] It was to high chief Keatonue's tribal me'ae that Robarts took Krusenstern and his company, who later briefly described the structure, which they erroneously identified as the me'ae of the tau'a.[40]

At such tribal me'ae, tau'a promulgated the public socioreligious taboos whose enforcement relied on assured godly punishment for infractions.⁴¹ Such god-given restrictions were recognized as belonging in quite a different category than the more mundane taboos issued by chiefs.⁴² Tau'a might was best exhibited at occasional public gatherings at the tribal me'ae or, infrequently, at koina festivities. These were the times for the gods to manifest themselves through a tau'a. First there was the trance for all to see: a wild look, quivering contortions, a brief sleep, and a sudden awakening. Then godly demands for human sacrifices or prophecies were expounded in a shrill, squeaky voice.⁴³

On occasions like this, when a tau'a was known to be about to pronounce a prophecy, chiefs and others of high rank would assemble, sometimes at the tohua, or dance court, of the priest. During such a performance a profound silence would prevail throughout the surrounding area.⁴⁴ On one occasion on Hivaoa, when intertribal war was a concern, a specific day for prophecy was announced. At that time all the males went to the tribal me'ae, each bringing one or two "old," probably meaning fully matured, coconuts as a gift to the tau'a. During this assembly the tau'a, flanked by two tuhuna priests wearing black feather headdresses, waistbands hung with human skulls, and their customary coconut leaf cloaks, walked to a temporary stage and sat down. The tau'a immediately went into his trance and soon demanded more human sacrifices, to be obtained through war.⁴⁵

Just as living tau'a demanded human sacrifices for their gods, such victims always being obtained from tribes other than their own,⁴⁶ so at their death their deified souls required similar offerings.⁴⁷ In fact, such sacrifices were required anytime that a tau'a became sick. From one to three victims might be necessary, depending upon the severity of the illness.⁴⁸ Upon the death of such a priest at least three sacrifices were required. Crook witnessed such a ritual on Tahuata. An ambush party was sent to Hivaoa to obtain the requisite victims. They returned with three males and one female. The bodies were taken to the tribal me'ae; two were baked in a pit oven and eaten, another was placed in an upright position on the me'ae, and the fourth corpse was deposited in a special house some distance away, where it was left to rot.⁴⁹ Robarts told Urey Lisiansky that three victims were required on such an occasion, two being hung up in the me'ae and the third eaten.⁵⁰ Krusenstern apparently was told that the three victims were not eaten but simply hung up in trees, presumably at the me'ae, and left there until the flesh fell away.⁵¹

Both the variation in the treatment of the sacrificial victims and, except for Crook's account, the seemingly specific requirement of three victims was never explained. The former may have reflected the ranking of the particular deceased tau'a, though which procedure signified what rank would be difficult to say. Although Crook's description would seem to negate the idea of a consistent need for three victims, this is not necessarily the case. Since the required victims were to be offered up at the tribal me'ae, and women were normally tabooed from entering such a precinct, it is possible that only male victims were suitable. In other words, the woman may simply have been at the site of the ambush and was killed along with the three males, all four being brought back to Tahuata. As described by Crook, three of the bodies were ritualized at the me'ae, while a fourth, which could have been the female corpse, was placed in a separate structure at a distance from the me'ae. Thus, the requisite three human sacrifices had been maintained.

In addition, Robarts told of an ambush for a similar purpose during which the captors, having exhibited their slain victim to his tribe, apparently announced the purpose of their ambush by giving three war whoops.[52] As mentioned earlier, Crook noted that there were three orders of superior gods: those of the sky, the sea, and the natural elements.[53] This suggests that the three war whoops employed on various occasions symbolically referred to the three superior gods to whom, in this case, the victim had been sacrificed. Krusenstern depicted the purpose of the sacrifices as conciliating deity so that the spirit of the tau'a would find ready acceptance among the gods.[54] Thus it can be reasoned that each of the three sacrificial victims was to placate the god of one of the three domains.

While Crook explained that ambush raids of neighboring tribes for tau'a death sacrifices did not necessarily precipitate avenging wars,[55] Robarts gave Lisiansky quite a different story. He claimed that such raids would result in wars lasting up to one year, the length depending upon the "nearest relation" to the deceased tau'a. By "nearest relation" he seems to refer to the particular family member designated to inherit the supernatural powers of his now dead relative. He explained that immediately upon hearing of the death of the tau'a, such a relative retired to a tabooed location where he was furnished food, and where he stayed until deciding to come out, an action said to terminate the war.[56] While avenging wars may well have been precipitated by the seeking of sacrificial victims, the sequestering of the "nearest relation" is left unexplained. It is at least a possibility that such represented a ritual tabooing of the heir apparent to the deceased tau'a's position, perhaps lasting until all appropriate funeral rites had been completed.

While tau'a communicated directly with the world of spirits, the class of priests known as tuhuna ota ogo conducted the formal rituals for appeasing the gods through prayers and offerings. Most notable of the latter were the human sacrifices that the gods demanded through the tau'a. In this arduous task, conducted at the tribal me'ae, the tau'a were aided by a number of assistants known as u'u.[57] Although tau'a, tuhuna ota ogo, and u'u were allowed to eat together, it would appear that inspirational priests held a comparatively superior position. Crook told of a principal tuhuna ota ogo having been clubbed to death by a high-ranking man during an altercation over property ownership.[58] Since such an act could not have been committed against a tau'a, who could not be touched and whose property was held inviolate by taboo, the superiority of tau'a over tuhuna ota ogo seems probable. Respect for the latter priests varied among the islands, those of Tahuata being shown less deference than those on Nukuhiva.[59] Nonetheless, tuhuna were more than just ritual specialists. Like the *matapule* of Tonga,[60] they represented the embodiment of tribal traditions, including oral histories and the genealogies of chiefs.[61]

Tuhuna ota ogo did not inherit their position but were ordained to it by a predecessor who had taught them.[62] It is not clear from what level of society potential priests of this class came. However, we do know that the high chief of Taiohae, Keatonue, was also a tuhuna ota ogo priest.[63] Regardless, there appear to have been steps in the training of such an individual, and since Crook refers to both a "head of priests" and a "principal priest" or tuhuna ota ogo, there must have been ranking within the group.[64] However, it seems that there was no differentiation in the elements of dress that identified these priests. At least on Nukuhiva, dress consisted of a loose coconut leaf cloak, one end of which was fastened around the neck by a cord, the loose leaves being allowed to hang across the shoulders and down the back of the wearer. While this was unique to the Nukuhiva tuhuna ota ogo, the headdress, made of a short segment of coconut leaf gathered at the back of the head, was also worn by other people of "distinction," and by common people as well during special, but unidentified, ceremonies.[65]

Crook concluded that there were more tuhuna ota ogo priests than there were tau'a,[66] which seems possible, since their duties were many and varied. They were involved in all ceremonial rituals, some of which, like those prior to intertribal war, lasted for days. They attended to all human sacrifices and had the right to eat anything that had been sacrificed to the gods. They attended all funerals, and were the only ones permitted to beat the sacred drums at the tribal me'ae. In addition, they were the practicing physicians who administered medicine to the sick and performed surgical operations.[67] However, it was during certain unidentified ceremonies that their knowledge of traditions and genealogies came to the fore. Such information, described by Crook as sacred songs, were delivered in a variety of ways. Some were chanted to the beat of the great drums at the tribal me'ae; others were said to be recitative, delivered with violent voice and action.[68] The full range of content of these sacred songs has not been recorded. However, some are known to have dealt with the genealogies of chiefs, while others consisted of a recitation of some forty-one island names, some with quite mythical descriptions. Atua from some of these islands were said to have visited the Marquesas in years gone by. Of special interest is the record that some of these songs were delivered in a language unintelligible to the common people.[69] This suggests an equivalent of the chief's language of Tonga and some other Polynesian islands in its restriction to a given class of people.

ME'AE

Although every Marquesan family was said to have had its own me'ae,[70] the early ethnohistoric record concerning such structures is limited. Me'ae were said to be repositories for the dead,[71] and since the souls of the dead became atua, such structures perforce had religious significance, at least for the families of the deceased. There were also mortuary me'ae that contained the bodies of sacrificial victims who, for unexplained reasons, had not been eaten by the priests but left intact for the gods.[72] However, the most important me'ae were those devoted to tribal religious rites. According to Crook's report to James Wilson of the *Duff*, one such sacred precinct was present in each district, which I take to mean a tribal district.[73]

While the architecture of such me'ae was not recorded,[74] James Wilson did leave a brief description of a chief's me'ae at Vaitahu, on

Tahuata. Built on sloping ground, it consisted of a level stone platform upon which two houses stood. One of these contained a tall drum at each end of the dwelling, while in the center stood an eight-foot-high escutcheon-like assemblage of reeds, some vertical, others horizontal, and still others laid obliquely, the whole appearing to form one face of a pyramid. Close by was the other house, in front of which stood two life-sized human figures carved in wood. Behind these figures, and leaning against the wall of this totally enclosed house were three similarly constructed escutcheons, the reeds composing them stained different colors. The central panel of this complex was noticeably taller than the other two and bore the figure of a bird at its top, possibly representing the small sacred bird mentioned by Crook.[75] Within the house was a cylindrical coffin containing the remains of chief Honoo, father of high chief Teinae of Vaitahu. It had been carefully bound with plaited coconut cord dyed various colors.[76] All such structures, including the tribal me'ae, were forbidden to women.[77]

Of a different nature was the sacred tribal me'ae of Taiohae, Nukuhiva, to which Robarts took Krusenstern, Lisiansky, and Langsdorff.[78] It was situated on top of a thickly wooded hill. Inside its precinct was a decomposed corpse laid out on a simple board that was raised off the ground by poles, the whole being covered by a roof thatched with leaves.[79] Krusenstern referred to an "outer circle" where a few anthropomorphic statues of wood were located. Near these were some "pillars" covered with coconut leaves and white "cotton stuff," probably a reference to bark cloth.[80] While Krusenstern implies that there was more than one "pillar," Lisiansky described only one and referred to it as a "monument." It was said to be handsomely covered on the outside with coconut leaves and contained an "altar" within the structure. He further observed that the ground within the precinct was covered with coconut shells, which Robarts identified as the remains of offerings for the dead. In fact, a fresh coconut was noted resting on the head of one of the figures.[81] The placement of this coconut was not necessarily unique or fortuitous. On the occasion of memorial feasts for the dead, it was customary to send a bit of all the types of food to the principal me'ae, where the food was placed on the head of one of the figures as an offering.[82]

Nine years later Porter appears to have visited this same me'ae—he stated that it was the chief place of religious ceremonies in the valley of Taiohae. He described it as situated at the foot of a mountain in a grove of trees. Its basic component was a platform upon which was a squatting anthropomorphic stone statue about the height of a man but more massive in build. The eyes and ears were said to be large and the mouth wide, features typical of many Marquesan carved human figures.[83] Arranged on either side of this statue, as well as in front of and behind it, were several such figures carved in breadfruit wood. On each side of this complex of figures stood a thirty-five-foot-tall obelisk of bamboo framing interwoven with palm leaves and decorated with streamers of white bark cloth. Around the base of each obelisk were hung the heads of hogs and turtles, which were explained to Porter as being offerings to the gods.[84]

The presence of anthropomorphic figures accompanied by tall obelisks decorated with palm leaves and white bark cloth conforms to Krusenstern's earlier description of this site, except that a stone sculpture either had been added or had replaced one of wood. Here it should be noted that Linton's 1920–21 information that these early descriptions of obelisks were in error, and that they actually represented the heightened roof of a tau'a house built on the me'ae, does not hold for this me'ae.[85] Krusenstern indicated that the priest's house was near, but not on, the me'ae, and the descriptions of these tall structures mention no dwellings from which they sprang. Linton's data in this regard may represent a case of mixed oral tradition that might have grown out of an early ceremony in which tau'a sat within these structures in the process of obtaining their prophecies. Certainly their shape and construction bring to mind the oracle towers that were located on certain *heiau* in Hawaii, which also were decorated with bark cloth.[86]

While the elements of the me'ae platform were basically similar to what Krusenstern described, Porter recorded a singular assemblage a short distance from the me'ae. There he found four, apparently full-sized, war canoes. Not only were they decorated with ornaments of human hair, shell, and other items, but in the stern of each vessel was a carved figure of a man holding a paddle. The figure was fully dressed with plumes, earrings imitating whales' teeth, and other ornamental fashions of the island.[87]

Such an assemblage was almost certainly symbolic and related to some ceremony. This seems likely in the light of Porter's description of a ceremony being conducted by Keatonue and others that so appalled him by its seemingly childish nature that he did not bother to relative, or anyone else, was residing in that particular object. To break such a taboo was to excite the wrath of that spirit, resulting in possible death.[93] A basically similar approach was used as a means of revenge against a thief. Suspecting a particular person of having committed a robbery, the victim would give people's names to the presumed culprit's breadfruit trees, pigs, and other possessions. These then became bewitched by the spirits of the named individuals and could never again be used by the presumed thief.[94] Bold spirits were also known to invade houses and, through whistling and other noises, make clear their wish for food, which was usually forthcoming.[95] So prevalent was this fear of individual spirits that Robarts confessed to Langsdorff that he occasionally found it worthwhile to threaten to release his own spirit on somebody in order to get that person to do his bidding.[96] To an extent, the concepts of spirits and gods, particularly parochial gods, were similar; the difference lay in perception. Among the upper classes the souls of the deceased became atua who spoke to them through tau'a and could be placated by rituals, offerings, and prayers. For the lower classes these same souls were perceived as implacable spirits, and thus best avoided.

While inspirational priests were believed to have powers of sorcery, such powers were not limited to them. Secular practitioners, working for themselves or for a client, were said to be capable of making people ill or causing their death. The simplest method was for the sorcerer to obtain some of the spittle of the intended victim. This was enclosed in a specially designed parcel made of leaves that was buried in the ground. It was believed that as the parcel gradually decayed, so the victim would gradually decline. The only cure was to find and dig up the parcel.[97]

More elaborate processes were also recorded. These included various ceremonial rites to be performed by the sorcerer. The primary requirement was having one or more packets containing something of the intended victim, such as spittle or a bit of food he or she had been eating. As long as these were buried, the victim's illness continued. Once the sorcerer was known, the cure became a matter of paying the miscreant sufficient pigs to get him or her to dig up the offending packets and thus remove the spell.[98] Whereas various forms of sorcery were widespread in the Pacific island world, I found no references to it in the early historic literature concerning Tahiti and Tonga. However, it may be significant that the use of spittle and learn its significance. Nor do we know the nature of the site at which it took place. The chief and his party spent hours singing and clapping their hands before what might be described as a miniature village scene. There were ten or twelve little houses about two feet long and eighteen inches high, decorated with strips of bark cloth. In each was a little wooden "god." Alongside these miniature dwellings were comparably small canoes complete with their paddles and fishing gear, such as harpoons and seine nets. Typical of sacred areas, a line had been drawn around the whole, including the singers, indicating it was taboo.[88] Since various forms, some imitating houses, were made from coconut leaves by priests as part of funeral feast ceremonies,[89] it is possible that what Porter saw was a memorial ceremony for some deceased relative.

Besides the tribal me'ae of the Taiohae basin, the only other early account of a similar type of religious site was that of Pedro Fernandez de Quiros, of Vaitahu on Tahuata. Set apart from a cluster of dwellings was a palisaded area with an entrance on its west side. Within this enclosure was a house containing carved wooden figures around which were offerings of food and a pig. Although the Spanish soldiers succeeded in taking the pig, the natives refused to allow them to take the remaining offerings.[90] If this was indeed a tribal me'ae, it suggests that there were differences in size, construction, and planning of such structures. With that in mind, the site of Paeke in the Taipi Valley of Nukuhiva may well have functioned as such a religious center. Certainly its size, relative remoteness, and numerous stone figures set into its platforms suggests such a possibility.[91]

SPIRITS AND SORCERY

Although the protection and wishes of the gods, as well as the proper functioning of priests and rituals, were important elements in the lives of those in the higher levels of society, this was not the case among the lower classes. They appear to have shown little concern for these more complex concepts and practices. According to Crook, the forces most likely to affect their lives had to do with human maliciousness and a dread of spirits and sorcery.[92]

So strong was the fear of spirits that if one wished to assure the security of a tree crop, or even a house, the customary taboo was strengthened by the owner's announcing that the spirit of a dead fragments of partially eaten food in Marquesan sorcery practices was duplicated in Hawaii. There, chiefs guarded their spittle by having their own spittoons always at hand and maintained a scrap bowl in which to deposit bones and fragments of food, lest these might be obtained by sorcerers and used against them.[99]

CHAPTER 5

Daily Life and Diversions

Like Tongans and Tahitians, Marquesans enjoyed bathing. They cleansed themselves each morning and again in the evening, and frequently in between as well.¹ However, beyond this pleasurable routine, the activities of the day must have varied with the social class to which one belonged. Certainly few could afford to follow the example of the upper ranks of the taboo class males, among whom regular productive labor seems to have been nonexistent. Men of this station started their day like the upper classes of Tonga, by drinking kava with other members of their rank. Unlike Tonga, however, the drinking took place at one of the taboo houses and lacked the formalized ritual of making and serving the drink, the cup of liquid simply being passed among those present. After a bit of food and perhaps a nap, the group might proceed to a beach for a little swimming, surfing, and fishing. This was followed by returning to the taboo house and spending the rest of the day telling stories, talking, and eating.²

Younger men seem not to have participated in the morning kava drinking. Instead, some spent the morning having additions made to the tatooed designs on their bodies. For others a favorite pastime was to assemble at one of their "playgrounds," probably meaning a tohua (dance court). Here they would spend the day singing, dancing, or conversing. With the approach of evening they returned to their "houses of rank," where they were further entertained by groups of young girls who indulged in songfests lasting well into the night.³

DIVISION OF LABOR

Such manifest lack of productive endeavor by many of the upper classes necessitated the presence of a considerable lower-level work force to maintain their casual lifestyle. Most, though not all, such meaningful work was done by servants and the lower classes of Marquesans. Physical labor was clearly divided between the sexes. Women produced innumerable yards of bark cloth, mats for a variety of purposes, fans, and twine cord, and took care of their homes and children. Women of the poor class also gathered shellfish at low tide.[4] As with Tongans, only men were concerned with all aspects of agriculture, as well as fishing and the building of houses and canoes. And again as with Tongans, there were male specialists known in the Marquesas as tuhuna (who were not to be confused with the tuhuna priests, whose full title was tuhuna ota ogo).[5] These men were specialists: barbers, tatooers, and fishermen. In the latter occupation, Edward Robarts included all fishermen, rich or poor, as tuhuna, but William Pascoe Crook specifically described tuhuna fishermen as those employed by "persons of property," who furnished them with canoes and used their catches for barter.[6] In addition, there were craft specialists who were also recognized as tuhuna. These included canoe builders, drum makers, ornament producers, and carpenters who excelled in the production of utensils and weapons. Such craftsmen were hired for various periods of time, during which their employer housed and fed them. The more adept traveled from island to island and were held in high respect.[7] Though not mentioned in the early literature, it would seem probable, given the fine stonework and wood and stone carving in the Marquesas, that specialists in these occupations would also have been recognized as tuhuna.

TOOLS AND DOMESTIC CRAFTS

Tools were few but adequate. Adzes fashioned from hard volcanic rock and mounted on the end of an elbow-shaped handle by means of coconut cord lashings varied in size, the largest weighing as much as twenty-five pounds.[8] Interesting from a time perspective was Pedro Fernandez de Quiros's 1595 description of adzes at Tahuata made of thick bones and shells.[9] Knives for butchering were pieces of split bamboo, or fragments of shell of various shapes and sizes, having one edge sharpened or modified to form a sawtooth edge. A sharp-edged stone might also serve as a knife, as did teeth from the upper jaw of a shark fixed on a stick.[10] Chisels were said to have been made of human bone, as were augers, while other bones were formed into points to serve as awls.[11] Although Krusenstern noted a pointed piece of stone used as a drill,[12] teeth from the lower jaw of a shark, fastened to a wooden handle, were quite capable of drilling material as hard as a whale's tooth.[13] Rough scraping and even sawing were accomplished through the use of fragments of various corals, and shark skin served to give a piece of work a final polishing.[14]

With these simple tools craftsmen were capable of turning out a variety of containers, probably the finest being those worked out of a solid block of wood. In their simplest form these were nothing more than crudely finished shallow troughs up to six feet in length, one use of which was to mash breadfruit, using a smoothly finished stone pounder whose shape Robarts likened to a hand bell.[15] However, their finest work was to be found in food bowls. Some of these were round and so perfectly shaped that Robarts found them equal to those turned on a lathe.[16] Others were oval, measuring one by two feet, with a knob at one end carved in the shape of a man's head. These were sometimes fitted with a lid. Both shapes were decorated by carved or engraved figures of men, fish, and birds.[17] Krusenstern also described some large covered dishes made of thin brown wood and carved in the shape of mussels.[18] One specialized bowl was designed for kava. Its shape was an elongated oval in which one end was narrower than the other (and thus may have served as a spout).[19] Carved wooden chests, some with lids, were also noted by visitors,[20] and Porter mentioned having seen a neatly made child's cradle carved from a single log.[21] Such items carved from solid wood required seasoned timber if cracking was to be avoided, and such seasoning appears to have been practiced.[22]

Gourds, or calabashes (*Lagenaria siceraria* (Molina) Stanley), were probably a more common material than wood for food containers. All that was needed was to pluck the ripe gourd, cut an opening at the top, and clean it out and let it dry; it then became an adequate container. Although they varied somewhat in size, Crook estimated that gourds averaged about ten inches in diameter.[23] Here, too, carvers applied their art by shaping and often decorating semiglobular wooden covers having lipped edges perfectly fitted to an individual gourd mouth.[24]

Gourd containers were slung in an openwork net of thickly braided coconut fiber secured at the top by a drawstring made of *fau* bark (*Hibiscus tiliaceus* L.). This string was decorated with drilled and carved human and other bones as well as *kokuu* berries.[25] Since Crook described the kokuu "berries" as being hard, black, and round,[26] they were probably the fruit of *Sapindus soponaria* L., or soapberry, a native of tropical America.[27] In regard to this latter identification, it should be noted that the naturalist G. H. von Langsdorff reported finding the Marquesans using the hard-shelled gourds of what he identified as *Crescentia cujete* L., the American calabash tree, as water containers. These, he claimed, were restricted to each individual of either sex.[28] This would seem to negate Forest Brown's contention that the latter was a late introduction, though on what grounds was not explained.[29]

Wickerwork baskets for storage were also among domestic furnishings, though whether they were made by men or women was never recorded.[30] The combs used by Marquesan women to dress their hair were probably of their own making, as was the case with women in Tonga.[31] As for fans, mats, and bark cloth, there is little question that these were major products of the women of the Marquesas. Fans were items of admiration and appear to have given a degree of prestige to the owners of very fine ones. A few were made of feathers, but the majority were formed by plaiting a material described as a bark or coarse grass into squares, lozenges, or semicircles, the curved edge of which formed the base. All were kept white by repeatedly applying a coating of lime obtained from burning mussel shells.[32] While women appear to have designed and plaited the fans,[33] it was probably the men who carved the elaborate handles of sandalwood (*Santalum* sp.), *toa* (*Casuarina equisetifolia* L.), ivory, or human bone.[34] This was probably the reason for Robarts's having included fan making as men's work.[35]

Mats woven of pandanus leaves varied according to their intended use. The finest were made for sleeping on or as bed covers, and were woven by "ladies of rank." Others were worn by fishermen or, when painted and trimmed with feathers, as costumes for dancers. Somewhat coarser ones served as floor covering or portable ground cloths for seating visitors. Other mats served as room dividers in large dwellings or as sails for canoes.[36] However important these various mats were, what was likely the nearly continuous daily activity of women was the making of bark cloth for clothing. However, since women were strictly tabooed from things religious, it is not surprising that Crook noted that such cloth was always made by women, "except for sacred purposes."[37] Unfortunately, he did not expand on this exception, which may have had to do with the clothing of priests or that used in religious ceremonies. Nor do we know who might have been permitted to make such sacred material.

Secular bark cloth was made from the bark of one of three trees: *ute*, from the paper mulberry; *hiapo*, from the banyan; *mei*, from the breadfruit.[38] The most favored of these, from which several grades of cloth were made, was that from the paper mulberry. Fineness of texture depended upon two factors: the age of the sapling from which the bark was taken, usually determined by its height, and the amount of beating employed in reducing and spreading the fibers of the bark. The most delicate cloth was made from the bark of saplings having a height no greater than about ten feet. Such cloth was used to make the finer turbans and loincloths. Somewhat coarser cloth was made from bark peeled from trunks having a height of about twenty feet and was used to make robes as well as loincloths.

Up until at least 1806, beating the bark was accomplished by using a cylindrical mallet or club whose rounded surface was scored or grooved lengthwise completely around the club.[39] However, by 1813 this had been superseded by one made of toa wood and having a round handle and a squared beating end whose four faces were lightly grooved.[40] Its similarity to beaters in Tahiti suggests a historic introduction from the Society Islands, probably via European vessels. In Robarts's time, the anvil upon which Marquesan bark was beaten could be either a smooth stone or the flat surface of a prepared log.[41] In 1813 Porter saw only a smooth toa log being used for a similar purpose.[42] Here it is worth mentioning that according to Simon Kooijman's study of Polynesian tapa, round-to-oval beaters, as well as square-sectioned ones, were used not only in the Marquesas but also in Fiji, Samoa, Easter Island, and Hawaii; in the latter two both stone and wood anvils were employed.[43]

How the bark was prepared prior to being beaten was not described in the early literature. What is known is that sufficient strips of bark to make a sheet of cloth were kept moist while being beaten, after which they were trimmed and laid aside for two days. They were then beaten again, and the longer edges of each strip were joined to others by felting them together through gentle pounding. On the following day the beating was done crosswise to the grain until the felted edges could no longer be seen. This resulted in the formation of a sheet of bark cloth said to measure from ten to twelve feet square. Such a cloth was washed at least once, after which it had to be beaten again to strengthen it. Should the garment be torn, the edges of the rip were moistened and felted together by moderate beating.[44]

Crook described two types of ute cloth used to make *kahu* (robes). The whitest of these was thick and rough, though pliable. It appears to have been a common practice to bind two of these sheets together at their edges with a form of cordage made from strands of bark cloth. Another type, less white, was beaten so thin that it was necessary to add a second layer of fine bark to increase its thickness.[45] Cloth derived from the youngest saplings was white and was beaten so fine that the best of it, reserved for making turbans, was described as resembling fine gauze.[46]

Hiapo bark produced a naturally scented, reddish cloth of medium thickness. Its use seems to have been restricted to loincloths, some of which were extremely large.[47] These latter appear to have had a specialized use—for instance, the overly large loincloth worn by an important man when inviting guests to the funeral feast of a high-ranking man of the taboo class.[48] Cloth made from the bark of breadfruit was given only minor notice. It was described as being brown, thick, and occasionally dyed yellow.[49] This latter color was obtained from turmeric, and a fugitive orange-red color derived from a specially prepared turmeric perfume was occasionally used on the garments of higher-ranking women, who regarded it as a luxury.[50] Other colors were infrequently used, but what they were and how they were obtained was never stated.[51]

MEALS AND THEIR PREPARATION

Of the various restrictions having to do with food and its consumption, the clearest was that between the two major class divisions, the taboo and the common people. The latter, which included members of the ka'ioi, male attendants of women, and women, could not eat any food belonging to members of the taboo class. Nor could they touch, let alone use, the food bowl of such an individual because they were regarded as inferiors.[52] Since there appears to have been ranking within the taboo class, this same food restriction seems to have held there as well. According to Crook, no one whose rank was inferior to a member of a particular taboo class man could eat any of his food. Nor were commoners allowed to eat turtle and certain kinds of fish.[53]

There were also restrictions pertaining to certain foods that involved class distinctions. Unfortunately, the two Crook references concerning the nature of these restrictions are confusing. In one he asserts that pigs, plantains (including bananas), bonito, squid, and certain other fish belonging to persons of a "superior class," which is not clearly defined, could not be eaten by those of an inferior class.[54] At another point, however, he explains that on Nukuhiva, hogs, plantains, and some kinds of fish could be eaten by men or women unless they had somehow become tabooed or belonged to members of a temporary society called *hio*. At the same time he says that at Tahuata, coconuts, as well as hogs, plantains, and some kinds of fish, were always restricted to persons who belonged to the same class as the owner of the items.[55] In other words, one was free to eat these particular foods, providing their owner was of one's own social status, whether that was high or low. There were also restrictions between women of different rank, those of lesser position being forbidden to eat the food of those of a higher class.[56]

Although women could not visit a taboo house, and thus could not eat there with their husbands, should their spouses be of that class, this did not preclude their eating together elsewhere.[57] However, even in eating together there were restrictions. Although a husband could eat the food prepared by his wife, she could not eat any food prepared by him, nor could she use his fire for cooking. In fact, this restriction seems to have applied to all women and men, whether married or not, with one exception. Women of "blood royal," presumably meaning those of the chiefly class, were permitted to allow a man to prepare their meals, providing he was of low rank.[58]

Although it was clearly stated by Crook and Langsdorff that women could not touch or eat from a man's food container,[59] it is possible that all such personal containers were tabooed to others. Langsdorff noted that the special calabashes used for holding water were restricted to each individual, and David Porter observed that although men, women, and children might eat together, each had his or her own food in a separate dish.[60] Such restrictions, however, may have applied only to the upper social ranks, or perhaps only at Nukuhiva, since Étienne Marchand reported that men, women, and children at Tahuata had frequently been seen eating together from the same dishes.[61] Important as all Marquesan taboos appear to have been, their breaking was not always calamitous. Crook noted that accidental rendering of items taboo by servants or commoners was often quietly kept secret, to avoid inconvenience.[62]

All food was prepared outdoors, near one's dwelling.[63] In this general area might be a fireplace for roasting, and almost certainly a pit oven. Pit ovens were of different sizes, but none were more than about two feet deep. Some were simply holes in the earth, but others were said to have been lined with large, smooth stones. Using a fire plow of two sticks, a fire was kindled in the pit and stones added to absorb the heat. When these had become red-hot, the fire and embers were cleared away. Some of the heated stones were placed on the floor of the pit, then covered with bamboo canes or leaves. The food, usually wrapped in banana leaves or the crushed, damp stalks of the coarse sedge (*Cyperus pennatus* Lamark), were laid in the pit and more hot stones added, after which the whole was covered with leaves and earth to seal in the steam needed for cooking.[64]

Pigs and an occasional fowl were generally cooked in a pit oven;[65] Crook complained that the pork cooked in such a way was only half done.[66] This should not have been surprising, since pork was occasionally eaten raw.[67] What must have been pieces of pork, as well as chicken, were also cooked in wooden vessels through the technique of stone boiling.[68] However, such food was not part of the normal diet, pigs being reserved for festivals or special occasions.[69] They seem to have been held in sufficient esteem that should one be found sleeping on a trail, it was forbidden to walk over it or awaken it.[70]

Certain types of seafood, such as lobster, conches, and particular fish, were always cooked. However, bonito and albacore, as well as certain other fish, were preferred raw.[71] Edmund Fanning appears to have been somewhat taken aback when he observed some Marquesans catching small fry of four to six inches and immediately eating them, starting with the head.[72] When fish were not available, Marquesans substituted seaweed dipped in salt water.[73]

Pit ovens and open fires were also used to prepare a variety of vegetable foods. The tubers of *pia* (*Tacca leontopetaloides* (L.) O. Ktze.) were baked and then beaten into a dough, after which coconut milk was added and the whole boiled by the use of hot stones until curds were formed, indicating that it was ready to eat.[74] Taro (*Colocasia esculenta* (L.) Schott) was either boiled or roasted. Also, perhaps because most was dry grown, the tubers were grated rather than reduced by mashing, and converted into a paste by adding coconut cream.⁷⁵ To the sweet root of *ge* (*Cordyline terminales* (L.) Kunth) was added that of an unidentified fern; the whole was placed in a large pit oven and cooked for about twenty-four hours.⁷⁶ Other mixtures might include sweet potatoes, pia, yams, or taro, to which coconut milk was added to produce a variety of puddings.⁷⁷

While these diverse plants offered variation in the diet, breadfruit remained the dominant, and most depended upon, source of vegetable food. In its simplest form, the fruit was roasted on an open fire, the hard rind peeled off, and the starchy pulp mashed into a paste over which milk of a mature coconut was poured.⁷⁸ A variation of this called for mixing the paste with coconut water to which grated coconut meat had been added. Yet another technique called for wrapping the (presumably peeled) breadfruit in banana leaves and baking it in a pit oven, after which it was eaten with coconut cream.⁷⁹ An epicurean delight reserved for feasts required several days to prepare. It consisted of several breadfruit that had been force-ripened by placing them in a bound tube made of two sheets of tree bark whose ends were sealed by coconut shells. After several days they became soft and sweet. They were then transferred to a long, young banana leaf wrapper, and a quantity of rich coconut cream was poured over them. After being cooked in a pit oven for five or six hours, the mixture was taken out and cooled. Robarts, who described this process, characterized the end results as being sweet and luscious.⁸⁰ Here it is interesting to note that while coconut milk, or the cream extracted from grated coconut meat, was almost always added to these mixtures, Marquesans were not fond of drinking either coconut milk or the bland water of green coconuts, their preference being fresh water.⁸¹

Fermented breadfruit, called *ma*, could be taken directly from its pit and mixed with water to make a refreshing drink that Langsdorff likened to buttermilk.⁸² However, to prepare it as a food required kneading it with water, after which it was wrapped in loaf-shaped leaf packets and baked in a pit oven. The cooked results were mixed with water and beaten in a shallow tray to form a soft paste or dough for eating. According to Robarts, this represented the principal food of Marquesans, who, in times of plenty, would make up enough at one time to last several days.⁸³

Marchand wrote that Marquesan families assembled twice a day, at noon and at dusk, to eat their meals.⁸⁴ However, neither Crook nor Robarts found this to be the case, claiming that Marquesans ate whenever they were hungry, which appeared to be often.⁸⁵ Since they were located well within the tropics, where meat spoiled rapidly, when a pig was cooked, they partook of it five or six times during the same day, assuring its consumption before any deterioration set in.[86] In the absence of personal food bowls or calabashes, leaves served the Marquesans as dishes,[87] and fingers, as effective eating utensils.[88] Finally, regardless of when a common meal was taken, it was customary to include one's deity. This was done by taking a bit of one's food and, after naming one of the gods, tossing the morsel to one side with the comment "This is for you."[89]

DIVERSIONS

Marquesan children had ample diversions from the everyday routine of life. There were kites of dried breadfruit leaves to fly, tops to spin, balls of unspecified material to juggle in the air,[90] and a device reminiscent of the cup-and-ball game. This consisted of a foot-long stick with a six-inch peg protruding vertically at one end. A ball of coconut cord was placed on the point of the peg and made to fly into the air by striking the stick with another piece of wood, the idea being to retrieve the falling ball on the pointed peg.[91] There were also stilts for young people to begin practicing for the day when they might participate in the adult sport of stilt racing at koina festivities.[92] A long rope tied to an overhanging tree limb, and having the middle of a stick securely fastened to its lower end as a seat, made a fine swing, and a cord with a weight fastened at one end served as a form of jumping rope when swung around and around just above the ground.[93] There was also the typical Polynesian game of string figures, or cat's cradle.

In a culture in which war was a dominant feature, it was not surprising that young men teamed up to participate in sham battles and practice the art of accurate throwing by hurling nuts and fruit at one another.[94] Finally, there was always the sea, where most had been introduced as infants to the joy of swimming.[95] However, the use of surfboards appears to have been a historic introduction, the first mention of them in 1813 by Porter, who likened them to those in Hawaii. Here one might suspect the source of this introduction to have been the Hawaiian named Owheve (called Tama by the Marquesans), who left the ship *Alexander*, commanded by Asa Dodge, in February 1798 to live with the Marquesans.[96]

Although wrestling was a simple sport among the young,[97] there is no mention in the early records that adult Marquesans perfected the formalized wrestling and boxing tournaments common in Tonga and Tahiti.[98] In fact, their only arranged public sport involving physical contact was stilt races conducted on tohua courts during festivities. These were popular races on which bets were laid, and a part of the action involved contenders attempting to trip their opponents and thus cause them to fall, much to the delight of the spectators.[99] In a culture imbued with the desire, if not the love, for battle with its neighbors, it is possible that publicly demonstrating one's proclivities in interpersonal fighting was not required, since one's prowess in fighting the enemy was bound to be known and respected. There might also have been the idea that fighting one's tribal kin, even as a public sport, had the potential of developing social rifts that might rupture the rapport required among a tribe's warriors to defeat its enemies. As the record stands, it would appear that, besides stilt racing, the warmongering Marquesans' sense of enjoyable diversions rested on such peaceable entertainments as singing and dancing, occasionally accompanied by drums, the whole often coming together in periodic festivals known as *koina.*

Although E. S. Craighill Handy's 1921–22 ethnographic studies in the Marquesas led him to conclude that both the mouth flute and the nose flute, as well as the musical bow and a form of jew's harp, were indigenous to those islands,[100] there was not a single reference to any of these in the early records with which we are concerned. Considering the length of time spent on those islands by Crook and Robarts, it is difficult to believe that had these instruments existed during their stay, one or the other would not have noted the presence of at least one of them. The evident conclusion is that they were post-1813 introductions. Prior to that date, the only instruments stated to exist were drums and trumpets.[101]

Drums were divided into those used only for ceremonies, war, and religious purposes, and those used during koina festivals. The former were made in two sizes and, like all drums, were carved out of a *tou* (*Cordia subcordata* Lamarck) log. The larger were from five to six feet tall with a fifteen-inch-diameter head made of the skin of a devil ray, or manta. The smaller drums were somewhat over three feet in height with a seven-inch-diameter head of shark skin. The larger instruments were played by striking forceful blows with the fingers held close together. The beat tended to be either regular and "solemn," or to consist of two or three beats followed by a rest. The smaller drums were either beaten with the open hand, the base of the palm striking the rim of the head, or beaten rapidly, using only one finger of each hand. This latter pattern was employed to fill in the rest moments of the larger drums.[102]

Crook described the drums used at koina festivals as being quite small, ranging from two to two feet, four inches in height, with a head diameter ranging from seven to as much as fifteen inches.[103] However, according to Langsdorff, there were others having a height of as much as four and one half feet, with shark-skin-covered heads ranging from one and a half to two feet in diameter.[104] Koina drummers were chosen for their skill, which must have been considerable, since Crook described their range of rhythms to be so varied as to seem quite confusing.[105]

All drums, whether large or small, had a similar design. Their interior, rather than being a hollowed-out cylinder, was formed into two hollow cones, the superior one accounting for three-quarters of the height of the drum. Where the tops of the two cones met in the interior of the instrument, a hole was cut for an air passage. Wide vertical slots were cut through the walls of the lower cone, thus forming, in effect, a ring base for the instrument. The skin forming the head of the drum was stretched across the opening of the upper cone while wet and initially bound by several turns of a flat, plaited coconut fiber rope. When dry, it was firmly laced in place with three-strand plaited coconut cord and the temporary binding was removed.[106]

Most trumpets were referred to as conchs, Marchand identifying one as *Strombus lambis* L.; Langsdorff identified another horn as *Murex tritonis*.[107] The one identified by Marchand had a calabash tube fastened to it as a mouthpiece; the mouthpiece of that noted by Langsdorff consisted of the shell of a candlenut fastened to the small end of the murex shell. Such trumpets were decorated with coconut fiber cord and braided or bunched strands of human hair.[108] Although perhaps it was not common, Marchand described another trumpet on Tahuata that consisted of a bamboo tube to which was fastened, at an acute angle, a smaller bamboo that probably served as a mouthpiece.[109]

At Nukuhiva and Uapou, trumpets were used only for events concerned with war.[110] However, at Tahuata the sound of trumpets was heard not only during war but also during religious ceremonies, including human sacrifices, and as signals of invitation to funeral and other feasts. Crook claimed that Tahuatans often blew their trumpets for sheer amusement; they were also known to blow them from the summit of a trail when visiting another valley, possibly as an identifying signal but also to enjoy the echoes of the horn reverberating off the surrounding slopes.[111]

Drums were not the only source of rhythm for dances and singing. Although apparently limited to males and male singing, different methods of hand clapping served as accompaniments. The loudest of these was produced by holding the left arm close to the body while bringing the forearm across the chest. The right hand was used to slap the hollow thus formed at the inner angle of the left elbow. An alternative that sometimes accompanied the elbow slap was striking the shoulder with the hollow of the bare hand. Another form of clapping, said to have been used in religious ceremonies, was produced by interlacing the fingers of the hands and bringing the hollowed palms sharply together in a rhythmic fashion. Simple clapping with the hands held flat was common for dancing as well as religious ceremonies.[112]

Male singing, depending upon the song and the circumstances, seems to have varied considerably. Krusenstern wrote that it sounded like howling, while Langsdorff described the singing at a koina as a wild sort of cry.[113] Crook, however, probably had it right when he described male singing of story accounts as "violently voiced."[114] At the opposite extreme, singing that appeared to have been of a solemn, ceremonial nature was said to have sounded like droning or humming done in a rather mournful manner, and included moments of silence between some words.[115] Indications are that women did not sing at ceremonies or at koina festivals. However, Robarts wrote of a number of enjoyable evenings with others when groups of young women would entertain them with songs sung a capella. At such times the women were seated, occasionally in circles, on mats and spent the early night hours entertaining with songs on topics ranging from love to war.[116]

Dancing was not limited to koina festivals at tohua dance courts. During a visit with an important chief and his entourage, Fanning noted that at a slight distance from his chiefly gathering was a dancing male dressed in gaudily painted mats decorated, as was his turban, with feathers. His performance continued unabated during the entire time of Fanning's visit with the chief. His performance was explained as being a "friendly dance" customarily performed on such occasions.[117] On another occasion, when an enemy captive had been strangled to death in front of a waiting army, women and girls were said to have performed a "dance of derision" upon his expiring. On more pleasant occasions, during evening singing entertainments by women, one or more males might rise and dance to the songs being sung.[118]

There is no clear indication in the early literature that group dancing in formalized patterns, such as was common in Tonga,[119] was present in the Marquesas. What brief descriptions there are, suggest that many of the dances, even where several dancers were involved, were individual presentations during which each dancer seldom, if ever, moved beyond the particular spot in which he or she was performing.[120] While some leg movements might be involved, most of the movements seem to have been restricted to the arms and fingers.[121] For instance, in one dance observed by Krusenstern, the principal movements consisted of raising the arms in the air and rapidly wiggling the fingers.[122] Langsdorff described one koina in which the dancers, without moving from their location, sprang upward and made quick, pantomimic gestures with their hands and arms. It appeared to him that these motions were attempts to represent common actions of life, such as fishing, slinging stones, swimming, and the like.[123] If his conjecture was correct, it would seem that at least some of Marquesan dancing had affinities with the well-known hula dances of Hawaii.

THE KOINA

Such features as drumming, clapping, singing, and occasionally the sound of conch trumpets as a special element of welcome came together in periodic koina festivals held on tohua courts. By 1921 the word "koina" had come to mean either a feast or a festival, and both functions were thought to have taken place on tohua courts.[124] However, in Roberts's time (1798–1806), a koina was identified as a "ball, play dancing,"[125] and the word for "feast" was quite different.[126] Although feasting might occur as part of a koina, that was not always the case. Crook wrote that visitors attending such a festival carried a scant supply of food with them, and usually received an equally scant amount at the site of the koina. This, he explained, was understandable in light of the fact that visitors might number as many as ten thousand. In addition, there was also the occasional problem that tribal land on which a koina was scheduled to take place might have been virtually denuded of food crops as the result of a recent incursion by an enemy.[127] This would suggest that there were preordained locations for particular festivals, regardless of local conditions. However, we do know that there were koina at the time of the major breadfruit harvest and at the terminating festival for a deceased tau'a or chief when large amounts of food were offered to the guests.[128]

As for feasts unassociated with koina, early records suggest that they were not held at tohua courts. For example, Robarts's description of the feast given upon the death of an important individual represented it as having been served on the family altar, meaning the taboo house. In addition, two other references by Robarts to feasts that did not include the koina type of entertainment appear not to have been associated with a tohua.[129] In fact, the raised platforms in front of many homes were said to be used on occasion as feasting areas.[130] In other words, feasts alone were not seen as equivalent to a koina, nor were they necessarily associated with a tohua, except when serving as an element of a koina.

Koina celebrated weddings, the birth of a prominent woman's first child, the initiation of tattooing of the son of a haka'iki, or high chief, and the arrival at puberty of the daughter of an upper-class family. Koina also constituted the final ritual following the death of a chief or a tau'a.[131] However, there were other koina mentioned by the early European visitors for which no specific reason was elucidated. Such was the one attended by Crook at Aakapa,[132] as well as those apparently required during specific periods that were important enough to serve as a respected reason to accept a temporary truce during a war.[133] At least some of these must have been of a religious nature and tied to periods of the year recognized by the Marquesans as critical to their well-being. Although the specifics of the Marquesan calendar were never explained, Crook noted that their year was divided into seasons based upon the ripening of breadfruit, as well as the passage of the sun directly over their heads in October and February. The first appearance on the horizon of certain stars and constellations also seems to have played a part in these determinations. Each successive moon appearance was given its own name, as was each day of a single moon period.[134]

That the seasons of breadfruit ripening were a determining time factor for certain koina was made clear by Langsdorff. He was told that on the occasion of the major breadfruit harvest, which would have been in January or February, chiefs and principal people arranged a number of koina.[135] It would also seem insignificant in this regard that the koina at Aakapa attended by Crook was in August.[136] This would have approximated the time of the third, and final, limited harvest of breadfruit, after which the trees "rested" before beginning to bear fruit again in October. That this particular koina was an important occasion of religious significance was reflected not only by the attendance of an estimated ten thousand people distributed among three tohua but also by the fact that the festivities were opened by a religious ceremony.[137]

The tohua in which koina were celebrated was essentially a stadium. Its dominant feature was a flat, rectangular dance space that might be paved.[138] While the location of some tohua took advantage of the flat floors of valleys, others were built on sloping ground and obtained their level surface by terracing. An additional feature was one or more raised platforms adjacent to the sides of the dance floor.[139] A simple tohua might have only one platform situated on one of its longer sides, while more elaborate ones were enclosed on both sides and ends by such structures, all of which served as seats for spectators.[140] Some of the larger and more important tohua had guest houses on these platforms. These were large, well built, and decorated, some being open across their front, presumably for better viewing of the dancers.[141] In some tohua, the local chief's house enclosed one end of the dance court.[142] Whether this constituted his permanent residence or was reserved for his personal use at times of a koina is not clear. Although the principal use of tohua was for koina celebrations, that of a tribal chief might also be used in times of danger as an assembly area for consultations with warriors.[143]

The singing and dancing at koina were regarded as the most pleasurable of Marquesan experiences. People would travel from the most distant part of an island to attend such festivities, and some who could manage it, might sail to other islands to attend similar events.[144] All visitors were welcome, even tribal enemies. However, the latter never came totally unarmed, a sling being worn around the head as a passive but available weapon. This, plus the tendency to group together rather than to mingle, was a precautionary measure against duplicity on the part of the hosts. While the event perhaps was not common, should a local tau'a suddenly be seized by a spirit and go into a trance, all entertainment ceased and, apparently, the avowed safety of all guests was immediately canceled, thus allowing hostilities suddenly to erupt.[145]

To prepare for participation in a koina, the women washed off the juice of the papa vine that they used to lighten their skin, and anointed their bodies with coconut oil. Occasionally this was mixed with the liquid expressed from turmeric, which heightened the fairness of their skin. The ka'ioi, or male dancers, occasionally used the papa juice to lighten their skin in preparation for a koina. However, when the time for dancing arrived, they covered their bodies with the customary mixture of coconut oil and turmeric and donned an especially large loincloth. When it was available, they would substitute for the oil mixture the orange color derived from baked turmeric, using it to paint various figures on their bodies.[146] To accomplish this they mixed the baked turmeric coloring with the shiny, soapy pulp, or saponin, from the fruit of the kokuu, or soapberry.[147] Both sexes adorned themselves with a wide variety of ornaments on their hands, feet, head, neck, and ears.[148]

Entertainment on the tohua court appears to have been during daylight hours, and consisted not only of dancing and singing but also of stilt racing, the runners having been well fed for the occasion and tabooed from intercourse with their wives for three days previous to the races.[149] Evenings, according to Crook, were spent enjoying entertainment in the visitors' houses or, as on another koina occasion, casually enjoying two or three individual dancers in the home of the local chief.[150] Although women seem not to have been altogether tabooed from dancing in the tohua, they may have had certain limitations, since Robarts explained how the women at one koina danced on fine mats in front of their houses while warriors danced on the main court.[151] However, it seems that they were definitely tabooed from that part of the court designated for the male singers and drummers.[152]

While it would seem that most koina dances were, in the eyes of Europeans, circumspect though strange, there was one female dance that Jean Baptiste Cabri seems to have overexaggerated in his description of it to Langsdorff. It was one in which, he insisted, women of rank danced naked and gave occasion for many "violations of decorum" for the entertainment of their guests.[153] This would appear to have been the dance earlier described by Crook. In this the women, wearing only the large kahu carefully gathered around them in folds, were virtually forced to let it fall open in front, revealing their nakedness, since the dance required the full movement of their hands and fingers. Crook explained that such a revelation was not considered lewd and that the women did not indulge in any of the "lascivious" movements encountered in the dances on other islands, which probably referred to those of Tahiti.[154] With the termination of the joys of a koina, Marquesans returned to their homes, looking forward to the next festival, wherever it might be located.

CHAPTER 6

From Birth to Death

By the very nature of birth there could be no question of whom a Marquesan child's mother might be. However, that could not be said with assurance when it came to identifying its natural father. At least that was certainly the case among the upper classes for which we have data. As will be described further on, this was not due to overly adulterous wives but mostly to the Marquesan system of unequal age betrothal and the socially acceptable custom of upper-class women maintaining a head servant and incidental sex partner, or several in sequence, both before and after marriage. What was important was that, regardless of male parentage, the husband of the mother accepted the newborn child as his own, with all of the privileges that went to an offspring. It was quite distinct from the Tahitian attempt to keep the chiefly bloodline clear through infanticide, or the Tongan system of giving a newborn the rank of the mother.[1]

As a woman approached the time for parturition, a small taboo house was built near her dwelling for the occasion, and various ceremonies were conducted for the purpose of easing her through labor. Should she be of a wealthy family, a tau'a, usually a woman, might be hired to recite incantations designed to ease the birth. This seems to have been an unnecessary precaution, for childbirth was said to have been easy, with labor rarely lasting over half an hour. A woman, who might be the pregnant woman's mother or a close relative, served as midwife. She and the expectant mother were placed on a large sheet of bark cloth; and the latter, or at times both women, were covered by a similar sheet during the actual birth.[2]

While G. H. von Langsdorff claimed that only women were allowed to be present at a birth,[3] at least in the case of the firstborn child of a woman of "distinction," this was hardly the case. Her principal male relations were on hand to participate in a unique and symbolic rite. Should such relations be of the taboo class, they would first render themselves common by anointing their bodies with coconut oil, after which they would prostrate themselves beneath the sheet covering the women. The purpose was to allow the expectant mother to sit upon their heads during parturition. Other members of the taboo class who had not made themselves common might also be present as witnesses, but did not participate in the rite.[4]

Immediately after birth the mother went to the nearest stream to bathe; the child was carried separately by a woman, probably the midwife, to the same stream to be washed. After this cleansing, at Nukuhiva, the child was covered all over with the dark green juice of the papa vine (*Rhynchosia minima* (L.) DC.). However, because this liquid was said to have a strong odor, the juice from the leaves of kokuu (*Sapindus saponaria* L.) or nono (*Morinda citrifolia* L.) were occasionally substituted. However, on the windward islands this use of the papa juice was more restricted, being limited to the child's navel, and continued only until the navel cord parted.[5]

Upon the birth of a child, the husband, being the acknowledged father, celebrated the event by baking a pig that only he was permitted to eat. Urey Lisiansky was told that from the time of birth until the parting of the umbilical cord, no one could enter or leave the dwelling that housed the child.[6] However, with the parting of the cord, a second pig was killed and friends were invited to partake of the meal.[7] It was probably this event that precipitated the koina said to have occurred upon the occasion of a woman giving birth to her first child. Such an outstanding celebration was undoubtedly limited to the wealthier upper class who could afford the extravagance. However, regardless of status, a Marquesan woman acquired a new name on the occasion of the birth of her first child.[8]

With the probable exception of the landless lowest class, at the birth of a child its parents presented it with an inheritance thought sufficient to give it a degree of security during its lifetime. In the case of the wealthy, this might be a parcel of land; for the less well-to-do, it could amount to one or two breadfruit trees; and if they were too poor to own a tree, the parents would immediately plant one for the child. The choice of breadfruit over other food-producing plants was based upon the surmise that the yield from one or two trees was sufficient to support an individual for one year.[9] Such trees were restricted to their owner; William P. Crook explained that by the time a daughter could clothe herself, she could no longer eat the fruit from her mother's tree, nor could her mother eat that from the tree of her daughter.[10] Whether a similar restriction applied to father and son or other members of the family was never discussed.

THE YOUTHFUL YEARS

A. J. von Krusenstern wrote that with few exceptions, mothers never suckled their young but simply turned them over to relatives.[11] However, his fellow traveler, Langsdorff, and some years earlier Étienne Marchand, presented quite the opposite view.[12] There seems to have been no fixed time for weaning, some babies being fed *popoi* and raw fish within a few months after birth.[13] Should the mother have trouble weaning her child, she encouraged the process by putting a bitter substance on her nipples or tying a bit of bark cloth around them.[14]

While still quite young, children were treated with tender fondness, and among families that could afford it, they were turned over to the care of servants. In the latter situation, attention to the youngster's well-being was assured by the knowledge that any neglect resulting in harm to the child could result in death to its appointed guardian. However, as the children grew older and could manage for themselves, parental care and restraint were relaxed, and the young were free to wander their neighborhood.[15]

During their early ambulatory years, children were taught by constraint not to render things taboo by their unwitting actions. As in some other islands of Polynesia, the head of an individual was not to be touched by others.[16] In the Marquesas this was extended so that anything passed over the head of an individual became tabooed and had to be destroyed or kept in a taboo house. To continue using such an object was said to result in exposing the person over whose head it had passed to a potentially fatal illness. However, there was an upper limit to this restriction, since food, for example, was deemed not to be contaminated if hung at an unspecified height above the head of an individual.[17] For women and children there was also the additional interdiction that avowed that anything they walked over, including the place where food was cooked, could no longer be used.[18] This was only the beginning of a longer list of restrictions that would be learned as a child matured.

By the age of six or seven, children's former freedom from clothing gave way to traditional forms of dress, the boys putting on or loincloth, and the girls a kahu, or bark cloth robe. At this those girls who had a "taste for appearance" became concerned with maintaining a light complexion. The process was a bit restrictive. The tanning effect of the sun was forestalled by spending much of the time indoors, or using the leaf of a banana or a fan palm (*Pritchardia pacifica* Seem. and Wendl.), occasionally decorated with colorful feathers, as a parasol when outdoors. Even the daily bath became a nighttime activity. To lighten the skin further, the bleaching effect of the juice of the papa vine, which was said to whiten even hair, was applied to the entire body each morning, a custom some women followed into old age. There was even a mixture of sap from three different plants to be applied if one's skin became too tanned. For unexplained reasons, the papa extract was invariably washed off when a woman was to participate in a feast, a public entertainment, or a religious rite.[19] While only a conjecture, the fact that the juice was dark green and was said to have a strong odor may have necessitated bathing when one was to join the company of others.[20] As Crook noted, the girls always washed off the liquid when the island was about to be visited by a foreign ship.[21]

By the time a boy reached the age of eight or nine, the operation of supercision was performed, using the sharp edge of a fragment of stone. The surgeon conducting the operation was tabooed until the prepuce of the young patient had healed. However, during his tabooed state the surgeon was well fed on pork, and at the conclusion was presented with a pig. How this operation was handled, let alone paid for, by the poorer class was never recorded. However, in this regard it should be noted that Crook explained that the operation was not compulsory, although those who had not conformed in this regard were called *pea*, or nasty.[22]

Although the operation of supercision was designed to expose the glans penis, revealing the latter in public when swimming or on any occasion requiring the removal of the loincloth seems to have been regarded as unseemly. In such situations the split foreskin was pulled over the glans penis and temporarily tied together by a bit of bark cloth.[23] I encountered this concealing of the glans penis from public exposure among my laborers on Easter Island in 1955, on the occasion of their gathering shellfish for me. In this instance the means of hiding the glans penis was simply to place the organ between one's legs, even though the result made wading in the rock-studded surf a

...revalent this custom was, or is, in Poly-
... supercision seems not to have been accom-
..., this was not the case when a young man
... became eligible for tattooing. However, based
... would appear that it was not the arrival of man-
...nificant but the inception of tattooing, which then
...sible. This was made clear by Crook's mention that
...men of fifteen or sixteen years of age were not yet tat-
tooe... ...at this was true of one chief's son whose age he reckoned to be tw... ...ty-three or twenty-four years.[24] In addition, David Porter gave eighteen or nineteen as the accepted age for men and women to begin being tattooed.[25] Since the tattooing artist had to be paid, it is understandable that some of the lower classes were never tattooed.[26] However, lack of means to pay alone would not seem to explain the observation that many of the natives on Uapou lacked tattooing, and that the natives of an entire valley on Hivaoa were not tattooed.[27] Nonetheless, for those who chose, or were required by class or tradition, to be tattooed, the commencement of this artistic ordeal was said to represent one of the most important occasions in the lives of at least the males.[28]

When the son of the high chief, Keatonue, undertook to be tattooed, it was cause for days of public festivities. He was placed with his tattooer in a house tabooed to everyone except those males who were allowed to enter by permission of the high chief. During the several weeks of his initial tattooing by his specialist, both men were fed the best foods. However, this was but the beginning of a lengthy ordeal, since from then on, additional sessions of tattooing would take place several months apart. Young men of less than superior rank had access to special tabooed houses maintained by tattoo specialists who were paid in pigs, the number depending upon the wealth of the customer's family and the extent of the design desired. Women, who were never extensively tattooed, were never offered a tabooed house, the tattooing being administered at home or wherever she might choose. The poor who owned no pigs with which to pay a specialist were forced to rely on apprentices who accepted less valuable payment in order to practice and improve their artistry.[29]

Whereas the commencement of tattooing, rather than puberty, was the time of celebrations for a man, for a young woman of the upper class such festivities occurred upon the appearance of her first menses. This time was attended with special rites, and she taken to an undescribed, tabooed location.[30] It may have been at this time or soon after that she was given a male servant to cohabit with her. Such a servant, known as a *pekio,* was thenceforth regarded as superior to other male servants. Should his mistress eventually marry a man of property, she could choose to take her pekio with her or acquire another to take his place.[31] It is thus no surprise that unmarried girls were reported to be quite free in their sexual activities.[32] However, Edward Robarts implied that there were other women of lesser rank for whom this freedom may have had a price. He explained that the loss of virginity was no hindrance in getting a husband, provided a girl was of rank.[33]

Robarts left the impression that life for the young and unmarried of the upper classes was one of singing, dancing, and partying.[34] This may have been the case for some, but there must have been periods for others to learn the practical as well as the esoteric aspects of their society. For those who would become tau'a there were techniques of deity visitation ritual to learn; for tuhuna ota ogo priests, besides formalized ritual patterns to learn, there were the many songs of traditional histories to be memorized. These are but two examples, and one can recognize many more cultural aspects that required some form of learning activity. Regrettably, such educational procedures failed to be either noticed or recorded. Only Robarts explained how, from time to time, warriors would train boys in the use of slings (with large nuts in place of stones) and teach them how to conduct themselves in war by arranging sham battles using blunted spears.[35]

While the less obvious educational endeavors went unrecorded, the dress and functioning of the young male public entertainers, known as ka'ioi, were sufficiently in evidence for Crook to have indulged his curiosity about them. However, Robarts seems not to have perceived them as a specialized group of males, which is what they appear to have been. According to Crook, they were, along with women and their male servants and pekio, restricted to the common class, as distinct from the elitist and privileged all-male taboo class. As such, they were free to eat with women and other members of their class but could not touch any food or food containers of the taboo class. While women's male servants and pekio were restricted to the common class because of their immediate and perhaps demeaning association with women, the reason for the ka'ioi restriction appears more tenuous. It would seem to be their occasional use of the papa juice employed by women to lighten their skin, which denoted a shared association with the opposite sex.

Over years of oral transmission, descriptions of the ka'ioi, their purpose, and even their makeup as a group have drifted far from the simple, and only, early explanation of their place in Marquesan society. In 1920–21 the ethnologist E. S. Craighill Handy was given to understand by his Marquesan informants that ka'ioi were an unorganized group of young unmarried males and females. They were described as overly addicted to painting themselves with a yellow dye and being primarily interested in moving throughout the valleys, searching for amusement, singing romantic and erotic love songs, enjoying abundant sex, being somehow connected with tattooing, and being involved with festivals.[36] However, at the time of ka'ioi existence, Crook found them to be made up of males from various social ranks and economic levels. Their specialties were singing and dancing at public festivals. On such occasions they wore large loinclothes and decorated their bodies with the yellow dye of turmeric or the deeper orange coloring derived from baking the rhizome, and adorned themselves with a wide range of ornaments.[37]

In essence, Crook's record describes the ka'ioi as men specializing in entertainment just as other Marquesan men specialized in crafts or rituals, their only difference being their exclusion from the ranks of the taboo class. As noted elsewhere in this volume, although young women enjoyed singing, and some participated in dancing at koina festivals, there is no early indication that they were a part of some generalized partygoing group known as ka'ioi. In that regard, the similarities of Handy's characterization of the ka'ioi to the Tahitian 'arioi society suggests the distinct possibility that accounts of this latter society had been introduced into the Marquesas in historic times and incorporated into the orally transmitted legendary explanations of the long-defunct group of ka'ioi entertainers.[38]

MARRIAGE AND DIVORCE

Some betrothals and marriages between the chiefly classes of different tribes were made as a critical element in solidifying an alliance of cooperation and peace. However, such marital arrangements did not always assure peace between two tribes. Nonetheless, they had the advantage of securing protection for members of the two families involved, in the event of hostilities. In case of capture, one would be recognized as a relative by marriage and allowed to go free.[39] Thus, the more tribes were included in betrothals and marriages, the safer it became for the members of the families involved to travel through territories other than their own.

In such alliances neither the consent nor the age or age difference of the couple to be betrothed or married was considered. Nor were such arrangements limited to the chiefly class. Crook mentioned cases where an adult woman was betrothed to a mere boy or even an infant. In such cases, the woman was allowed to accept as many pekio in succession as pleased her, and all resulting children were regarded as belonging to her future husband.[40] There were also betrothals of couples who had not yet reached the age of puberty. One alliance described by Crook involved the betrothal of the eight-year-old son of the Tahuata chief, Teinae, to the daughter of the chief of the Piggena tribe of Hivaoa, who was still being breast-fed by her mother. Such a betrothal, at least in this case, involved a series of discussions and exchanges of presents, and ended with a final gift of valuable articles being taken by Teinae and his entourage to the Piggena tribe on Hivaoa.[41]

The only general description of a wedding between two chiefly families was left us by Robarts. It involved the marriage of the three- or four-year-old son of one chief to the already pregnant daughter of the other. The match was inaugurated by the groom's family sending notice of the desired union to the parents of the intended bride. Upon acceptance, several days were devoted, probably by both families, to preparing food, making bark cloth, and gathering flowers and sandalwood, the latter most likely to scent coconut oil. On the day of the wedding, the groom's entourage made their way to the bride's dwelling, where their approach was signaled by the beating of a drum as all were ushered into the home. In the meantime the bride's mother, in a gesture symbolizing great respect, had laid her usually untouchable robe upon the floor for her daughter and future son-in-law to sit on. As they did so, the sacred me'ae drum was brought by several tuhuna ota ogo priests and their assistants; while one beat the drum, the others offered appropriate ceremonial songs in their priestly dialect. After several hours of this rite, the bride's relatives brought forth a large feast including pig and fish, after which the assembly was called by drum to a tohua. Here they danced until sundown. The day ended in the bride's home, where all enjoyed singing throughout the night.

Within a day or so the father of the groom, along with other attendants, returned to the site of the wedding to visit the bride and groom and to distribute a variety of gifts. This was reason for yet another feast that lasted several days. It was now time for the groom's father to take his son and daughter-in-law home to his estate. There the groom's relatives provided yet another feasting and festival occasion during which the different ranks of ladies of the estate welcomed the bride. At the close of this final celebration, the bride went through the final act of choosing her pekio. A young man was appointed as a potential pekio, and the two retired beneath the robe of the bride, who was supplied with a bowl of food. As the two proceeded to eat from the same bowl, the young man was required to act as if he were her servant. If she accepted him, she signified her decision by offering him a part of some food in her hand that she was about to eat. If this did not happen, it was a sign that he was rejected and the bride was free to choose another as her pekio.[42] All pekio of married women were regarded as belonging to both the husband and the wife. While some appear to have been of the servant class, others were well-to-do and of a higher station. For example, Keatonue's pekio was said to own large properties and was also toa, or head warrior, of Keatonue's forces.[43]

While the above obviously described a wedding of the upper class, marriage based upon affection between couples of comparable ages also took place; Porter claimed that girls seldom married before the age of nineteen or twenty.[44] Lisiansky suggested that some marriages were based upon mutual consent of the two parties. However, he went on to explain that if the girl refused such an arrangement, the young man might go to her parents to request her hand. Their consent required that he live in the home of the girl and her parents for a given length of time. Should all go well, the marriage was concluded by the couple leaving her parents and setting up their own home.[45] Quite probably the rite of marriage varied with the rank and wealth of the families involved. In some cases where a man and a woman agreed to live together as a married couple, the only formal act was an exchange of gifts between the groom and the bride's parents. In yet another report, the ceremony of marriage consisted simply of a feast.[46]

Although women were free to have sex with whom they pleased prior to marriage, any adulterous acts on their part after marriage, except with the pekio, could result in severe punishment by their husbands.⁴⁷ Since women seem to have had no comparable redress against a wayward husband except resentment, some employed an act seemingly designed to generate social pressure against their husband's infidelities. They attempted suicide by swallowing the poisonous berry of the 'eva.⁴⁸ Had the berry been chewed, the effects would have been fatal. However, by swallowing the fruit whole and calling attention to such an act of desperation, the woman knew that a tuhuna ota ogo priest would be called and, by administering a concoction of the flowers of 'oute (*Hibiscus rosa-sinensis* L.), would induce vomiting and thus cause the berry to be expelled with no harm done.⁴⁹ How common male infidelities were is not known. However, Crook noted that the haka'iki, Keatonue, boasted of having children by other men's wives; two of them lived in his family, and a third had been adopted by another member of the chiefly class.⁵⁰

Adoptions appear to have been common in the Marquesas and were not limited to children; Crook was adopted by the Tahuata chief Teinae, with all the perquisites of that position.⁵¹ Yet another form of acquiring a child was described by Robarts. Should a young unmarried woman be known to be pregnant, a family having an unmarried son and desiring an additional child would send their son to the girl with a present and a family request for the forthcoming child. If she agreed, the young man slept with her that night and left the following morning, perhaps never returning. This act was accepted as a symbolic recognition that he was now the father of the forthcoming child. Food and more gifts were sent to the woman during her pregnancy. Upon the birth of the child, the son's mother immediately accepted the newborn as, in effect, her grandchild and took it to live with her. Without even the dismissal rite of divorce, the real mother was now free to marry whom she pleased.⁵² In fact, divorce was said to be a simple matter of a husband dismissing his wife,⁵³ although Langsdorff and Lisiansky claimed that such a separation was a matter of consent by both parties.⁵⁴ Perhaps economic position and rank made the difference in method.

ILLNESS AND MEDICAL PRACTICES

Only Crook left a record of the variety of ills suffered by Marquesans. Boils were common, and an occasional breaking out of pustules between the fingers was thought to result from the spell of a sorcerer. Some natives suffered from kidney stones or gallstones, and an occasional attack of dropsy was said to occur as a result of having eaten tabooed fruit. There were two frequent and seriously debilitating diseases. One consisted of a thick scaling of skin, especially around the ears, which was accompanied by a gradual loss of the use of one's limbs as well as a strange backward bending of the fingers. The other appears to have been leprosy, since Crook described it as affecting the fingers and toes in a manner that gave the appearance of their having been cut off at the joints.[55] Strengthening this identification of the disease is Robarts's claim a few years later that leprosy was present.[56] For Marquesans the occurrence of leprosy was caused by a person's having come in contact with a woman's menstrual discharge.[57] In addition to these ailments, Crook mentioned an unidentifiable disease called *mokeyo,* and also noted the loss of eyesight among a few natives.[58]

What remedies, if any, were employed in efforts to cure the above maladies is not known. However, there were treatments for other ailments. Robarts mentioned women massaging his weary muscles, and having the pain of his sunburn blisters alleviated by liquid obtained from the crushed leaves of an unidentified plant,[59] and Crook described how the yellow juice pressed from the bud of the *mi'o* (*Thespesia populnea* (L.) Sol.) was used on the chafed skin of children.[60] Seawater taken internally was a popular medicament.[61]

Unrecognized illness was attributed to sorcery or the actions of displeased atua, or gods. Since tau'a were capable of being in direct contact with such gods, they were called upon to intercede on a patient's behalf.[62] Sometimes this was simply a matter of the tau'a determining what had infuriated the pertinent god and deciding the penance required of the patient.[63] In more drastic cases different action was called for. In one instance Crook described how a patient had been placed in water, after which the tau'a invoked the god while beating the water with tree branches and pouring additional water over the head of his patient. Such god-inflicted misery was a time for women to assemble in the home of the ill person and sing the same mournful songs as when greeting a wounded warrior or seeing off a departing friend. If the patient took a turn for the worse, they dispensed with the singing and indulged in a ritual of wild, naked dancing replete with lamentations and the cutting of their bodies with sharp stones.[64]

Except for cases of spiritual healing, all important medical assistance, including surgery, was performed by tuhuna ota ogo priests.

Some, like the high chief Keatonue, who was also such a priest, were experts at setting broken bones and employing protective splints.[65] Their surgical instruments were minimal, a bit of bone serving as a probe and a shark's tooth satisfying the diverse purposes of lancet, splinter extractor, and, in the case of a fractured skull, a trephine.[66] Since surgeons were also priests, it was no surprise that before undertaking an operation, they would raise their instruments upward to the atua in a gesture of dependence upon supernatural assistance in the success of their operation.[67]

DEATH AND BURIAL

Robarts listed the natural causes of death in the Marquesas as old age, leprosy, childbirth, and starvation during periods of drought and resulting famine.[68] However, intermittent warfare, the need for human sacrificial victims on certain occasions, interpersonal strife, and an occasional suicide accounted for others. The latter, usually the result of a quarrel, was accomplished by hanging, jumping from the top of a coconut palm, or chewing the poisonous fruit and seed of the 'eva.[69] For those captured and slain as a result of warfare or the need for human sacrifices, there were no personal funeral rites with corpse preparation and final deposition. However, in cases where a corpse was lacking there may have been some form of recognition of the departed. Robarts wrote of having made a voyage to Tahuata and, returning to Nukuhiva later than expected, finding the "Old Queens" house dressed out in mourning in the belief that he had been lost at sea.[70]

For those other than a high chief and a tau'a, the recorded rites pertaining to death and disposal varied. Primarily, this was in the treatment and final disposition of the corpse, and in the location and (probably) the size of the accompanying feast. As with other aspects of Marquesan life, such differences probably reflected the status and wealth of the departed. The initial activity upon the death of an individual was to wash the corpse and place it upon a bier that might be a wooden plank or a platform of bamboo raised inside the deceased's dwelling.[71] Then the women assembled for the acts of ritualized mourning of weeping and cutting themselves. To the consternation of European observers, such actions were periodically suspended, at which time the women carried on normal conversations, as if nothing had happened.[72]

At, or immediately after, this mourning rite, tuhuna ota ogo priests arrived with their sacred drums and began offering incantations in their special dialect. During this time the most important social event of a funeral, the feast, was being prepared and guests were being invited to gather and partake of the offering. The size and personal ranking of such an assembly, as well as the amount and kinds of food offered, must have varied with the position and wealth of the deceased's extended family. In addition, if the deceased had been a member of the tabooed class, the feast and remaining rituals would be conducted in his tabooed house and grounds, from which women were excluded.[73]

Crook has left the most complete description of what must have been the funeral feast of a high-ranking man of the taboo class. As the feast was being prepared, a "principal" man assumed the duty of inviting the proper guests for the occasion. The fan he carried in his hand, as well as his costume—consisting of bark cloth, various ornaments, and an especially large loincloth—symbolized his position and purpose. Thus dressed, he proceeded to the homes of the priests and members of the upper classes, inviting them to the feast.[74] In the meantime, one of two types of coffins may have been completed. One type consisted of a log that had been hollowed out except for its ends and that could be closed by a neatly fitted lid held in place by bindings of coconut fiber cord.[75] The other type, said to be just as acceptable, was a board whose upper surface had been made slightly concave.[76] If one of these had been completed, the corpse was placed in or upon the container and carried to the sacred taboo grounds, where it was laid in a small house or a loft raised off the ground by several posts. Since Crook mentioned that such a loft might be placed near the house of the deceased, rather than in tabooed ground, and Porter specifically states that a female corpse was placed in a house vacated for that purpose, it would appear likely that the bodies of women, if not all commoners, were forbidden to be placed in areas normally tabooed to them when living.[77] If a coffin had not been completed in time for the feast, the corpse was carried to its appropriate place and at the termination of the feast was committed to its special container.[78]

As the assembly gathered, the men congregated at the taboo house of the deceased while the women, all finely dressed, were restricted to the grounds beyond the tabooed area, where they served as spectators. In the meantime the tuhuna ota ogo priests, continuing their chanting, proceeded to construct small shrines in front of the taboo house. Using the white wood of *Hibiscus tiliaceus* L., twisted leaves of coconut palms, and bits of white bark cloth, they created various forms, some imitating their own houses. To these they added miniature urns of coconut leaves that they placed along the sides of the shrines, and coconut shell containers filled with food for the departed spirit were placed within the shrines. During all of this time the chanting continued, and no one could touch the edibles or even light a fire within sight of the priests until they had completed their chant. Only then could the feast begin.[79]

The feast was always on the day of death or the following day, a practice once shared by the people of Easter Island.[80] It featured quantities of pork, at least for those wealthy enough to have pigs. It also included varieties of puddings, taro, and breadfruit served on leaves.[81] The master of the family cut up the pig and saw to the proper distribution of its parts.[82] The head was dedicated to the propitiation of the gods, as a means of assuring a safe passage for the spirit of the deceased to its final destination in the "lower regions." Probably for this reason the head was given to the officiating priest, who put it aside and was given a different cut of meat for his immediate use. The statement that he later consumed the head suggests he may have taken it to his me'ae for final ritual dedication.[83] At least this would explain the finding by Yosihiko Sinoto of more than ten pig skulls buried in front of a me'ae in Hane Valley, Uahuka.[84] The hindquarter of the hog was reserved for the tribal chief, who, if not present, was sent that portion.[85] In addition, Robarts claimed that portions of the feast were sent to the priests of the principal me'ae, who placed samples of each food on the head of a particular sacred wooden image.[86] The remaining joints of the pigs were distributed to the "principal" people, who shared their allotment with others of, presumably, lower rank.[87]

A special feature of the funeral feast was the requirement that it continue until all food had been eaten. Thus, when one became surfeited, it was only necessary to set aside what was left of one's food and return some hours later to continue the meal. Such a routine, which often required additional cooking of the usually undercooked pork, might occasionally last into the following day.[88] If the deceased had been a member of the taboo class, his funeral ritual and feast were at his tabooed platform, which thus excluded women and, presumably, other members of the common class.[89] While never made clear, it would seem probable that the funeral feast for a member of the common class would have been available to women and other commoners.

With the termination of the funeral feast it was the duty of the nearest relatives to maintain a vigil over the remains.[90] For some this meant carrying the body to the family burial ground, or me'ae, where it was left exposed on a wooden platform until it wasted away. In other cases the nearest kin spent weeks rubbing the corpse with coconut oil as a means of limited preservation. Unlike comparable Tahitian practices, no evisceration seems to have been employed.[91] Near some burial shelters, or lofts, where bodies were maintained were several plain or carved low wood or stone pillars, on top of each of which rested a flat stone disk. This latter served as a platform on which were placed small shrines and provisions for the spirit of the deceased and, no doubt, functioned as an effective rat guard as well.[92] Symbols of the deceased's occupation or rank when living may also have been included. Deceased warriors lying in state had their weapons placed nearby.[93]

Unfortunately, there is a paucity in the early historic records regarding the final disposition of the dead. Krusenstern, apparently referring to exposed bodies, reported that twelve months after the first funeral feast, a second one was given. At this time the remaining bones of the corpse were broken into pieces and placed in a box made of breadfruit wood that was then sequestered in the me'ae.[94] Porter recounted a modified version of this, stating that the remaining bones were cleaned, after which some were kept as relics and the remainder deposited in the me'ae.[95] Although Robarts claimed that only the corpses of lepers were buried,[96] Lisiansky and Langsdorff were made to understand that in the event of war, the dead were buried in order to keep the enemy from taking the bones for their personal use.[97] However, such records do not fully account for the skeletons Robarts encountered in caves, the numerous preserved coffins placed on protected ledges that were seen by Linton, or the primary earth burials reported by Sinoto.[98] Time, rank, circumstances of death, and even tribal or island differences may well account for this range of customs. Whatever the final dispositions may have been, the people of high status did not forget their dead. It was their custom occasionally to offer feasts in memory of those who were long departed.[99]

Although there are no early accounts of the rituals involved with the death of a high chief, or haka'iki, and only fragments of information about those involving the demise of a tau'a, we do know that both terminated with a koina.[100] As described in the chapter on religion, a tau'a death demanded human sacrifices. In addition there was a seven-day tabooing of his valley during which no fires could be lit and women were not allowed to leave their homes.[101] While friends and relatives attended funeral feasts of the secular dead, only tau'a, tuhuna ota ogo priests, and their assistants could partake of the food of a tau'a funeral feast.[102] What followed the rites of human sacrifice and the traditional partaking of food is known only to the extent that rituals of some sort continued for two or three months. At their close, preparations for a terminating koina were declared.

While tohua, or festival courts or plazas, must have existed in many, if not most, major island valleys, Robarts implies that in this situation the construction of a new court was required. This, along with other preparations, required at least six months.[103] This was a time for young women to assemble at the ends of the new court to learn or practice their dances, and for their mothers to prepare great quantities of white bark cloth for their daughters' fanciful costumes. On the day of feasting, a young woman of special beauty opened the festivities by being ushered onto the tohua grounds with the beating of drums, the blowing of conch shell horns, and a ritualistic war whoop given the customary three times. As young women began dancing on fine mats in front of their guest houses, numerous warriors, rather than the celebrated ka'ioi professional dancers, took to dancing on the court. All around, and in the surrounding guest houses, people from throughout the island, even enemies from other tribes, mingled as welcome guests. For three days the feast of whole hogs, fish, and plant foods was free to all. Or was it? Robarts finished his description of this special koina by noting that during this time, men of rank guarded the mountaintops and passes to prevent the "common people" from committing depredations.[104]

CHAPTER 7

The Quest for Food

DOMESTICATED CROPS

Although James Cook's naturalist, George Forster, set foot only on the island of Tahuata in the Marquesas, his observation that "Their food consists of the same variety of fruits and roots which are common at Tahiti, except the apple (*Spondias*)"[1] was essentially correct for the other populated islands of the archipelago. Crook also found the "apple," *Spondias dulces* (Soland. ex.) Parkinson, still lacking in the Marquesas in 1797–98. In 1804 G. H. von Langsdorff reported its limited presence on Nukuhiva, thus suggesting a historic introduction of this fruit.[2] The Marquesans shared with Tahitians an inordinate fondness for breadfruit. However, unlike them, the Marquesans appear to have lacked an inherent urge to cultivate their land beyond what they deemed necessary, a judgment that often proved to be inadequate.[3] To clear new land in the valleys and adjacent slopes, they set fire to the tall reeds and bush growing there, and in the higher, more moist lands they killed unwanted trees by scorching their roots.[4] Using their only cultivating tool, a sharpened stick,[5] they planted their crops in the spaces between the dead trunks.

Of root crops, early European visitors noted the pia, or Polynesian arrowroot (*Tacca leontopetaloides* (L.) O. Ktze.); *kape* (*Alocasia macrorrhiza* (L.) Schott.); *ti* (*Cordyline terminales* (L.) Kunth.); turmeric (*Curcuma longo* L.); at least three kinds of yams: *puahi* (the greater yam, *Dioscorea alata* L.), *hoi* (*D. bulbifera* L., said to be eaten only in times of famine), and *titou* (which may have been *D. pentaphylla* L.); sweet potatoes (*Ipomoea batatas* (L.) Lam.); and taro (*Colocasia es-*

culenta (L.) Schott.).[6] Of these, only taro and, to a lesser extent, sweet potatoes appear to have been common.[7]

Where sufficient running water was available, wet taro cultivation was practiced,[8] but dry taro plantings were probably more common. William P. Crook described large fields of taro mixed with banana plants growing on the steep slopes of lower ridges of mountains,[9] and David Porter, in describing the type of soil planted to taro, seems to confirm the presence of dry taro cultivation.[10] Wet or dry, taro was grown in sufficient quantity for A. J. von Krusenstern to note its presence in the plantations surrounding dwellings.[11]

Edward Robarts's claim that sweet potatoes and yams were not planted, but grew wild in the mountains, may have been correct for those higher elevations.[12] However, sweet potatoes must have been planted in the lowlands, for Crook wrote of traveling to neighboring valleys to obtain sweet potatoes for his own garden.[13] As for yams, especially the greater yam, *D. alata*, it is not surprising that they were grown in the more moist mountains uplands, just as they were grown in such locations in Tahiti.[14] However, the apparent lack of interest in the yam, especially the greater yam with its large, starchy tuber and dry storage capabilities, seems curious, given the periodic droughts and accompanying famines on these islands. While yams could have been a late and relatively unacceptable introduction, and thus left to grow wild in the uplands, it seems equally probable that the reverse was true. That is, they may have represented one of the earlier foods that were largely displaced by the introduction of the starchy breadfruit by later migrants.

Although Captain James Cook obtained some yams in 1774, as did Edmund Fanning in 1798,[15] it was not until 1804 that they had become common enough to be listed by Langsdorff as one of the principal vegetables, along with the sweet potato.[16] This would seem to suggest that the increased presence of the yam, as well as of the sweet potato, was due more to the demand by European vessels for these crops than to a change in native dietary preferences.

While taro and other root crops required constant replanting to maintain continuous production, this was not true of the prime staples preferred by the Marquesans: breadfruit, coconuts, and bananas.[17] These had the advantage that once planted and set, no further attention was required, since they could be depended upon to produce edibles constantly or seasonally for long periods of time before replanting became necessary. According to Crook, there were numerous varieties of both breadfruit and bananas, and Porter claimed there were nearly twenty recognized varieties of the latter.[18] There were other, less important plants that also required little attention once planted and doing well. Besides the apple (*Spondias dulcis*), other tree crops included the Malay apple (*Syzygium malaccense* (L.) Merr. and Perr.) and the *noni* (*Morinda citrifolia* L.). There were also the nuts of the *ihi* (*Inocarpus edulis* Forst.), which produced a crop in May and in November, as well as candlenuts (*Aleurites moluccana* (L.) Willd.), the latter more often used to produce candles than for dietary purposes.[19]

Although such trees as *Terminalia catappa* L., *Cordia subcordata* Lam., and *Pandanus* spp. are mentioned in the early literature as being used for various purposes, there is no reference to their nuts or fruits being used as food.[20] Whether their use as a source of nutrition never came to the attention of the early visitors, or they were never exploited except in times of famine, is not known. Nonetheless, their food potential was at least available to Marquesans. In addition to these arboreal crops were such plants as sugarcane (*Saccharum officinarum* L.), the *huou* (*Solanum repandum* Forst.), and the pineapple (*Ananas comosus* (L.) Merr.), the latter of American origin. According to Crook, pineapple was introduced by Captain Josiah Roberts in 1791. However, by 1813 the credit for its introduction had been transferred to Crook, who was also now said to have introduced the castor bean (*Ricinus communis* L.).

Of additional interest was the *nano*, said by Crook to have been likened to the soursop, or guanabana (*Annona muricata* L.), which is of American origin. He described the plant as being a small tree having smooth, dark green, oval leaves and producing its fruit from the sides of its branches. This fruit was said to be the size and shape of a large egg, the outside of which was covered with protuberances. The interior flesh was white and slightly bitter, and contained numerous hard seeds. Although the pulp of guanabana is quite edible in its ripe, raw state, Crook said that the Marquesans beat the fruit, roasted it in embers, and threw the seeds away. However prepared, Crook's description of the plant would certainly seem to confirm its identification as *A. muricata*. Furthering this is the fact that the botanist Forest Brown found *A. muricata* still growing in the Marquesas in 1923, though he presumed it to be a recent arrival.

Although Crook mentioned the American chili pepper (*Capsicum* spp.) growing in the Marquesas, he gave no indication that it was used as a condiment. Nor did he disclose any use of the nut or its enlarged base, commonly referred to as the fruit, of the cashew (*Anacardium occidentale* L.), which he found growing on Nukuhiva, as did Brown in 1923 (he presumed it to be a recent introduction). Besides the above plants, the Marquesans also grew the kava plant (*Piper methysticum* Forst.) for its roots, which were used in preparing a drink.[21]

Although unenclosed groves of breadfruit and coconut palms were mentioned in the early literature,[22] there is nothing to indicate that other tree crops were treated in a similar manner, which suggests that their secondary role did not require such specialized stands. However, many of the root crops, as well as the smaller, more delicate plants, including the paper mulberry (*Broussonetia papyrifera* (L.) Vent.), used for making bark cloth, were planted in stone- or fau (*Hibiscus tiliaceus* L.)-fenced enclosures surrounding the homes of the landed gentry.[23]

While this range of food resources added variety, or served as complements to Marquesan dishes, it was breadfruit, with its ability (through fermentation) to be stored for extended periods of time, that was of prime importance to the culture. So vital was it that if for any reason a man or woman was heard to curse the tree or its fruit, nothing could save the person from an ordained death except flight to another island.[24] However, there seems little, if anything, to support Langsdorff's information that almost all fish were tabooed as food during the period of growth of young fruit. This was supposed to have been based upon the belief that if fish were eaten during this time, all the young breadfruit would drop off the tree. Even Langsdorff admitted skepticism about the validity of this information.

Breadfruit trees were found from the lower valleys well inland. The inland change of environment, probably the cooler temperatures, resulted in smaller trees and a somewhat later fruiting season than at lower elevations near the coast.[26] This may account for Crook's statement that the major, or "great," harvest that occurred around January was quickly followed by a smaller one.[27] As Robarts observed, the breadfruit harvest seasons varied somewhat.[28] This seems evident, since Crook and Urey Lisiansky gave January as the major harvest season, while Robarts claimed that harvest occurred in February and March. All three observers gave June as the second season of breadfruit, which, however, appeared to offer the poorest returns. There was a third, equally limited, season variously stated to be in August or September, occasionally extending into October.[29]

These short Marquesan breadfruit seasons, each lasting only a month or so, are perplexing compared with those of Tahiti, which lasted from January to May, or Tongatapu, which extended from November to June.[30] There is no botanical evidence indicating that the numerous varieties of Marquesan breadfruit tended to ripen all of their fruits during periods of only a few weeks when those of other islands extended their ripening seasons over several months. In the light of this, the lengths of the historically recorded Marquesan breadfruit seasons appear not to have represented the total length of each natural season but, rather, the periods of intensive harvesting for storage purposes. This would be especially true of the one season in or about January, referred to by Crook and Robarts as the "great harvest."[31] According to Crook, Marquesans picked breadfruit before it was fully ripe,[32] and, as will be noted shortly, force-ripened it before storage. Thus the fruit chosen for storage were not necessarily all ripe, but sufficiently advanced that they could be picked.

This intensive harvesting for storage of not fully ripened breadfruit was the exact opposite of the approach to similar activity in Tahiti, where massive harvesting and storage took place near the close of the breadfruit season.[33] In the case of the Marquesans, the early harvesting represented a vital security measure against the known occurrences of droughts and famines, and thus took precedence over other considerations. For Tahitians the late harvesting was simply an efficient way to gather and preserve their remaining fruit for use during the following months, when fresh breadfruit was unavailable. Since individually cooked breadfruit seems to have formed part of a normal Marquesan meal,[34] it appears that fresh fruit was available for longer periods than the so-called seasons would imply. There is only a hint that from October to January there was a dearth of fresh fruit; Crook noted in October that young breadfruit were only then appearing and thus promising a good crop in January.[35]

The great breadfruit harvest was said to mark the beginning of the new year.[36] As in Tahiti, this probably referred to the agricultural year, the difference being that in Tahiti the major harvest in March marked the end, rather than the beginning, of a year.[37] How the required workforce was obtained was never addressed in the early writings. For small holdings having a limited number of trees, the harvesters may have consisted of kin groups. Larger landholders with labor dependents drew upon the latter. Feasting may also have been a method of enticing help. Crook described how he was advised by a

Marquesan friend to obtain a large quantity of fish and some other edibles, and to offer the food to others if they would help him fence his property.[38] Robarts indicated that loyalty to a favored chief could result in the chief's acquisition of a large labor force from among the poorer people.[39] In this regard, Fanning noted that some district chiefs holding large groves of breadfruit would mark a certain number of trees by tying bundled grass around their trunks as a sign that their fruit was available for the picking.[40] Such a gesture was bound to have been appreciated by the landless, who had no such resource.

However the harvesting force was obtained, picking, preparing, and storing of a large crop required many hands. There were those who climbed the trees and, using a long pole forked at one end, under which a small net was suspended, broke off each fruit, which then dropped into the net. From there it was transferred into a larger net bag lashed around the perimeter of a wooden hoop and suspended by a rope from one of the upper tree limbs. Once filled with a certain number of fruit, the bag was lowered to the ground, and the fruit was transferred to the storage pit.[41] This load would appear to have been the *pona* mentioned by Crook, which contained a specific number of fruit that varied, in multiples of ten, from one island to another. Although Crook failed to mention the number of fruit in one pona, he went on to explain that ten pona made one *ou*, ten ou made one *manno*, and ten manno made one *tinne*, which, depending upon the island, was equal to either forty thousand or eighty thousand.[42] Thus, working backward, one pona contained either forty or eighty breadfruit, though which figure was used on which island is not known. What is important is that a harvest count appears to have been required. Furthermore, this kind of record gives some idea of the size of the larger harvests. Crook reported that some chiefs were known to obtain several manno in the course of one harvest, which would have amounted to several thousand fruit having been picked. He was also told that there were cases where a chief had received one tinne of breadfruit during a single harvest.[43]

With one or two pona lashed to a carrying pole, the fruit was transported to the temporary campsite of the harvesters, located near a chief's storage pit. Using the ground-off end of a shell as a scraper, the skin of each fruit was removed, a job that continued day and night until the harvest was completed. The cleaned fruit were then piled in a hole lined with coconut leaves and securely covered. This forced ripening of the fruit took only one night, after which the core of the now-soft fruit was easily extracted. Unlike the pit storage of breadfruit in Tahiti, which was designed to last, at best, one year,[44] the greatly extended storage life desired by Marquesans required an extra process before final storage. This consisted of placing quantities of the cleaned fruit in two-foot-square, leaf-lined cavities and compressing them, in effect squeezing the liquid out of the massed fruit by placing stones on top of them for several days.

During this final operation new storage pits were dug or old ones cleaned out. The size of such ma pits depended upon the projected size of the harvest,[45] some being as small as four by eight feet and five or six feet deep.[46] However, that of the operation here being summarized from Robarts's description[47] was no less than twelve feet square and between twenty-five and thirty feet deep. This estimate of the depth may not be too far off, since Crook estimated other pits to have had depths of twenty feet.[48] Although some ma pits were stone-lined, the one described by Robarts had been dug in the earth and its sides cut smooth by using the edge of a large pearl oyster shell.[49]

Final preparation of the earthen storage pit consisted of lining the bottom and lower walls with what were essentially ti leaf thatching panels, the leaves, three deep, being held together with bamboo pins. With the breadfruit now compressed into a firm yellow mass, it was passed down into the ma pit, where a man treaded it down. As the top of the mass rose higher and higher, additional leaf lining was added to the walls of the cavity. Such pits seem never to have been filled to the brim with breadfruit, since room was needed for proper sealing. This was accomplished by first covering the mass with leaves over which was placed a one-foot layer of clay sprinkled with water and compacted by treading. The final act was to add stones and fill the remainder of the cavity with water brought to the site through a ditch. The latter procedure would appear to have been employed either to allow the clay sealant to plasticize and further seal the pit or, perhaps, to identify any seepage points, since the water was later withdrawn, the upper leaf lining checked and replaced where necessary, and the whole again sealed over.

These large storage containers with their specially processed contents were designed for extended preservation of food that could be drawn upon as a vital resource during years of famine. With proper maintenance and occasional additions of fresh fruit, they were said to last up to forty years.[50] However, there must have been smaller fermentation pits for making the more common ma customarily used at meals, since Robarts explained the difference in taste between common ma and that which had been stored for many years.[51]

Although breadfruit was the prime food to be stored against famine, it was not the only crop that was set aside to be used in times of scarcity. According to Porter, coconuts were picked, presumably before they were ripe enough to fall to the ground, and hung in bunches on the trunks of the palms, where they were left to dry and cure. Those which sprouted were collected and planted; the remainder were stored because they would remain edible for at least three or four months, according to Porter, and up to a year, according to Robarts.[52] There seems to have been no attempt to preserve bananas through pit fermentation, as was done in Tonga,[53] although forced ripening of bananas by sealing them in a grass-lined cavity for three or four days was a common practice.[54]

ANIMAL HUSBANDRY

By the late eighteenth century, chickens and pigs were the only domesticated animals of the Marquesans, and only the latter could be said to have been given much attention. Archaeological evidence indicates that the dog had arrived with the earliest settlers, though perhaps as a companion rather than a food source.[55] However that might have been, by historic times it was no longer present. Although chickens, said to have been a large breed,[56] were present, they were not numerous; not only did the Marquesans eat their eggs when they could find them, but the young chicks were often eaten by rats.[57] There is nothing to indicate that fowl were regarded as a valued source of meat. On the contrary, Langsdorff claimed there was little interest in them as food; they were more prized as a source of feathers for headdresses and the like, some cocks being plucked clean for this purpose.[58] The value placed upon this source of decorative plumage may have been the significant factor that caused the Marquesans to offer up fowl to the gods and as sacrifices to those particular tau'a thought to be living gods capable of controlling the weather.[59]

While chickens were dominantly for plucking, there was no doubt that pigs were for eating, though only on special occasions—and even then, not always for everybody. Though not yet clearly proven to have arrived during the initial settlement period, A.D. 300–600, they were definitely present on the islands by A.D. 600–1300.[60] Early historic descriptions say they were a small breed, which suggests that they were probably descendents of the China pig.⁶¹ As early as 1774 George Forster, who was already well acquainted with this smaller breed, reported acquiring some "large hogs" on Tahuata in exchange for some highly valued Tongan red feathers fastened to bits of bark cloth.⁶² While his size judgment was subjective and related to the comparative size of other pigs obtained, it may be significant. It offers the intriguing, but historically unconfirmed, possibility that a European hog had either been left on that island by Mendaña's expedition in 1595 or had been allowed to breed with a pig during the expedition's two-week stay, when their animals must have been temporarily landed to allow them to feed off the land.

A similar encounter on that same island in 1791 was reported by Marchand, who wrote that a chief had brought "one of the biggest hogs yet seen," which he offered to trade for a cat but was refused.⁶³ Insofar as I have been able to determine, the first European pig, an English sow, reported to have been left in the Marquesas, specifically at Tahuata, was given to a chief by Richard Hergest in 1792.⁶⁴ Intriguing as the above possibility might be, it is counterbalanced to some extent by reports by Crook and Porter that Marquesans occasionally castrated some boars and spayed some sows, which probably would have increased their weight.⁶⁵

Considering that pigs were almost wholly vegetarian in their diet and the islands suffered periods of drought and famine, it is not surprising to learn from Crook that they were not, in his eyes, overly plentiful and that even some of the principal families did not possess any.⁶⁶ While castrating and spaying may have produced heavier pigs, it did nothing to add to the porcine population—which, perhaps, was an additional reason for the operations. Young pigs were distributed to various families, probably relatives, for feeding and raising. It was in the feeding of these piglets that Marquesans found a use for the islands' rat population, other than as occasional human famine food.⁶⁷ The little animals were caught by hand and hung alive before a fire until dead, after which they were broiled, mashed up, and the flesh mixed with fermented breadfruit and fed to the young pigs.⁶⁸ Once grown, the pigs were allowed to fend for themselves.⁶⁹

Pork seems never to have been a common dish. Instead, it was reserved for special occasions, the nature of which determined the number of pigs to be killed.⁷⁰ As in Tonga and Tahiti of the same period, no blood was drawn in killing a pig or, as already noted, even a rat.⁷¹ Such critical occurrences as the birth of a child, the tattooing of a member of the upper classes, weddings, funerals, and the ceremonies honoring a deceased individual were occasions for serving varying quantities of pork,[72] as was the case of a man honoring his wife on some special occasion.[73] Since the lower classes, and certainly the landless elements of the society, probably could not afford pigs, similar events in their lives probably did not include pork. However, public dances and festivals, as well as sacrifices, could also be times for killing innumerable pigs, so many that they would become a scarce commodity for some time afterward.[74]

Although there seems to have been no time when men could not eat pig, this was not the case with women. When Crook first landed on Tahuata and reported back to James Wilson of the *Duff* on what little he had learned during his first days on the island, he included the information that women could not eat pork.[75] This same information was later repeated by Langsdorff.[76] However, the latter amended this by explaining that if a husband wished to honor his wife on some special occasion, he would give a feast including pork, which was then available to her. Also, if a husband gave his wife a pig, she and her female friends were free to eat it, though it was forbidden to him.[77] However, in 1813 Porter claimed that women were not prohibited from eating pig except during periods of taboo. Even then, if men were not present or, if present, conveniently averted their eyes, the women could consume some pork. Although unexplainable on the basis of data on hand, he further recounted that there were certain tribes who were not tabooed in this regard, and among them men and women were free to eat pork together.[78] Thus, either the earlier observations of these restrictions were incomplete in their coverage, or restrictions pertaining to women eating pork had been modified through time, perhaps as a result of European attitudes brought to the islands.

FISHING

Although the Marquesas Islands lacked barrier reefs and their fish-laden lagoons, their surrounding waters and bays seem to have offered more than sufficient piscatorial resources for the human population. Crook listed over twenty varieties of fish, as well as whales, porpoises, turtle, squid, crabs, lobsters, shrimp, and various shellfish, including the conch, pearl shell oyster, and the "gigantic oyster," a possible reference to the giant clam. In addition there were freshwater shrimp, eels, and large prawns.[79] While cavalla and two unidentified fish named *uua* and *kennatato*, as well as turtle, could be eaten only by the superior classes on Nukuhiva (though the latter was reserved for tau'a priests on Tahuata[80]), there remained an ample range of fish for others. Although albacore, bonito, and a fish called *atu* had to be eaten with others of a similar social class and at a single time, at least they were available to all classes on that basis.[81]

Fishing was man's work, but the gathering of shellfish was done by women from among the poor.[82] The early historic records of the social ranking of fishermen appear ambivalent. On the one hand, Crook and Robarts mentioned poor fisher folk, some living in caves near the coast, who did nothing but fish and barter their catch with people living inland in return for food and other necessities.[83] Krusenstern maintained that Marquesans who owned even a small bit of land hated fishing and left that occupation to the poor as a means of maintaining themselves.[84] That this could not have been wholly accurate was indicated by Langsdorff's information that tribal raids for human sacrifices on another tribe's valley were often undertaken during rainy weather because that was a time when great numbers of people went to the shore to fish, and thus the raiders were less likely to be heard or seen.[85]

On the other hand, while some poor families, presumably landless, maintained themselves through fishing, there were also respected fishing specialists, or tuhuna, usually employed by a person of property who furnished a canoe. Although any catch made by such a tuhuna belonged to the landowner, who traded it to others, the fisherman was assured of continued maintenance as well as needed supplies from his patron.[86] In clear contradistinction to the view that fishing was a lowly occupation was Crook's account of one of the sons of the high chief Keatonue being renowned as a fisherman and, with another, owning more canoes than his father. He owned not only shore property on a bay but also the fishing rights to the waters stretching out from his property.[87] He appears not to have been the only well-placed individual to own such property with adjacent fishing rights. Crook mentioned others and described how such rights were protected by driving a stake in shallow water and affixing a small bit of bark cloth to it, indicating that it was *ahui*, restricted to the owner.[88] The use of ahui, though little employed on Tahuata, was common on Nukuhiva not only for fishing grounds but also for crops when deemed necessary.[89]

Returning to the apparent ambivalence regarding the ranking of fishermen, an important difference between poor fisher folk and the tuhuna and chiefly class fishermen was that the latter two had canoes, or access to them. It thus seems probable that the poor were purely coastal or shoreline fishermen whose occupation required little skill and equipment. The others were deep-water fishermen whose knowledge of watercraft operation and deep-water fishing raised their occupation to the level of respectability. In addition, they were possibly the only ones who were allowed to catch those fish and turtles that were restricted to use by the upper classes, a factor that may have heightened their social esteem.

There was little written about any special techniques employed by Marquesans in fishing. Upon the spotting of a school of porpoises, canoes were dispatched to see if the porpoises could be diverted into a shallow bay where they would become stranded and easily killed. To accomplish this, the fishermen would get on the seaward side of the school and strike stones together beneath the water. The clicking sound drove the porpoises away from the canoes and toward the shore. Fishermen were also known to dive for lobsters and catch them by hand, and conger eels were lured out of their holes with bait, then were secured by slipping a noose around them.[90] Night fishing with hand nets, especially for flying fish, was common, with bundles of tall reeds used as torches.[91] The Marquesans also employed at least two kinds of vegetative poisons. One was the fruit of the *hutu*,[92] *Barringtonia asiatica* (L.) Kurz., which, at least in Tahiti, was crushed and spread on the surface of the water.[93] The other was described as a root that was crushed and spread on the seafloor, probably in the quieter waters of a bay.[94] This could have been either *Wikstroemia foetida* (L.) A. Gray or *Tephrosia purpurea* (L.) Pers., both reported growing in the Marquesas and both known to have been used in a similar manner in Tahiti to poison fish.[95]

Beyond these special features the better-known Polynesian fishing methods were hook and line with, or without, fishing pole,[96] and netting. Lines were made of the fibers from coconut husks as well as those from branches of *Hibiscus tiliaceus* L.[97] Most hooks were either of one piece and made of pearl shell, or of two pieces, a shaped shank of pearl shell to which was attached by thread a straight, unbarbed hook described as being of bone.[98] To fasten hooks to lines, fine filaments were scraped from the papa vine, *Rhynchosia minima* (L.) DC., and used to form the necessary snood.[99] Crook also described the use of a hook made from a thorn of the "prickly palm," possibly the pandanus, used to catch small fish called *popo*. The hook was baited and fastened to one end of a short line, and a small wooden float was secured to the other end. Once hooked, the fish was soon exhausted from dragging the float and could be caught.[100] Although no one wrote of fishing spears, Porter mentioned the use of bone and wood harpoons.[101]

Fishing nets were made of the same materials as fishing lines.[102] However, there was one mention of nets having been made from the fibers of a nettle.[103] Since the fiber of the nettle, *Pipturus argenteus* (Forst.f.) Wedd., was used to make fine netting in Tahiti, and several species of *Pipturus* have been reported growing in the Marquesas, it was probably the fiber of one of these that was employed.[104] Although the particular use to which various nets were put was never described in the literature, the types were noted. These included seines and straight nets, the latter up to one hundred feet in length. There were said to have been casting nets, scoop and sweep nets, and what was called a bell-hooped net.[105] Thus, although lacking the fruitful fishing grounds of lagoons with barrier reefs, the Marquesans seem not to have been deterred from obtaining sufficient seafood to offset their otherwise limited sources of protein. Certainly the wide variety of fishing gear and the range of seafood reportedly obtained would seem to support this view.

DROUGHT AND FAMINE

The dependence upon domesticated food resources was interrupted from time to time by irregular periods of drought, one of which was said to have lasted three years.[106] Such extended dry spells appear to have been limited largely to the elevations below the cloud zone. This is indicated by Urey Lisiansky, who was told that during a recent drought, numerous people had been forced to search the mountains for wild plant foods.[107] In addition, Crook explained how in times of famine the *pahei* fern, which grew on the summits of ridges, was sought for its edible roots.[108] In this regard, it was probably subsurface drainage patterns from the high cloud zone that accounted for an interesting phenomenon noted by Robarts. He observed that in various valleys some breadfruit trees would continue to bear fruit while others not far away would be drought-stricken.[109]

Regarding these odd situations of spotty desiccation, Robarts commented that those whose trees still produced fruit had something to eat, while neighboring owners of drought-stricken trees had nothing.[110] He seemed to imply that even in times of famine, property rights and other restrictions remained in effect, despite starvation. On the basis of what few data are available, it would appear that the only food distribution occurring during droughts was that of chiefs and other land-wealthy individuals who were capable of maintaining large breadfruit storage pits. However, such distribution was limited to the avowed henchmen and, presumably, the household servants of these individuals.[111]

As for the destitute, primarily the poor,[112] they attempted to survive on fern roots, Polynesian chestnuts (*Inocarpus edulis*), the bitter yam (*Dioscoria bulbifera*), the corms of plantains and bananas, rats, and fish.[113] Robarts's claim that yams and sweet potatoes grew wild in the mountains suggests that these hardy crops, though not dominant staples, had once been purposely planted in the uplands and allowed to go feral to serve as an additional source of food during famine.[114] Finally, though Robarts was said to have told Lisiansky that cannibalism purely for food was a reality in times of famine, and Krusenstern enlarged on that theme,[115] there is no mention of it in Robarts's personal account, nor did Crook hear of such instances during the famine he encountered.[116]

During severe droughts, such as the one experienced by Robarts, whole valleys were vacated by their former inhabitants, and in the area of Taiohae alone 200 to 300 deaths occurred in one year.[117] Robarts seems to suggest that at least some of these deaths by starvation were the result of individuals having recklessly accepted a drought as a temporary phenomenon and thus relied on reducing their activities during such food shortages rather than foraging the mountains for wild supplements. With an extended drought, they became so weakened that they could not climb the steep trails to places where such resources existed.[118]

There were also others, lured by tau'a priests' visions of distant verdant islands, who would load their large canoes and sail off in search of these better lands.[119] Although other vision-related voyages of discovery took place from time to time,[120] one may reasonably suspect that the irregularly recurrent droughts on these islands may well have been the major catalyst for the Marquesan prehistoric dispersions within Polynesia that Yosihiko Sinoto's archaeological evidence indicates.[121] Since it is likely that the technique for long-term breadfruit storage had not yet been developed in the early periods of occupation, extended droughts might well have inspired some to search for other, more propitious lands.

CHAPTER 8

Transportation and Trade

With no coastal plains on any island of the Marquesas, and valley walls steep and often precipitous, land travel from one part of an island to another was arduous at best. Valley floors formed natural pathways for only limited distances inland, and at their heads were nearly perpendicular cliffs that had to be scaled or crossed along their bare rock walls. Other trails ascended toward the mountainous high interior via the crests of narrow ridges and crossed the major island divides through narrow natural gaps or passes.[1] There is nothing in the records to indicate that these trails were well maintained. On the contrary, James Wilson described the path on Tahuata leading to a high chief's home as being crossed with tree roots and partially blocked here and there by large boulders, all of which made walking difficult, at least for the uninitiated.[2]

While trails such as these were taken in stride by those who had grown up using them, they could not have been particularly conducive to the casual, ready communication between valleys that might have induced amalgamation of discrete valley populations. Given this effect of the rugged terrain, coasting by sea from one valley mouth to another probably offered the easiest and most often used means of communication, at least between those living near the sea. By the same reasoning, it also afforded easier access to enemy valleys by warring parties.[3]

CANOES AND VOYAGING

Although simple log rafts were quickly constructed as the occasion demanded, dependable water craft in the Marquesas were limited to single and double canoes. However, only a few of the latter may have been designed as permanent double-hulled vessels. War canoes, for example, were described as single and supplied with outriggers, yet when necessary they could, as Edward Robarts explained, be fitted together to carry 140 warriors. The same was true for vessels built for voyages of discovery. Fishing vessels, too, appear to have been single canoes but were occasionally made into double canoes for certain types of fishing.[4] However, vessels for interisland sailing seem always to have been double canoes.[5] Whether permanent or temporary, the structural arrangement consisted of two canoe hulls fastened abreast of one another by poles stretching from one vessel to the other that kept the two hulls about six feet apart.[6]

While some canoes undoubtedly served a variety of purposes, others seem to have been designed for specific functions. The smallest of what were probably general-purpose canoes were described by Captain James Cook as being between sixteen and twenty feet in length and fifteen inches wide,[7] while others were estimated to be between twenty and thirty feet long with a width varying from twelve to eighteen inches. The hulls of those designed for interisland sailing were said to have a maximum length of thirty feet and a beam of three feet, and those constructed for the purpose of sailing forth to discover new islands were somewhat larger.[8]

Fishing canoes varied in size, depending, quite probably, upon where they were intended to be used. The smallest, for which we have no measurements, were described as dugouts with no washstrakes and, like all single canoes except those of Fatuhiva, which may have carried paired outrider floats, were furnished with outriggers. Others were said to be equivalent to those used for interisland voyaging, while the largest, possibly designed for open, deep-water fishing, were described as being larger than war canoes and having a width of six feet.[9] It was probably this larger type of fishing craft that Robarts was describing when he wrote that it was between fifty-five and sixty feet long, and four men could sit on each seat.[10] As for war canoes, David Porter gave their length as fifty feet with a beam of two feet.[11] Although primarily used for warfare, they also served as pleasure craft and, given ostentatious decoration, functioned as a tribal chief's proper vessel when making a formal call on another tribal chief.[12]

Marquesans found at least five different trees suitable for making canoes. Breadfruit, mi'o, and *tamanu* are clearly identifiable in the historic record.[13] Another, described by Robarts as producing a kind of almond, and written down by Urey Lisiansky as *toomoomyee*, was probably *maii*, or *Terminalia catappa* L.[14] A fifth tree said to grow near the seashore, and to produce a soft wood used to make small canoes, was probably the tree identified by Captain Cook as being of soft wood and growing near the sea; its bark, so he understood, was used for making canoes.[15] This was probably *Erythrina indica* Lam., for the botanist Forest Brown described this tree as growing near the shore and producing a soft wood that, he was told, was used to construct light canoes.[16] Of these five trees, only the wood of tamanu was, according to Lisiansky, limited to the construction of war canoes.[17] This assertion, however, must remain in some doubt because the broad-beamed apparent fishing canoe described by Robarts was also made of that wood.[18] Nonetheless, if Lisiansky's information was correct, it is possible that, as in Tahiti,[19] the tree had sacred significance.

For the purposes of this study, the features and construction of Marquesan canoes are based upon the early historic records. Those interested in more detailed structural information covering a longer period of time should refer to Haddon and James Hornell's classic study, *Canoes of Oceania*. As for the early records, the general European assessment of Marquesan canoe construction was hardly complimentary. They were said to be clumsily built, and so poorly sewn together that they required constant bailing.[20] However, A. J. von Krusenstern judged them to be sturdily built; and Robarts, who made numerous voyages in them, never disparaged their construction, though he admitted to their need for constant bailing.[21]

Basically, each canoe was made up of three sections. In its simplest form, the hull was nothing more than a dugout carved from the trunk of a tree. To this was added a prow consisting of a horizontally projecting flat board.[22] Some prows were decorated on the top end surface with a simple carving of a face variously described as that of a human or an animal, while others had the carved figure of a man holding up a flat board.[23]

Another prow decoration, mentioned by George Forster and illustrated in an engraving of a painting by William Hodges made during Cook's visit to Tahuata in 1774, consisted of flat upright pieces.[24] Both James Hornell and Edward Dodd have doubted the authenticity of these prow uprights in Hodges's illustration, regarding them as an error on the part of the engraver.[25] However, George Forster's inde-

Outrigger canoes at Vaitahu, Tahuata island. Drawn by William Hodges in 1774. Courtesy of Special Collections, University of Arizona, Tucson.

pendent description of a similar decorative device on a Tahuata canoe during the same expedition confirms their authenticity. It was also at Tahuata that Edmund Fanning saw a double war canoe whose bow planks were ornamented with four human skulls.[26]

Attached to the stern of a canoe hull was an elongated, slender projection. Some took the shape of an elongated, reclining S figure.[27] Others were formed into a simple upward curve that Porter likened to the runner of a sleigh or fore part of a Dutch skate.[28]

For the great majority of canoes the log dugout segment served as the underbody of the vessel.[29] On top of its sidewalls and ends were washstrakes fastened to the underbody with coconut fiber rope. The resulting joints were caulked either with the fibers of coconut husk held in place by strips of bamboo lashed to both faces of the joint or with moss that was sealed with resin obtained from breadfruit trees. In some canoes, thin plank bulkheads were inserted within the hull to stiffen its sides.[30] Besides containing seats or thwarts within the hull,[31] some vessels had a rectangular bench raised above the level of the gunwales at the bow where an important person might be seated, as well as another in the stern for the steersman.[32] According to Porter, a third such platform might be placed amidships in a war canoe to serve as a seat for a tribal chief.[33]

All single canoes, with the possible exception of those observed by Pedro Fernandez Quiros at Fatuhiva in 1595, carried outriggers to which a float was attached. Hornell argued rather successfully from the data he had on hand for the absence of double outriggers in the Marquesas.[34] However, they may have been used on some vessels, perhaps as a temporary device, just as some canoes were temporarily made double for particular purposes. This suggestion is based upon a comment made by Otto von Kotzebue when viewing the canoes of Tongareva. He wrote, "Their boats, which are badly constructed, resemble those in the Marquesas, being furnished with an outrigger on each side."[35] Although Kotzebue's own voyages never included the Marquesas Islands, he had been a member of the earlier Krusenstern expedition of 1803–06 that visited this archipelago.[36] His comparison, then, must have been based upon his observations of at least one type of canoe in the Marquesas during that voyage. Thus, unless his statement is to be totally negated, and there seems no reason to do so, he confirmed the existence of double outrigger canoes in both the Marquesas and Tongareva. The fact that his artist, Louis Choris, had earlier made a sketch of a double outrigger canoe at Easter Island,[37] suggests that there may have been an early introduction into Polynesia of this type of canoe, which, by historic times, had largely been replaced, perhaps by the more stable double canoe.

However this might have been, the number of booms of single outriggers varied from two to three.[38] Although Crook mentioned fau (*Hibiscus tiliaceus* L.) as used for making outriggers,[39] the lightness of this wood suggests that he was referring to the float rather than the booms. Thus, it is not clear what kind, or kinds, of wood were used for the majority of outrigger booms. However, Étienne Marchand did mention one canoe at Tahuata that used bamboo for this purpose.[40]

The float attachments of Fatuhiva canoes, as described by Quiros in 1595, appear to have been unique in Polynesia and are therefore of special interest. Using Hornell's more precise translation of Quiros's pertinent text, we find that he wrote of Fatuhiva canoes: "there came out 70 small canoes, not all the same size, each made out of a tree trunk, with counterpoises of canes on each side, after the manner of the outboard rowing galleries of galleys, which reached down to the water on which they rested to prevent capsizing."[41]

As Hornell has pointed out, these canoes were represented by Quiros as small dugouts and would have had little freeboard. Thus, bundles of canes, probably bamboos, fastened to each side of a vessel and reaching to the water would help to keep such canoes from capsizing.[42] Hornell gave the known distribution of such outrider floats as the Philippines, Burma, Siam, and the Solomons to the west, and the coast of Colombia to the east—which, from my personal observations in early 1940, should be expanded to include the northern coast of Ecuador. It was these latter South American canoes, known in Ecuador as *imbaburas*, which had light balsa wood logs lashed to each side of a dugout, that Hornell concluded were probably a Spanish introduction.[43] However, since that writing, a study of a ceramic model of such a canoe belonging to the prehistoric La Tolita culture of northern Esmeraldas Province, Ecuador, has been published by Jacinto Jijón y Caamaño.[44] Thus, while the outrider float device of Fatuhiva canoes could be a case of independent development, it seems more likely, if Hornell was correct in his interpretation, that the concept was the result of an introduction from Colombia or, considering the more favorable ocean currents, Ecuador through a casual prehistoric contact.

However, an alternative interpretation of Quiros's attempt to describe the canoe balancers in terms of the galleys of his day is possible. It might have been a reference to double outrigger booms extending from each side of the canoes that he saw as resembling the oars extending down to the water on each side of the galleys.

The triangular mat sail of the Marquesans was set with its apex pointing downward and its top spread wide. One edge was fastened to an upright mast stepped forward of midships, and another to a boom that extended out at a high angle from the horizontal.[45] Its overall configuration caused some observers to describe it as a sort of lateen sail,[46] from which it might well have derived in ages past. When not sailing, canoes were paddled. Made of mi'o wood (*Thespesia populnea* (L.) Sol.), the paddles were short and had a slender handle with a knob at the top. The edges of the blade spread out from the handle at a low angle until slightly below the midpoint of the blade. They then turned in sharply and terminated in a knoblike point that extended a little beyond the blade proper.[47] There was also a much longer handled paddle having an oval blade, one use of which appears to have been as a steering oar.[48]

Although there is no indication that regular working canoes were jointly owned by several people, that was not the case with war canoes, which were the property of important, high-ranking families.

Porter explained that the numerous segments of a war canoe, even its paddles, were separately owned by individuals, probably relatives. It appears that when such vessels were not in use, they were taken apart, the owner of each segment assuming responsibility for its proper care. In the event of war or other need for these vessels, each owner brought his part, along with the material needed to attach it in its proper place. Such an exercise in mass assembly could be accomplished in a remarkably short time; one high chief told Porter that a total of twenty such canoes could be made ready for him in six days.[49]

Two-way voyaging, although reportedly limited to the islands of the archipelago, was an ordinary but nonetheless hazardous undertaking. Swamping of a vessel was common, as was upsetting, either of which could be rectified, after righting the vessel, by industrious bailing. Should this fail, all hands were lost unless land was within reach by swimming.[50] Nor were double canoes altogether safe; Crook recorded the breaking apart of such a vessel.[51]

While the easterly trades were the dominant winds throughout most of the year, there were days during the summer months of November and December when the islands experienced westerlies.[52] These were not always of broad expanse nor of long duration; their being accompanied by heavy clouds suggests that they were transient shreds, or spurs, from the warm western equatorial air mass on its temporary eastward migration during the summer relaxation of the easterly trades.[53] Whatever their source, the Marquesans of Nukuhiva, and probably Uapou, used them to sail to the windward islands of Hivaoa and Tahuata, a voyage said to take three days, which probably was made via Uahuka.[54] With the disappearance of the temporary westerlies, Nukuhivan visitors to Hivaoa or Tahuata were assured of returning to their own island with the reappearance of the easterly trade winds.

It was the Nukuhivan use of these temporary winds to sail east with the assured knowledge that the rejuvenated easterlies would bring them home again that caused Crook to arrive at a rather cogent conclusion. He saw this phenomenon as proof that Polynesians must have spread from the west to the east by means of this technique, rather than the reverse.[55] Although these westerlies within the low latitude of the Marquesas appear to have derived from an equatorial event, the same periodic occurrence of westerlies in somewhat higher latitudes, due to wind shifts with the eastward passage of cyclonic disturbances, would have offered the same potential for eastward exploration, which thus further strengthens Crook's early conclusion.[56]

Although Crook's logical view of how Polynesian expansion from west to east could have taken place, Marquesans, at least at the turn of the century, seemingly failed in this presumed fail-safe approach and others sailed forth in other directions and were never heard of again. Or perhaps the negative results of previous voyages of discovery to the east resulted in later expeditions searching for unpopulated islands in directions that did not offer hope for a safe return to the homeland. All that is known from early accounts is that such voyages were still occurring at the turn of the century, with no record of their participants having returned to tell of their results.[57]

The reasons for such errant searching for new land were said to be family quarrels, famine due to occasional droughts, and war.[58] There was also the seemingly inexplicable intrusion, from time to time, of a tau'a tempting others with visions of lush, uninhabited islands just waiting to be settled. To further inspire additional voyaging, tau'a would claim to have learned of the successful landfall of previous unheard-from expeditions, thus explaining away their participants' long absence.[59] As the record stands, within the period we are dealing with, there is no indication that Marquesans were making two-way voyages to islands beyond their own archipelago. Nonetheless, the number of intentional migratory sailings was far greater than any noted in historic reports for any other Polynesian islands. On Nukuhiva alone, 800 people were claimed to have left that island, though over what length of time is not known.[60]

What is most important about these sailings is that such voyages were equipped for settlement. Porter told how one chief sailed forth with four large canoes, taking with him several families and a stock of provisions including pigs, chickens, and young plants.[61] Thus, while many such voyages may have ended in catastrophe, those that did find new islands were fully prepared for a successful settlement. Considering the archaeological evidence presented by Yosihiko Sinoto for the Marquesas having been a prehistoric center of dispersal,[62] this cultural drive to search for new land not only was of long standing in the Marquesas but also was still maintained at the time of European contact. Societal situations would seem to have initiated some of these voyages, yet since the full range of agricultural potential, especially in the upland plateau remnants, remained unexploited, it seems probable that the sporadic famine-producing droughts were likely the more basic factor promoting migrations.

Although Marquesans lacked two-way contact with lands beyond their archipelago, Crook noted their having names for up to forty-four different islands, all but three appearing in their sacred songs. To this number, Porter added a few more.[63] While some of these islands were probably legendary, the names of others must have been obtained from voyagers who arrived in the Marquesas by accident. Such names as *boaboa* and *huaheine* surely refer to Bora Bora and Huahine in the Society Islands, and *tamoe* might refer to Timoe, just east of Mangareva in the Gambier Islands. They also must have had a contact from one of the coral atolls of the Tuamotus, for they described the island of *hornatiputa* as being a lagoon island.[64]

Those who arrived from distant, unknown lands were referred to as atua, or gods, since they had come "from the back of the sky," or, as Crook explained it to Fanning, "from the clouds."[65] These expressions are reminiscent of the Tongan reference to foreign arrivals as "men of the sky,"[66] and Marquesans referred to Europeans in a similar manner.[67] What new concepts or traits the pre-European men from the back of the sky may have introduced into Marquesan culture will be difficult to ascertain. Nonetheless, the possibilities for introductions by such casual contacts should be borne in mind rather than dismissed out of hand. As noted elsewhere, the introduction of the coconut into the Marquesas was said to have been the result of one casual contact.[68]

TRADE

With only the islands within the Marquesas group as trading partners, transactions were indeed limited. As Robarts aptly explained it, there was little to offer another island that it did not already have.[69] However, there were some differences in product availability. Uapou, for example, found it advantageous to trade a variety of goods for the large oceangoing canoes produced on Nukuhiva.[70] At the same time, Tahuata seems to have favored the turmeric grown on Uapou and to have traded ornaments and pigs for it.[71] However, by far the most valued and sought-after trade item was the specially prepared and baked turmeric perfume produced on Nukuhiva. This, however, was not an islandwide product. On the contrary, perhaps one of the reasons for its high trade value was that its manufacture was under the control of members of the Hapa tribe, who lived in the inland valley of Muake.[72]

The manufacture of turmeric perfume appears to have been a seasonal occupation undertaken at certain "peculiar" springs. This suggests that the mineral content of the water employed in the operation may have had something to do with the special and desirable scent of the final product. When the time for production arrived, the men involved would build temporary huts by the springs; during the entire operation they were forbidden to have any relations with women. It is possible that these producers of the perfume were not the owners either of the raw material or of the final product but, like tuhuna craftsmen, were paid in food. This is suggested on the basis that food was sent to the workers at the same time that the raw rhizomes of turmeric used in the manufacturing process were delivered to them.

Upon delivery, the rhizomes were spread out on a platform of reeds, and dirt, rootlets, and the like were removed by having young boys trample the material. The cleansed rhizomes were then finely grated and deposited in a large wooden trough carved from a coconut log. Here the gratings were subjected to numerous washings, presumably with water from the local springs, until the inner fleshy material had separated from the remnants of outer skin. The latter, it would appear, was skimmed off or otherwise removed from the trough, and saved for use as insulating material during the baking process. The finely grated flesh was poured into another container for settling. This now somewhat condensed material was transferred to an open mold, presumably of wood or a gourd, that was shaped like a hat block and had a small hole at the base to drain off excess water. The mold and its contents were wrapped with leaves to protect them from burning and placed in a pit oven that had been lined with hot rocks. The whole was tightly covered with the rhizome skins to hold in the heat. After about two hours of baking, the mold was removed and the cooked loaf of orange turmeric perfume turned out on a clean sheet of bark cloth, where it was allowed to dry and harden in the sun.[73]

Not only did the monopolistic control and seasonality of production limit the quantity of perfume available, but the obvious need for a considerable quantity of rhizomes to make each loaf added to the value of the finished product. And that value was considerable. On the windward islands of Hivaoa and Tahuata, large canoes and other finely worked crafts, as well as hogs, were readily traded for these loaves of Nukuhivan perfume. Little wonder, then, that Nukuhivan traders in this product would have their canoes ready and loaded to take advantage of the westerly winds of November and December to sail to the windward islands for a bit of lucrative trading.[74] If the "peculiar" waters of the Muake valley springs did, in the process of washing, add an element to the pleasing scent of the perfume, the restricted locale of its production would be understandable. The use of an open type of casting mold to form the loaves of perfume would appear to be unique in Polynesia and raises a question as to its origin. The shape and use of the mold calls to mind early European molds for steaming puddings and the like, which presents the possibility that Marquesans may have seen such a mold in use on board a vessel and adapted the technique to their own needs.

CHAPTER 9

Warfare

War was a way of life among the Marquesans. If the cause for war was not a quarrel, especially over landownership, or an outright attempt to invade and conquer another tribe's valley, a simple challenge to a battle would do. Tau'a priests occasionally used divine prophecy to instigate war.[1] Lacking these, there seems always to have been a traditional tribal enemy to fight, the reason for such enmity resting in legends kept alive by constant repetition.[2] Families, tribes, and alliances of tribes on a single island found reasons to battle, and interisland wars, notably between Tahuata and Hivaoa, increased the spread of such potential mayhem.[3]

Considering the extent of warfare, there is little in the early records to indicate that there was a specifically defined warrior class or group. There was, however, the position of toa, or chief warrior, whose title was more a reflection of his prowess in battle than his ability as a commander of troops. A high chief, or haka'iki, might also carry the title of toa; if he did not, he would have a special warrior with that title whose rank would be second to the high chief. In some cases the relationship between the two men could be quite close; the land-wealthy toa of High Chief Keatonue of Taiohae had served as pekio to Keatonue's wife.[4] While the title of toa did not carry with it the authority, per se, to command warrior tribesmen, the prestige afforded him by his recognized fighting ability undoubtedly lent power to any advice he might choose to offer. Warriors, though perhaps not recognized as a distinct social class, certainly must have constituted a part of the landed gentry, inasmuch as any land taken in intratribal battle was divided among them.[5]

WEAPONS

Clubs, lances, javelins, and slings were the weapons of war and were crafted by men.[6] Both Étienne Marchand and G. H. von Langsdorff specifically mentioned that they found no evidence of the presence of bows and arrows, and concluded that Marquesans were unfamiliar with them.[7] However, Pedro Fernandez de Quiros reported that the natives of Tahuata threw stones and spears at the Spaniards, and some used arrows as well.[8] Thus, unless the reference to arrows represents an error in the English translation of the original Spanish text, bows and arrows were present in the Marquesas in 1595 but had been totally discarded by the late eighteenth century. Their early presence in the Marquesas should not be surprising, since bows and arrows were still in use in the eighteenth century in Tongan warfare, as well as in the sport of rat hunting.[9] Also, though they may once have served as weapons of war in Tahiti, by the late eighteenth century their use had been redirected to hunting birds and serving in a sporting contest that had religious associations.[10] Although this is purely hypothetical, the demise of bows and arrows as weapons of war in eastern Polynesia could have been caused by the introduction of the less cumbersome sling, which may have proved more effective as a long-range offensive weapon.

Most Marquesan slings appear to have been woven of coconut fiber cord and were designed with a broad, flat band at the midpoint of the sling to hold the stone. Others were made of another fiber that Langsdorff thought might have come from a nettle.[11] The smooth, egg-shaped, waterworn stones used in slings were obtained just offshore by diving some twenty or thirty feet to the ocean floor to gather them.[12] Although warriors swung the charged sling only once around before releasing the stone, they were said to send the projectile a considerable distance, though their aim was not always accurate.[13]

Lances and clubs were made of toa wood (*Casuarina equisetifolia* Forst.), and throwing spears, or javelins, were of toa or an unidentified lighter wood. Lances, or thrusting spears, ranged in length from eight to as much as fourteen feet and were about one inch thick in the middle and sharp at both ends. Some were described as plain and well polished, while others, like the clubs, were decorated with carving or with bands of woven human hair said to have been taken from an enemy.[15] Although javelins were mentioned by several of the early

Mouina, a Nukuhiva chief warrior, wearing a whale tooth pendant and carrying a conch shell trumpet and the short fighting club. Decorations around his ankles and wrists and the end of the trumpet were probably of human hair. Engraving by W. Strickland after David Porter. Courtesy of Bishop Museum, Honolulu.

observers, only David Porter described them as being smaller than lances. He further added that at some distance back of the point was a series of holes drilled around the circumference of the weapon. Thus, when the point entered an enemy's body, the weight of the shaft was sufficient to cause it to break at the weakened spot, leaving the point embedded in the flesh. Apparently all spears that had drawn blood in killing an enemy were given the name of that man, and his blood was allowed to remain on the weapon.[16]

Clubs for close fighting were of two types. The larger weapon, six or seven feet in length, was variously described as being shaped like a paddle, a spade, or an oar.[17] The shorter clubs were from four to five feet in length and had an enlargement at the distal end. The shorter club was likened by William Pascoe Crook to a mallet that, in some cases, was decorated with carved figures, including representations of the human head.[18] On Tahuata the enlarged distal end of the clubs was simply a knob or large knot.[19] Although any one of these weapons could do lethal damage in battle, whether they did so depended upon the nature of the particular war being fought, since in the Marquesas not all wars were meant to be mass killings.

THE NATURE OF WARS

In terms of the number of individuals involved, the most limited wars were those resulting from private quarrels between individual families battling over landownership or the murder of a relative. Such wars appear to have developed only where contesting families lived some distance apart. Where contentious opponents lived within a general neighborhood, open fighting seems often to have been avoided by allowing the quarreling parties to express their arguments and feelings publicly. This was accomplished by bringing together a large audience and, after placing the two malcontents some distance apart, permitting them to vent their wrath publicly, in the loudest manner and with all appropriate gestures. Eventually one or the other was induced to relinquish whatever claim of injustice had precipitated the quarrel.[20] However, when it came to ownership of land being contested by two high-ranking individuals, a private war could result.

One such battle over landownership recounted by Crook involved the Tahuata chief, Teinae, and a distinguished "principal man" named Pahoumouma. As wars go, it was a miniature affair involving mixed family relationships. Pahoumouma was supported by six fighting men, one of whom was a brother of his opponent, Chief Teinae. The number of warriors on the side of the chief was not revealed, but the group consisted of other brothers of the chief, his brother-in-law, and all of his cousins in Pahoumouma's family. How long the battle lasted is not known, but at its termination no one from either side had been killed. However, since Chief Teinae and his warriors were judged to have been holding the advantage when the battle ended, the contested land became his rightful property. Pahoumouma, having lost his claim as a result of the superior fighting prowess of Teinae and his men, now resorted to peaceful negotiation. In the end he gained title to the disputed land by persuading Teinae to relinquish his war-won rights in exchange for six long fighting clubs, two hogs, three headdresses and, most valued of all, a sperm whale's tooth. So delighted was Teinae with this arrangement that he gave his erstwhile opponent a cat.[21]

This Marquesan concept of initial trial by battle, followed by a negotiated exchange settlement if defeated, was clearly defined to David Porter by the Hapa tribe when they insisted on trying their battle strength against his forces. When he warned that he would not readily make peace and would demand indemnities, they matter-of-factly assured him that they had ample fruit and hogs to purchase his friendship if, by chance, they were defeated. For Marquesans it would seem that trial of strength by battle was usually a first option.[22]

Wars within a chiefly family also could result in loss of land, since warriors of the winning side were free to divide among themselves the land of the defeated.[23] In a case of this sort described by Edward Robarts, a high chief had conducted a successful campaign against his eldest sister, resulting in the loss of all her inherited lands to the warriors of the chief. In this instance no attempt seems to have been made to buy back the lost terrain.

While Robarts's account gives himself the role of having precipitated and participated in two different procedures designed to gain the return of the conquered lands to the chief's sister, it seems apparent that once he gained permission of the high chief to proceed with his efforts, the traditionally prescribed rites for such action were explained to him. Thus, the following brief résumé of his account of these procedures should be of ethnographic value.

The initial procedure appears to have been a symbolic gesture signaling the desire of the family, represented by the high chief's and eldest daughter's mother and the daughter, for the return of the latter's land without actually requesting it. To accomplish this, a day was chosen when the mother, called the "old queen" by Robarts, escorted her daughter to a piece of land upon which the ruins of her former home still remained, and which was now owned by the high chief's son as a result of the war. Here she was seated among the remains of her former home, not a word being spoken.

Now that she had symbolically made her wishes known, it was up to those who now lived on her former property to accept or reject her wishes. Had they been accepted, one person would have brought her a branch and others would have followed, bringing various materials to build a temporary dwelling. However, they refused her wish, though no direct statement to this effect was made to her. Instead, the warrior owners talked among themselves in voices loud enough for her to hear, stating that there was no land for her and that they would keep their well-won property. Through all of this her brother, the high chief, who had precipitated the war, quietly stayed at a distance from the scene, watching the proceedings. When the warriors' wishes had been made clear, he returned alone to his home, and mother and daughter left the area together.

While this initial procedure did not involve direct confrontation, the second approach most certainly did, and was backed by a threat of war. In this arrangement, which occurred some time later, the husband of the "old queen's" granddaughter, a chief of a neighboring tribe, purposely entered into a quarrel with the warriors holding the desired land. This apparently offered sufficient reason to precipitate a war, if necessary. This time the high chief's mother and her eldest daughter, along with most of her chiefly family, as well as other sympathetic parties, assembled at one of the tohua, or dance courts, whereupon the war drums beat a signal for war. With that, the warriors of the granddaughter's husband appeared on the mountains, answered with a war whoop, and descended halfway down the slopes. With this, the mother of the high chief again took her daughter and set her in the ruins of her former home, after which she waved her mantle and asked of the audience, "Who is on my side?" At this point in Robarts's account, he took over as negotiator. Since he was the adopted son of the granddaughter and her husband, his service as negotiator would have been as a member of that chief's family and, through his adoptive mother, as a relative of the high chief as well.

With this show of force, the war drum was placed nearby to signal a battle, if necessary. At this sudden show of armed strength, one of the bewildered natives came forward and, prostrating himself before Robarts, performed the obeisant act of placing Robarts's leg on his shoulder and then asking him what the war was all about. The reluctant warrior proprietors of the eldest daughter's land were now made cognizant of what was desired of them if war was to be avoided. They immediately brought a hog and material to build a house, thus showing their capitulation. Since this, in itself, did not assure that the concession was by general consent, it was demanded that the return of the land be ritualized by a tau'a in a traditional ceremony. At the close of this rite the names of all the plots of land that were to be returned to their former owner were to be recited.

During this entire performance the high chief again kept at a distance and did not participate until after the tau'a ceremony and the naming of the land to be returned. On the first recital of the land involved, only the plot upon which the elder sister sat was categorized as being returned. With this announcement Robarts, without conversing with the high chief, sent him a broken stick indicating that only a part of the land was to be returned. In a similar silent manner the high chief sent Robarts a complete stick indicating that all of the former land of his sister should be returned. It was then the negotiator's duty to explain to the warrior tenants that all of the sister's land, including springs, sea beaches, and trees with attached fruit, must be returned. In addition, all food stored on these lands by the warriors during their tenure should be removed, or a war would follow immediately. These terms were accepted by a second, and now complete, recitation of all the plots involved.

With the completion of this final recitation, the negotiator sent a signal of peace, consisting of a bunch of coconuts and a piece of white cloth, to the warriors on the mountain. Another piece of white material was sent to the chief of those warriors, which served as an invitation for him to come and witness the final ceremony. Yet another white cloth with ten knots in it was sent as a request for the principal men of the chief's party to come down and serve as witnesses to the final traditional ceremony completing the transfer of the lands. The ceremony was not described, but it terminated with the now former owners shouting in unison that they were returning the land and had no further claims to it. With this act, the small dancing drums were beaten to terminate the event, and a number of live hogs that had been brought to the scene were given to the chief and his party, who, by having threatened war, had forced the transfer of the property.[24]

The war that resulted in the above procedures for the return of the land involved public sibling confrontation within the highest-ranking family of one particular tribe. Since the position of high chief, or haka'iki, was customarily inherited by the oldest son, and the involved sister was the oldest daughter, it also represented a confrontation between the highest age ranking within each gender of siblings. Thus, while the above procedures may have held for all land disputes involving particular families of the chiefly class, it is equally possible that it was specific only to such events involving the highest-ranking chiefly family of a tribe, as was the situation in this case.

What stands out in these procedures is that neither of the two siblings verbally expressed his or her desires during the two sessions. Both the request for the return of the land by the eldest sister, and the agreement by her high chief brother that this be done, were accomplished symbolically. This suggests the possibility that for such a high-ranking individual as the eldest sister verbally to request the return of her land would hold the undesirable possibility of losing face if, as in the above initial procedure, she was refused by the lower-ranking warrior tenants. The same might also apply to the high chief, who, by verbally agreeing that the land should be returned to her, might have lost face for having essentially taken away what his warriors had rightfully gained in his war against his sister. Since the actions of both brother and sister in these procedures were purely symbolic, no one could accuse them of having openly expressed their desires, thus leaving the decision up to the warrior holders of the land. While the high chief ostensibly held power over the people of his tribe, it was his unostentatious mother, the "old queen," whose opinions, according to Robarts, had the force of law.[25] She therefore seems to have been above reproach and was thus able, in the final procedure, to voice her personal desire that the land be returned to her daughter.

Land acquired by intertribal warfare could, on occasion, be recovered by the losing tribe through a negotiated purchase. However, this was not always, or necessarily usually, the case.[26] The extreme to which war could go was an event on Tahuata mentioned by Crook in which two individually weak tribes formed an alliance to make war on the largest tribe on that island. All but a few members of that large tribe were said to have been slaughtered and the tribe's extensive landholdings occupied.[27]

Not all wars were oriented toward the acquisition of territory, nor is it clear that increased arable land was a dominating survival need for most tribes, since some areas were left abandoned.[28] Robarts wrote of a battle with another tribe that was undertaken merely on the basis of a challenge given, he said, in a most insulting manner.[29] There were also interisland wars between tribes of Tahuata and Hivaoa, resulting in deaths and the taking of prisoners but involving no attempts to occupy land or demand tribute.[30] In some of these aggressive encounters the winner, rather than occupying the productive lands of the enemy, made a concerted effort to destroy their productive capacity. This was accomplished by girdling the breadfruit trees, beating down the central heart of growth of coconut palms, and destroying gardens, as well as the burning and looting of houses.[31] However, the wars that appear to have resulted in the least devastation were those waged against what were described as traditional enemy tribes. To a degree these undertakings appear to have verged on the ceremonial and may have required periodic recurrences.

Wars with traditional enemies were essentially pitched battles in unpopulated upland areas of the mountains on terrain that gave neither side a distinct advantage; the Tovii plateau of Nukuhiva was one such site. Such a war was preceded by religious ceremonies in taboo houses, and the time and place of battle, though not officially announced to the enemy, was nonetheless indirectly relayed to them.[32] However, not all such wars followed the same pattern.

Both Crook and Porter seem to suggest that each such war consisted of a single battle. While Crook claimed that all warriors in such a fight were decorated with ornaments,[33] this was not true in the battle seen by Porter. He noted that only one or two, who seem to have led the field, were richly decorated with shells, tufts of hair, ear ornaments, and the like.[34] These two decorated men may have been toa warriors representing their chiefs. Crook noted that when High Chief Keatonue's toa went to war, he was decorated with his chief's personal ornaments, perhaps thus symbolizing his presence.[35] However, Robarts, who seems to have participated in one of these traditional wars but, to the consternation of the enemy, had misunderstood the pitched battle requirements of the exercise, reported that four separate confrontations were required to fulfill the tribe's tau'a prophecy. In this case, only in the fourth and final battle, which included fighting, dancing, and general goodwill, were the warriors ornately dressed.[36]

Warrior ornamentation, which might include the skull of an enemy,[37] was limited to these traditional enemy battles. Crook described how the bodies of Hivaoa warrior enemies were brought back to Tahuata along with all of their ornaments.[38] However, it is not clear whether such decorations were worn during all types of wars, or whether they were worn only by chiefs and toa warriors.

These traditional battles, which women were allowed to watch and to bring small nets of stones for the slings,[39] often did not result in bloodshed or death. Customarily, the battle was fought at a distance with slings. Should a stone strike a man down, the enemy would rush forward in an attempt to kill or carry him off, but would be resisted.[40] Should the course of a war threaten to interfere with a prescribed koina festival of either tribe, a truce was called. Both warring parties would then join forces to prepare and participate in the event, after which the war might be renewed.[41]

It is possible that not all traditional tribal enemies resorted to lethal weapons during these occasional meetings. Robarts wrote of spending a pleasant day on a beach on Hivaoa where the warriors of two traditional enemy tribes, although wary of one another, spent the time in what was essentially a sham battle. Besides exchanging "hostages" of equal rank, they took turns throwing green nuts at one another. The event terminated with a dance, after which the warriors exchanged spears and fans.[42]

In Marquesan wars the only unharmed prisoners were those of the upper class, most probably of chiefly families, who were related by marriage or adoption to some member of the captor's tribe. Such people were allowed to go free and return to their families.[43] Crook noted yet another class of prisoners who, on certain occasions, were scalped and then allowed to return to their tribe. It seems probable that such scalping was limited in extent, since Crook was told that the victims usually survived the operation.[44] While he did not specify the circumstance that allowed this action, he may have inadvertently revealed it. At one point he described how four members of an enemy tribe had been captured, but since they had been taken prisoner after the termination of a battle, rather than being killed and, according to Crook, eaten, they were scalped and sent back to their people.[45] As for others taken in war, the records of Crook and Robarts are at variance and could reflect differences in treatment between the windward and leeward islands.

In describing what had happened to Hivaoa prisoners brought back to Tahuata, Crook claimed that they were killed and eaten, as were corpses of the enemy in intertribal fighting on the island of Tahuata.[46] However, Robarts, who appears to have been describing the war pattern at Nukuhiva, claimed that the war dead of the enemy were sacrificed on the tribal me'ae or at taboo houses. If captured alive, they were taken to the taboo houses and tortured.[47] However, this did not mean that cannibalism was absent on Nukuhiva. Robarts told of having been escorted over the mountains by warriors of an enemy tribe to which he was related by adoption, and hence should have been safe. However, he explained that had he been alone and caught by the "lower classes" of that tribe in the mountains while not following the prescribed trail out of their valley, he would have been killed and eaten on the spot.[48]

In spite of the tales that Robarts and Jean Baptiste Cabri told the Russian explorers in 1804 of Marquesan men eating their wives, children, and friends in times of famine,[49] there is nothing in either Crook's or Robarts's accounts that supports these claims. Such statements would thus seem to have been overly enlarged stories designed, quite probably, to enhance the two men's fearlessness in the eyes of the Russian contingent. As the records stand, cannibalism was restricted to tribes other than one's own for the purpose of religious rites and to enemies killed or taken prisoner in war. As explained to Robarts by a Marquesan friend, their forefathers had taught them to eat their enemies, though there were many among them who would not eat human flesh.[50]

FORTIFICATIONS

In spite of all the intertribal and interisland wars of the Marquesans, there is no indisputable historic record of the existence of fortifications until Porter's visit in 1813. The Quiros account of the 1595 visit of the Spanish states that the natives of Tahuata had run to the hills and entrenched themselves there.[51] Captain James Cook's visit to the same island in 1774 resulted in an assortment of speculations concerning a structure on a high mountain observed through telescopes. Cook was convinced it was a stronghold,[52] while George Forster described it as consisting of a row of closely set stakes with what looked like huts nearby. However, after being told that the native women had gone there to mourn their dead, he came to suspect that it was a burial ground.[53] His father, John Forster, was a bit more specific in describing the structure as being composed of several houses placed together on what he interpreted to be a "kind of elevated fortification" that was enclosed by stakes.[54] Rather than a fortification, the elevated area with buildings on it and the whole enclosed by a fence comes closer to a me'ae platform and housing assemblage. However, by 1791 the question of its function had become moot because the French expedition made an effort to verify its presence but found no evidence of its existence.[55]

The fact that neither Crook nor Robarts, who was involved in several wars, ever mentioned the presence of fortifications strongly supports the view that they did not exist on the islands until at least 1806. Nonetheless, it is worthy of note that in 1804 Krusenstern saw at a distance what appeared to be a roofless square stone building on top of the mountain that he thought might be a fort.[56] Here again it is just as likely that what he saw was a raised masonry platform.

Not until 1813 was a reasonably clear description of a hilltop fortification given by Porter. Its defensive palisades were tall, upright logs tightly fitted together and held in place by cross timbers. On the inner side of the palisades was a raised scaffolding topped by a platform for the defending warriors to stand on and throw spears and stones at the enemy. One of the forts had been built on top of a ridge and was further protected from advancing troops by a sizable fosse cut through the ridge crest.[57] In the valley of Taipi, Porter saw a massive stone-walled fort complete with protected sally ports.[58] Thus, unless eighteenth-century, or earlier, dates can be established for the appearance of Marquesan forts, historical records would seem to favor an early-nineteenth-century development, perhaps as a response to the introduction and use in warfare of European guns.

SIGNS OF PEACE

With wars seeming to be interminable affairs in the Marquesas, this chapter should close by noting that Marquesans did have symbols denoting peace, or at least a desire for peace and friendship. The arrival of Europeans, and possibly any foreigners from outside the archipelago, was greeted by specific material symbols. In some cases it was a piece of white bark cloth,[59] or a green bough accompanied by a bit of white cloth,[60] or occasionally a pig that was brought to the ship.[61]

Although most historic accounts do not identify the type of bough presented, it seems to have varied. George Forster identified the branch brought to Captain Cook's vessel as being tamanu (*Calophyllum inophyllum* L.),[62] while Crook identified the bough brought to Edmund Fanning as being toa (*Casuarina equisetifolia* L.).[63] The use of such a green symbol, regardless of what species, appears to have been a request for peace. During the visit of the French to Tahuata, the accidental discharge of a blunderbuss into a group of natives resulted in the frightened Marquesans immediately presenting the French with several green boughs.[64] In another potentially dangerous situation, a green plantain leaf was quickly found and presented to the Europeans, along with a pig.[65]

The piece of white cloth was explained to Porter as being a symbol of friendship,[66] which would seem to explain the combined display of a green bough and white cloth as a desire for peace and friendship. The same appears to have been true where a bough was accompanied by a pig.[67] However, within Marquesan society the coconut leaf or nut was the appropriate green symbolic emblem. As noted earlier, when the final agreement had been reached in the negotiations for the return of land to the high chief's eldest sister, thus eliminating the need for war, Robarts sent a bunch of coconuts and a piece of white bark cloth to the waiting warriors to indicate that peace had been reached.[68] In another instance, when Robarts was angrily threatening battle with some natives, the sister of the high chief's mother brought him a symbolic request for peace that consisted of a coconut leaf and an open coconut for him to drink as part of his acceptance of the request.[69] A coconut branch planted in the earth in the mountain fighting grounds was a symbol of a truce,[70] and when placed between two men upon their first meeting, it represented a desire for friendly relations.[71] Whatever the symbol, peace in the Marquesas tended to be an evanescent event.

CHAPTER 10

In Retrospect

MARQUESAN ROOTS

This synthesis of early ethnohistoric observations of the culture of the Marquesas must be seen as a limited view of the end product of some fifteen centuries of human occupation. However, to accept the whole of it as the result of independent evolutionary and inventive creation of a single founding population arriving, according to archaeological evidence, around A.D. 300, strains belief in human genius. The possibility, if not probability, that the Marquesas were peopled by more than one migrant group of settlers, not to mention occasional castaways, must be born in mind when considering the content of late-eighteenth-century Marquesan culture.

Any effort to relate the people and culture of one island group to that of a geographically more distant group faces a range of alternative explanations of how apparent similarities of material or social culture may have come about. This is especially true in Oceania, where culture histories are inadequate or absent. Varying environmental and social forces acting on cultural aspects of two separate societies can, through time, create discrete similarities without contacts between the two ever having been made. Similarly, comparable environmental potentials for two separated societies may result in the two unrelated cultures developing their economies and associated tools along essentially parallel lines. And then, too, there is the human genius to create—to invent, if you will—new tools or ways of doing things; and the simpler the new creation, the more likely that other, unrelated people will originate a comparable device or solution to a problem.

The above sources of cultural similarities can lead to unwarranted assumptions of cultural contacts or previous associations. However, the chances of similarities having resulted from contact or diffusion are enhanced where island cultures share a basic cultural pattern and there is evidence of migratory movements through time from early occupation to relatively later periods. Such is the situation in Polynesia, as elucidated by Roger Green in "The Immediate Origins of the Polynesians."[1] Given this originating homeland ranging from Vanuatu to, and including, Tonga and Samoa, it seems reasonable to expect contact cultural diffusion to at least some of the Polynesian islands to the east. Thus, since basic Marquesan culture is believed to have derived from this Polynesian homeland, at least some of its early cultural content might be expected to include ethnographic remnants reflecting a source in this originating area. It is with this in mind that the following comparisons are presented.

Archaeologically, the earliest phase yet discovered on the Marquesas islands, dating from A.D. 300 to 600, contained pottery, a certain style of adze, tattooing combs, and the worked stone sinker of an octopus lure, all of them similar to comparable items in western Polynesia. These have rightly been regarded as indicating that western Polynesia was probably a source of the early migrants. However, that same early phase also included a rectangular house foundation.[2] Since such foundation shapes have not yet been found in either Tonga or Samoa but are present, at least historically, in eastern Melanesia, the source of these migrants could have been a bit further west than western Polynesia. As might be expected, these few features exhibiting similarities to comparable ones to the west were gradually altered through time as this initial, seemingly isolated culture modified its portable tools to meet new environmental requirements and idiosyncratic desires. Excepting the rectangular house foundation, they soon could no longer be compared with cultural tools to the west. It was not until 1300 that architectural innovations appeared. Initially, these took the form of stone masonry house platforms, which were soon followed by more complex forms, such as the identifiable tohua courts and tribal me'ae.[3]

While only a few items of the earliest known archaeological assemblage showed relationships to western Polynesia and, possibly, eastern Melanesia, late-eighteenth-century Marquesan culture exhibited additional parallels with those islands to the west. Although house shapes were not identical to those of eastern Melanesia, their rectangular floor plan remained similar. Of far more importance was the basic similarity of the Marquesan socioreligious men's taboo complex, including its internal ranking and specially restricted houses, to the northern Vanuatu men's *suge* organization with its all-male *gamal* house described by R. H. Codrington.[4] A further Marquesan parallel with eastern Melanesia was the death feast given very soon after the demise of an individual.[5]

Scattered within the ethnohistoric descriptions of the western Polynesian cultures of Samoa and Tonga were several traits with parallels in early historic Marquesan culture. Among these are the treatment of some of the dead in Samoa. Missionary George Turner, who first visited Samoa in 1841–42, and lived there from 1843 to 1882,[6] reported that, as in the Marquesas, some bodies were placed in hollowed-out log caskets, while others were preserved for a length of time by evisceration and extended oiling of the remains.[7] While oiling was reported for the treatment of certain of the dead in the Marquesas, there was no reference to evisceration. However, this may have occurred, since some of the dead were eviscerated prior to oiling in eighteenth-century Tahiti. And although Marquesans lacked the formal ceremonies associated with the drinking of kava in Samoa and Tonga, the upper classes did follow the Tongan custom of starting each day by joining friends of their own class in drinking a few rounds of the beverage before beginning the day's activities.

Although early ethnohistoric data for comparisons are lacking for Samoa, it is worth noting that such early data for Tonga and the Marquesas show that these latter shared several features. One was the recognition and employment of craft specialists.[8] There was also a close similarity in the functions of the Marquesan tuhuna ota ogo and the Tongan matāpule. Both were expected to perform and be cognizant of certain religious ceremonies, as well as to serve as the authoritative sources of genealogies and their society's traditions.[9] It may also be significant that in both these island groups a special language unfamiliar to the masses was employed in religious contexts. The Tongans used a special language when addressing their most sacred Tui Tonga,[10] and in the Marquesas the tuhuna ota ogo conducted certain of their religious ceremonies in a special language not understood by others.

On a somewhat different level, the blowing of conch shell trumpets on certain occasions and the touching of noses as a form of greeting were common in the Marquesas and Tonga.[11] Here it should be noted that conch trumpets appear to have been lacking in Tahiti until after the beginning of the nineteenth century, and the touching of noses as a form of greeting was not reported until 1786; both traits appear to have been historic introductions.[12] Of no small interest in terms of suggesting a relatively late prehistoric introduction into the Marquesas are two specific forms of obeisance practiced in Tonga and the Marquesas in early historic times. One of these consisted of a woman kissing the hand of an important person and then placing that hand upon her head.[13] The other involved a man prostrating himself before a person of high station and placing that individual's foot or leg on the prostrated man's head or shoulder.[14]

The relatively late appearance, post A.D. 1300, of such architectural features as house platforms, tohua courts, burial me'ae, and tribal me'ae pose the question of their origin. Only in the case of the tohua can one hazard a reasonable hypothesis as to its origin. On the basis of known historic attributes and function, the Marquesan tohua may be seen as an elaboration of the Tongan *mala'e*. Both served as open areas for public gatherings, amusements, and ceremonies. In their simplest form each had a large open building along one edge of the performance area.[15] In this view, the Marquesan addition of paving, which was not always present even in historic times, and peripheral raised platform substructures for guest houses may be seen as elaborations on a basic design. Although one can discern certain functional parallels between Tongan *fa'itoka* and Marquesan burial me'ae,[16] far more detailed architectural studies of Marquesan masonry structures need to be made before the original function of various platforms can be clearly determined.

Unless one is to regard the early historic ethnographic Marquesan parallels with eastern Melanesia and western Polynesia as inconsequential, or the result of parallel evolution, it would seem probable that much of historically known Marquesan culture derived from these two sources. Furthermore, it can be expected that some non-material features would be retained for extended periods of time in both a mother culture and its separated offspring. This would be especially true of the more conservative elements.

Accepting that such retentions could have been maintained into the historic period, it must then be reasoned that, along with the western Polynesian similarities, the east Melanesian parallels connote yet another, separate source in the cultural amalgam of the

Marquesas. Thus, following Green's cogent argument for an eastern Melanesian source for the immediate origins of the Polynesians,[17] the eastern Melanesian parallels already cited must represent the earliest cultural intrusion into the Marquesas prior to the advent of the obviously Polynesian elements derived from Tonga and Samoa. However, the presence of these traits does not, per se, mean that their source at the time of their arrival in the Marquesas was that geographic area. If Green's theory holds, they could have come from what is now known as western Polynesia at a time when eastern Melanesian culture had reached those islands but had not yet completed the presumed transformation into what was to become known as western Polynesian culture.

Begging the question of when an eastern Melanesian is a Polynesian, there would appear to have been a recognizable physical difference between the lowest class of Marquesans and those of higher rank. Just as Joseph Banks and George Forster described the low-class *teuteu* women of Tahiti as being smaller than their upper-class counterparts,[18] so G. H. von Langsdorff noted that the lower class of women in the Marquesas who came aboard his ship were "little puny creatures" compared with those of the upper classes.[19] A. J. von Krusenstern described the hair of the lower class as being different from that of others in being woolly and coarse, though not quite so much so as that of the African blacks.[20] Crook described this class of people as having no interest in the religious beliefs and ceremonies of their superiors. Instead, they were obsessed with fears of spirits, witches, and ghosts,[21] concerns that certainly paralleled those of the Melanesians.[22]

Accepting that the lowest class of Marquesans were recognizably different from those superior to them, let us present the following hypothesis. The founding population of the Marquesas, essentially eastern Melanesian in culture, subsequently was overwhelmed and eventually subjugated by a later migration of western Polynesian settlers. Should that have taken place, one could reasonably expect a degree of cultural loss, acceptance, blending, and trait retention by the two groups. By early historic times this would seem to have taken place. The art of pottery making had been lost, but the rectangular-foundation house had become the customary dwelling. A modified version of the eastern Melanesian suge and gamal, or tabooed house, was in place, and the death feast had become a part of funeral rites.

Although the earlier founding population had become subservient to the later Polynesian element, they seem to have retained a few of their more personal eastern Melanesian traits. Not all males opted for the operation of supercision, even though not to do so resulted in their being ridiculed as "nasty." However, in Vanuatu, Codrington found that the lack of supercision was common among many of the men and apparently was not regarded disdainfully.[23]

It should also be noted that in a culture in which the upper-class males prided themselves on being extensively tattooed, there were others, albeit of the poorer classes, who had no such decorations. Although European observers assumed that such absence was owing to an inability to pay a tattooer, this was not necessarily the case. For example, Marchand noted that on Uapou only a few men were tattooed,[24] and Crook mentioned men of one whole valley of people on Hivaoa who were not adorned with such artwork.[25] A tattooing comb was uncovered in the earliest deposits known for the Marquesas, but this does not necessarily mean that it was used on male members of that early culture. As Codrington pointed out, in eastern Melanesia women were tattooed, but he does not mention men having been so decorated.[26]

The above is, perforce, a hypothesized attempt to account for the early presence in the Marquesan culture of features known to have been present historically in either western Polynesia or eastern Melanesia. This has been necessary since, as Janet Davidson has pointed out,[27] there remains a substantial gap in the prehistory of western Polynesia that, if Green's theory of the immediate origin of the Polynesians is correct, should represent the time when the transition from an eastern Melanesian to a western Polynesian culture was taking place. Thus, until the cultural content of that time gap has been revealed, one can only hypothesize as to its nature and when, and how many, eastward dispersals took place.

Of a different nature is the question of why the Marquesas served as a point of cultural dispersal, even during the early phases of its settlement—witness the early diffusion to the Society Islands.[28] As noted in Chapter 1, the force that initiated such dispersals appears to have been the La Niña phenomenon, which, apparently operating over centuries, has caused unpredictable, devastating droughts on those islands. For a horticultural society such famine-causing droughts would represent the most realistic cause for initiating early, as well as later, migrations in search of more suitable islands.

POTENTIAL SOURCES OF USEFUL AMERICAN PLANTS IN THE MARQUESAS

As has been noted, the missionary William P. Crook reported the presence of seven useful plants of American origin during his stay in the Marquesas from 1797 to 1798: the chili pepper (or capsicum, as he called it), the cashew, the pineapple, the soursop or guanabana, the soapberry, the sweet potato, and cotton. Crook was not the first to report the presence of cotton, that having been done by Captain Josiah Roberts, who visited the islands in 1792–93.[29] Nor was he necessarily the first to mention the sweet potato; Étienne Marchand had encountered a "sort of sweet potato" in 1791.[30] It may even have been noted as early as 1774, for George Forster implied its presence when he wrote of the food plants on Tahuata: "Their food consists of the same variety of fruits and roots which are common at Tahiti, except the apple (Spondias)."[31] And, contrary to Roland Dixon's claim that sweet potatoes were of slight importance in Tahiti, and thus not common there,[32] John R. Forster of Cook's second voyage wrote that they and the greater yam, *Dioscoria alata* L., were regularly planted and regarded as the best "eatables" during the season when breadfruit was not available.[33] Thus, had the sweet potato not been present on Tahuata, Forster would have noted its absence along with that of the apple. In addition to Crook's list of American plants, the naturalist G. H. von Langsdorff[34] reported the calabash tree as growing in the Marquesas in 1804.[35]

Since Crook was certainly no naturalist, his position prior to becoming a missionary having been a gentleman's servant,[36] one might doubt his ability to identify those plants for which he gave common English names. However, had he not been familiar with them before leaving England, he probably did encounter them when the missionary ship *Duff* arrived in Rio de Janeiro on its way to the Pacific. During their week-long stay in this port, Captain James Wilson reported the collecting of various seeds and plants for distribution in the Pacific, not to mention adding local provisions.[37] Besides the English-named crops, it was probably during this stay that Crook learned the Portuguese word for *Anacardium occidentale* L., or *cadju*, which he spelled phonetically as "cashu."

Two of the American plants in the Marquesas were unfamiliar to Crook, who simply gave their Marquesan names. One of these he wrote as *kogu* and described how its liquid was rubbed on the umbilical stump of a newborn child;[38] it was also used by ka'ioi dancers as an aid in applying the yellow turmeric stain to their bodies.[39] This I have identified, I hope correctly, as the kokuu that the botanist Forest Brown identified as *Sapindus saponaria* L., commonly known as the soapberry.[40] As for Crook's fruit, the nano, his description of its characteristics matches so well the botanical description of the fruit of *Annona muricata* L., commonly known as the soursop or guanabana, that there can be little doubt that nano and *A. muricata* are the same. In fact, Crook wrote that nano had been compared to that plant.[41] Furthermore, Brown found this fruit growing in the Marquesas in the early twentieth century; unfortunately, he failed to record its Marquesan name.[42] As for the identification of the calabash tree, *Crescentia cujete* L., I have accepted as accurate naturalist Langsdorff's identification. Like the other plants already mentioned, Brown reported it growing in the Marquesas in the early 1920s.[43]

Of importance in considering the source of these plants is the fact that all, with the possible exception of the particular variety of cotton, were available along the west coast of South America from Peru northward to, and including, Ecuador. The soapberry (*Sapindus saponaria* L.) has been found in prehistoric sites in Peru,[44] as have *Capsicum annum* L., *C. frutescens* L., and *C. pubescens* Ruiz et Pau;[45] and Juan de Velasco reported several varieties of the chili pepper growing in Ecuador in 1789.[46] The fruit of the soursop (*Annona muricata* L.) was modeled on the black pottery of the Chimu in northern coastal Peru.[47] Although prehistoric remains of pineapple (*Ananas comosus* (L.) Merrill) have not been found in Peru, small ones were said to have been growing in northern coastal Peru in 1585, and Velasco reported two varieties present in coastal Ecuador.[48] While the calabash tree (*Crescentia cujete* L.) appears not to have been native to the coastal valleys of Peru, prehistoric specimens of the fruit have been found in Peruvian coastal sites, and Teodoro Wolf found them to be common in the humid zones of coastal Ecuador during his geographic explorations of that country from about 1870 through the 1880s.[49] Root specimens of the sweet potato (*Ipomoea batatas* (L.) Poir. ex Lam.) have been recovered from a variety of prehistoric sites on the Peruvian coast from Nazca in the south to the Mochica sites in the north, and Velasco mentioned both purple and white varieties growing throughout Ecuador.[50] The lint-bearing cotton (*Gossypium barbadense* L.) was common in the prehistoric archaeological deposits of Peru, and Velasco reported cotton plants the size of trees growing in the humid areas of coastal Ecuador.[51] As for the cashew (*Anacardium occidentale* L.), I can find no evidence that it grew on the dry coast of Peru. However, both Velasco and Wolf reported it as common in the humid areas of coastal Ecuador, where I found it still present in the 1940s.[52]

Since the Marquesans had had no fewer than eight contacts with European vessels by the time Crook arrived in 1797,[53] an immediate possible answer to how these American plants reached the Marquesas would be via one or more of these ships. However, in the case of the sweet potato, Pacific anthropologists continue to accept Roland Dixon's argument that it was a prehistoric introduction into Polynesia,[54] although there is no definitive archaeological evidence supporting this position. Thor Heyerdahl's well-known view is that this root was carried into the Pacific by South American Indians using the trade winds to sail to Polynesia.[55] An opposing scenario has Polynesians sailing east to the South American coast and returning with the sweet potato.[56]

Although this latter concept appears to require that the Polynesians sailed eastward against the dominating trade winds to reach the continental coast, the latest view put forward by Ben Finney does away with this difficulty. He has suggested that such a voyage took advantage of the occasional eastward-flowing El Niño anomaly to reach the South American coast.[57] This is certainly not without merit. As has been described, Marquesans of Nukuhiva did take advantage of the brief annual periods of westerlies to sail to Hivaoa and Tahuata, returning home with the advent of the recurring easterlies or trade winds. It is thus possible that at some point in the prehistoric past, a Marquesan canoe was caught up in a strong El Niño event and may well have reached the northern coast of South America.

In this regard, it is worth calling attention to the historical record brought to light by the cultural geographer Carl Sauer. He noted that on the occasion of Vasco Nuñez de Balboa's march across Panama on his way to discovering the Pacific in 1513, he encountered several black, frizzy haired men held as slaves by the Quareca Indians. They were said to be members of a larger group of similar people living on the Pacific coast south of the Golfo de San Miguel, Panama, who were accustomed to making canoe raids on coastal Indians. Confirmation of the existence of these people was later made by Francisco Becerra. Not knowing of Melanesians at that time, the Spaniards presumed them to be blacks who had sailed across the ocean from Africa. Sauer concluded that these reports could represent the earliest intimation that there may have been landings in the Americas by people from distant parts of the South Seas.[58]

It has always seemed to me a bit strange, if not profligate, that if American Indians tried to settle in Polynesia, or Polynesians made a round trip to the coast of South America, they failed to bring with them other useful American plants rather than just the sweet potato. If any, or all, of the American plants already noted were introduced into the Marquesas in prehistoric times, the prospect that either, or both, types of voyages had occurred would be greatly strengthened. Since, with the possible exception of the sweet potato, the American plants noted could be expected to produce adequate amounts of pollen, a search for such prehistoric evidence should be conducted. However, such a search has yet to be undertaken, and until it is, and the results prove positive for prehistoric introductions, a more careful study of the potential for a historic introduction is desirable.

As noted earlier, Marquesans told Crook that Josiah Roberts had introduced the pineapple during his lengthy stay in the islands in 1792–93, but by 1813 their account had been modified; they then told Porter that Crook had introduced that plant. Thus, for all we know, the pineapple could have been introduced by Captain James Cook in 1774, since he was known to have introduced it into Tahiti and Tonga.[59] As for the remaining plants, there appear to have been no traditions regarding their origin, or perhaps Marquesans were never asked how they had received them.

Although there is the record of Mendaña supposedly having sown maize on Tahuata,[60] which apparently did not sprout or was not accepted, neither Cook nor Marchand mentions having left any seeds or plants on the islands. Nor is it likely that most of the other eighteenth-century vessels preceding Crook's arrival in the *Duff* would have carried such an odd assortment of seeds and plants as the soapberry, soursop, chili peppers, sweet potato, and cotton, as well as the calabash and cashew trees. This would be especially true of the latter, since the sap in the walls of the cashew nut is very caustic, thus requiring that it be boiled or roasted before it is safe to eat. However, such an assortment would not have been altogether odd for the Mendaña expedition of men and women bent on colonizing what they hoped would be the Solomon Islands.

The Mendaña expedition was made up of 378 people, of whom 280 were said to be capable of bearing arms.⁶¹ The rest were colonists who included women, a few children, and, presumably, the three priests who accompanied the party. Not all of the women were married at the time of departure, for Quiros reported fifteen marriages having taken place during the voyage to the Marquesas.⁶²

Sailing from Callao, Peru, Mendaña turned north along the coast, stopped at the port of Cherrepe for supplies, and then advanced as far as Paita. Here the group was close enough to the rich Piura Valley, as well as the humid coast of Ecuador, that tropical crops from those areas could have been readily available in the marketplace. In Paita, a large supply of fresh water was taken on and, one may safely presume, a final rounding out of supplies was completed. If, among the crop supplies, the sweet potato had been included, it is possible that, rather than the more delicate tuber, its seeds were taken. As D. E. Yen has pointed out, the incidence of seed is not rare, and during his own collecting of sweet potato seeds in South America, he obtained some along the coast of Peru at Trujillo and at Piura, the latter just inland from the port of Paita.⁶³ While the bulk of the supplies were obtained by Mendaña, his soldiers and intended colonists purchased others as they saw fit or desirable. Regrettably, no record of the range of these purchases was noted by Quiros.⁶⁴ Leaving Paita on April 9, 1595, Mendaña's four vessels sailed westward, sighting the island of Magdalena (Fatuhiva) on July 21 and anchoring in the bay of Vaitahu on Santa Christina (Tahuata) a week later.⁶⁵

On the following day, July 29, Mendaña and his soldiers landed and walked through the cluster of houses at the head of the bay. At that time he was said to have sown maize. After Mendaña had returned to his vessel, his soldiers, who had been left behind in the "village," created havoc with the natives, who deserted their cluster of houses and took refuge in the surrounding mountains. With the "village" now deserted, the Spaniards disembarked the people and, almost certainly, the livestock, since all had been at sea for over one hundred days. While there is no record of the livestock carried by the vessels, there is a mention of a calf that a native had picked up by one ear, and a small dog taken by another.⁶⁶

While Dixon made much of Mendaña's having sown only maize, little attention has been given to the potential for intentional or inadvertent introductions by the colonists of plants or seeds during their week-long rest on land. Nor has it been noted that at one point Mendaña considered founding a small colony in the Marquesas, which may have induced some of the colonists to begin planting a few crops in anticipation.[67]

Other than maize, there is no record of the seeds or plants carried by Mendaña's expedition, except a casual note that while at Santa Cruz the soldiers gave some cotton to the natives.[68] However, in 1606, only eleven years after Mendaña's second expedition, Quiros again sailed west from Callao on yet another attempted colonizing expedition. In this instance he listed some of the crops planted at Espíritu Santo on Vanuatu. This gives at least an inkling of the kinds of seeds Mendaña may have carried on board his ill-fated voyage. Quiros wrote of planting maize, cotton, onions, pumpkins, melons, beans, pulse, "and other seeds of our country."[69] His chief pilot, Gaspar de Leza, added to this list lentils, peas, "calabashes of Peru," and potatoes.[70] The latter were almost certainly sweet potatoes, since the Irish potato (*Solanum tuberosum* L.) is a temperate crop unsuited to the tropics.

As may be seen, a wide range of practical plants of both Old World and American origin could be expected to have been carried by Mendaña for use by his prospective colonists. Thus, any or all of the plants of American origin noted by Crook, as well as the calabash tree recorded by Langsdorff, could have been carried by Mendaña's people. They could have been intentionally or incidentally deposited during the week that the colonizers cooked, ate, slept, and wandered about the vacated native settlement.

All of the American plants were useful to colonizers. The fruit of the soapberry, with its saponin content, made a fine substitute for soap.[71] Though many such foreign plant introductions may not have been acceptable to Marquesans, as must have been the case with cotton, those that were readily acclimated to island conditions were apt to survive as feral indicators of such contacts. This was the case in Tahiti, where lemons, limes, and chili peppers survived, though unaccepted as food.[72] In this regard it would seem that no Old World plants, if introduced even casually, survived except one. The red and black seeds of what must have been the introduced Old World plant *Abrus precatorius* L., known commonly as the rosary pea, were used for decorative purposes by the Marquesans. Given the Spaniards' strong emphasis on religious matters—three priests accompanied the colonists, and a mass was said upon landing at Tahuata—it would not be surprising if this plant had been accidentally introduced at the time of their visit.

Regardless of the possibilities of plant introductions into the Marquesas by Mendaña, Polynesianists remain essentially adamant in their assumption that at least the sweet potato arrived in Polynesia well before the Spaniards reached the Marquesas. Radiocarbon dates of archaeologically recovered specimens of *I. batatas*, which had ranges of A.D. 1545–1725 and A.D. 1425–1605 for those found in Hawaii, and A.D. 1526 plus or minus 100 years for one found on Easter Island,[73] do not clearly support its prehistoric introduction. Nor does its claimed pre-Columbian age in New Zealand rest on solid evidence, since it is based on the highly questionable interpretation of early prehistoric storage pits as having been used to store sweet potatoes during the winter months.[74]

In spite of these failings, the plant's widespread occurrence observed in the last half of the eighteenth century would seem to suggest such an early prehistoric introduction. Besides being found in Tahiti, it was encountered to the north in Hawaii, to the east at Easter Island, and to the southwest at North Island, New Zealand, but was absent in the southern Cook Islands until introduced there by missionaries.[75]

Since it has been assumed by those supporting a pre-Columbian introduction that it was the result of a single episode, this extensive distribution logically implies that the plant's arrival at its entry point had to be at a very early period. This is indeed reasonable, given the assumption that the introduction was the result of a single event. However, an equally valid assumption could be made for more than one discrete introduction having taken place prior to European voyages of the latter half of the eighteenth century. Such multiple points of introduction would help to explain the wide distribution of that tuber as reported in the latter half of the eighteenth century. Thus, the Spaniards may have been responsible for the introduction of the sweet potato into the Marquesas in 1595, and again in 1606 at Espíritu Santo, Vanuatu, at the extreme eastern edge of Melanesia. Since the sweet potato had become an important introduced crop in Japan by the last half of the eighteenth century,[76] its possible introduction from that source prior to Captain Cook's first landing on Hawaii in 1778 is certainly a possibility. This could have been accomplished by way of derelict voyages from Japan of the type that reached Hawaii in later years, as recorded by John F. G. Stokes.[77]

As for a possible prehistoric introduction into the Marquesas, one might here interject the previously discussed question concerning the construction of the canoes of Fatuhiva as described by Quiros. If the balancers of those canoes were lashed along each side of a canoe, as argued by Hornell,[78] their resemblance to the Imbabura canoe type of Ecuador, now known to be prehistoric, could be important. It might suggest that Fatuhiva was the point of introduction not only of the sweet potato but also of the unique float device that could have been adapted from the type of Ecuadorian oceangoing canoe that might have brought the plant to Polynesia. Or was Hornell wrong, and what Quiros was attempting to describe were double outrigger canoes, as I earlier suggested?

As may be seen, one might reasonably ascribe the presence and use of some of the American plants in the Marquesas, including the sweet potato, to a pre-Columbian introduction. However, before doing so too quickly it is worth recalling the result of thirty years of known introductions made in Tahiti. There, after a number of recorded attempts to introduce a wide range of foreign crops, by 1797 the only ones that remained were the American pineapple, maize, and possibly the squash, as well as the feral chili peppers and tobacco plants, and the planted, but unwanted, Old World lemon and lime trees.[79]

The end result of this brief work is to illustrate how both contrasting hypotheses have degrees of validity, given their assumptive nature. It thus appears evident that until firmer evidence is forthcoming as to the sources, times, and means of the introduction into Polynesia of the sweet potato, as well as other American Indian domesticates, a more balanced approach than has been apparent in the past is justified. It would seem more rational to consider both views when attempting to gauge the cultural impact of a prehistoric, or historic and thus recent, introduction of such crops on the islands involved.

Glossary

ahui: A taboo or restriction against fishing in certain waters or harvesting particular crops.

'arioi: A Tahitian society of male and female entertainers, all of whom appear to have belonged to the chiefly class.

atua: A god.

'eva: Probably the plant *Ceodes brunoniana* (Endl.) Skottsb.

fa'itoka: A Tongan chief's burial mound, often rectangular and faced with stone masonry.

fau: The tree *Hibiscus tiliaceus* L.

gamal: In eastern Melanesia a house restricted to males and belonging to the *suge* men's ranked society.

ge: See *ti.*

haka'iki: High chief of a tribe.

hami: Loincloth.

hiapo: Bark cloth made from *Ficus prolixa* Forst.

hio: A temporary social group whose purpose was not explained.

hoi: The yam *Dioscorea bulbifera* L.

huou: The plant *Solanum repandum* Forst.

hutu: The tree *Barringtonia asiatica* (L.) Kurz.

ihi: The tree *Inocarpus edulis* Forst.

ka'eu: A woman's short skirt of bark cloth fastened between the thighs.

kahu: A bark cloth robe.

ka'ioi: Male dancers and entertainers.

kape: The crop plant *Alocasia macrorrhiza* (L.) Schott.

koina: A celebration of singing and dancing held on a *tohua.*

kokuu: The tree *Sapindus saponaria* L.

ma: Fermented breadfruit.

maii: The Indian almond *Terminalia catappa* L.

mala'e: A Tongan grassy clearing used for meetings, dances, and ceremonies.

manahune: Originally the Tahitian class name for landowning commoners.

manno: A quantity unit equal to ten times that of an *ou*.

matapule: A Tongan traditionalist, adviser, spokesman, and ceremonial attendant of a chief.

matta puovo: Highest-ranking group of men on Nukuhiva.

mattatoetoe: A class name for high-ranking wealthy families who may, or may not, be of chiefly affiliation.

me'ae: Family, *tau'a*, and tribal religious places also used as tombs.

mei: The breadfruit tree *Artocarpus altilis* (Parkinson) Fosberg.

mi'o: The tree *Thespesia populnea* (L.) Sol.

moa: A religious aide to a *tau'a*.

nano: The soursop *Annona muricata* L.

noni: The fruit tree *Morinda citrifolia* L.

nono: See *noni*.

ou: A quantity unit equal to ten times that of a *pona*.

'oute: Hibiscus rosa-sinense L.

papa: The vine *Rhynchosia minima* (L.) DC.

pekio: Male servant, sex partner, and secondary husband.

pia: The crop plant *Tacca leontopetaloides* (L.) O. Ktze.

pimata: The tree *Cheirodendron marquesense* F. Brown.

pona: A quantity unit consisting of forty or eighty breadfruit, the number varying from one island to another.

popoi: Cooked and mashed breadfruit.

puahi: The greater yam *Dioscorea alata* L.

rata: The tree *Metrosideros collina* (Forst.) Gray var. *toviana* F. Brown.

suge: A ranked male society in eastern Melanesia.

tahonga: A wooden ball-like ornament formerly worn by Easter Islanders.

tamanu: The tree *Calophyllum inophyllum* L.

tau'a: An inspirational priest.

teuteu: Formerly the landless lowest class of Tahiti.

ti: The plant *Cordyline terminales* (L.) Kunth.

tinne: A quantity unit equal to ten times that of a *manno*.

titou: Possibly the yam *Dioscorea pentaphylla* L.

toa: The tree *Casuarina equisetifolia* L.

toa: A chief warrior of a tribe.

tohua: A prepared dance court.

tou: The tree *Cordia subcordata* Lam.

tuhuna: A craft specialist.

tuhuna o'ono: See *tuhuna ota ogo*

tuhuna ota ogo: A noninspirational priest who performed ceremonial rituals and prayers.

tutu: The shrub *Colubrina asiatica* (L.) Brongn.

ute: Bark cloth made from the paper mulberry *Broussonetia papyrifera* (L.) Vent.

u'u: An assistant to a *tuhuna ota ogo*.

Notes to the Chapters

1. THE ISLANDS

1. Menard 1986, 36, 90.
2. Chubb 1930, 14, 18; Adamson 1936, 37.
3. Climatic records for Atuona for 1937–50 are published in Taylor 1973; those for 1951–60 are from *World Weather Records*, vol. 6, 1968; and those for 1961–90 are from NOAA, vols. 14–43. Rainfall data for Taiohae are from Taylor 1973.
4. Crook c. 1800, 145; Robarts 1974, 240.
5. Wilson 1799, 130–31; Robarts 1974, 95, 273–74.
6. For examples of this, see Taylor 1973 for Taiohae in 1947, 1958, 1969, and 1971.
7. Crook c. 1800, 149; Robarts 1974, 101, 148, 261.
8. For the 1941, 1957, and 1982–83 El Niño events on the west coast of South America, see Rasmusson 1985, 169–70, 175, Fig. 6. For precipitation data for the same years at Taiohae and Atuona, see Taylor 1973.
9. Philander 1989, 451–59 and Fig. 4.
10. Robarts 1974, 273.
11. Adamson 1936, 35.
12. Crook c. 1800, 129, 140; Robarts 1974, 150, 244.
13. Adamson 1936, 34–38.
14. Sinoto 1979, 112–17; Bellwood 1979, 253.
15. Sinoto 1979, 117–19.
16. Sinoto 1979, 117–19.
17. Crook c. 1800, 165.
18. Marchand 1801, 1:242–45.
19. Fanning 1924, 154–55.
20. Porter 1823, 93–94.
21. Crook c. 1800, 144, 147, 159.

22. Crook c. 1800, 141, 159.
23. Adamson 1936, 55.
24. Crook c. 1800, 165.
25. Crook c. 1800, 141.
26. Crook c. 1800, 142–43.
27. Crook c. 1800, 143.

2. THE MARQUESANS AND THEIR DWELLINGS

1. For comments on male stature, see Cook 1955–67, 2:374; Marchand 1801, 1:145; Robarts 1974, 249; Porter 1823, 96. For female stature see G. Forster 1777, 2:30; Wilson 1799, 140; Krusenstern 1813, 1:154.
2. Langsdorff 1813, 1:111.
3. For skin color of males, see Quiros 1904a, 16; J. R. Forster 1778, 232; G. Forster 1777, 2:8; Marchand 1801, 1:146; Robarts 1974, 250; Porter 1823, 78. For that of females, see Crook c. 1800, 117; Fanning 1924, 148; Wilson 1799, 129, 146; Sparrman 1953, 118; Robarts 1974, 53, 73; Lisiansky 1814, 85.
4. Porter 1823, 79.
5. Cook 1955–67, 2:373.
6. Crook c. 1800, 120.
7. For general range of hair color, see Marchand 1801, 1:143, 145; Crook c. 1800, 117; Fanning 1924, 148; Robarts 1974, 86–87, 250; Langsdorff 1813, 1:108; Lisiansky 1814, 85.
8. Quiros 1904a, 22.
9. G. Forster 1777, 2:15, Marchand 1801, 1:145; Robarts 1974, 91, 250.
10. Greg Dening in Robarts 1974, 59, ftn. 19, identified this plant as *Phaseolus amoenis*. However, Brown 1935, 116, 118 reported the word *papa* as being used to identify both *Phaseolus adenanthus* E. May. and *Rhynchosia minima* (L.) DC. Since the latter is a small creeping vine, and Crook c. 1800, 132, described the *papa* plant in similar terms, it seems probable that the proper identification is *R. minima*
11. Crook c. 1800, 132.
12. G. Forster 1777, 2:108; Marchand 1801, 1:145, 146, 151–52; Robarts 1974, 53, 73, 86–87; Lisiansky 1814, 85.
13. Krusenstern 1813, 1:158.
14. Marchand 1801, 1:151–52.
15. Marra 1775, 161; Marchand 1801, 1:151–52; Wilson 1799, 146; Crook c. 1800, 118; Krusenstern 1813, 1:158; Langsdorff 1813, 1:170; Lisiansky 1814, 86; Porter 1823, 114.
16. Quiros 1904a, 16; Cook 1955–67, 2:373; Wilson 1799, 146.
17. Fanning 1924, 148; Robarts 1974, 53, 73, 86–87; Porter 1823, 114; Krusenstern 1813, 1:119, 159; Lisiansky 1814, 87.

18. Fanning 1924, 147.
19. Marchand 1801, 1:151–52; Crook c. 1800, 118; Lisiansky 1814, 86; Porter 1823, 114.
20. Ferdon 1987, 8–9.
21. Ferdon 1981, 174.
22. Marchand 1801, 1:152.
23. Marra 1775, 161–62.
24. Marchand 1801, 1:152.
25. Marchand 1801, 1:152; Langsdorff 1813, 1:108.
26. Krusenstern 1813, 1:158.
27. References to the removal of hair are Crook c. 1800, 118, 132; Porter 1823, 113–14; Krusenstern 1813, 1:162; Langsdorff 1813, 1:114–15.
28. Robarts 1974, 269.
29. Langsdorff 1813, 1:174.
30. Ferdon 1981, 21–22.
31. G. Forster 1777, 2:8; Crook c. 1800, 119; Robarts 1974, 250; Krusenstern 1813, 1:114.
32. Quiros 1904a, 16; Marchand 1801, 1:148; Wilson 1799, 146; Crook c. 1800, 120; Langsdorff 1813, 1:122. For a specialized study of Marquesan tattooing see W. C. Handy 1922.
33. Krusenstern 1813, 1:155; Langsdorff 1813, 1:117.
34. Crook c. 1800, 142.
35. Langsdorff 1813, 1:121–22.
36. Porter 1823, 114–15.
37. For female tattooing, see Marchand 1801, 1:150–51; Wilson 1799, 146; Crook c. 1800, 117; Robarts 1974, 250; Porter 1823, 114; Krusenstern 1813, 1:119, 132; Langsdorff 1813, 1:120–21.
38. Fanning 1924, 147.
39. Langsdorff 1813, 1:121.
40. Marchand 1801, 1:147; Langsdorff 1813, 1:117–21.
41. The nuts were from the candlenut tree, *Aleurites moluccana* (L.) Willd.
42. Marchand 1801, 1:147–48; Langsdorff 1813, 1:118.
43. Marchand 1801, 1:147–48.
44. Langsdorff 1813, 1:118.
45. Langsdorff 1813, 1:119.
46. Crook c. 1800, 118; Krusenstern 1813, 1:156.
47. Crook c. 1800, 116.
48. Sparrman 1953, 119; Wilson 1799, 146; Krusenstern 1813, 1:158.
49. Crook c. 1800, 116; Robarts 1974, 269; Langsdorff 1813, 1:136.
50. References to the wearing of a *kahu* are G. Forster 1777, 2:30; Marra 1775, 158; Wilson 1799, 146; Crook c. 1800, 116; Porter 1823, 97; Krusenstern 1813, 1:158.

51. For white *kahu*, see Marra 1775, 158; Fanning 1924, 129. For yellow, see Krusenstern 1813, 1:119, 132; Langsdorff 1813, 1:92; Lisiansky 1814, 75.
52. Crook c. 1800, 117.
53. Langsdorff 1813, 1:123.
54. Crook c. 1800, 117; Fanning 1924, 129, 142; Porter 1823, 97.
55. Crook c. 1800, 116; Robarts 1974, 269.
56. For Tahiti, see Ferdon 1981, 24–25; for Tonga, Ferdon 1987, 7–8.
57. Marchand 1801, 1:173; Fanning 1924, 129–30; Crook c. 1800, 129; Krusenstern 1813, 1:158; Langsdorff 1813, 1:114; Lisiansky 1814, 75, 86.
58. Marchand 1801, 1:173; Porter 1823, 82.
59. Langsdorff 1813, 1:175.
60. Ferdon 1981, 85–86; 1987, 98.
61. Langsdorff 1813, 1:138.
62. J. R. Forster 1982, 3:491; G. Forster 1777, 2:16; Sparrman 1953, 119; Langsdorff 1813, 1:171.
63. Brown 1935, 113.
64. G. Forster 1777, 2:16; Sparrman 1953, 119.
65. Krusenstern 1813, 1:158.
66. Crook c. 1800, 119; Robarts 1974, 143; Porter 1823, 83.
67. J. R. Forster 1982, 3:485–86, 491; G. Forster 1777, 2:16; Marchand 1801, 1:154; Porter 1823, 83.
68. Sinoto 1979, 113–29.
69. Sinoto 1979, 127.
70. Ferdon 1981, 25; 1987, 10.
71. Krusenstern 1813, 1:158.
72. Métraux 1940, 233.
73. For necklaces, see Marchand 1801, 1:154, 161; Crook c. 1800, 119; Krusenstern 1813, 1:158; Langsdorff 1813, 1:86–87; Lisiansky 1814, 86–87.
74. Marchand 1801, 1:153–54; Crook c. 1800, 117, 119; Lisiansky 1814, 92.
75. Crook c. 1800, 119.
76. Cook 1955–67, 2:375; Marchand 1801, 1:154–55, 161; Crook c. 1800, 119.
77. Crook c. 1800, 119.
78. J. R. Forster 1982, 3:491; Crook c. 1800, 119; Porter 1823, 77; Krusenstern 1813, 1:157–58; Langsdorff 1813, 1:170–71.
79. Crook c. 1800, 119; Krusenstern 1813, 1:157–58.
80. J. R. Forster 1982, 3:491; G. Forster 1777, 2:15; Marchand 1801, 1:152; Crook c. 1800, 118; Fanning 1924, 125; Krusenstern 1813, 1:157; Langsdorff 1813, 1:171.
81. J. R. Forster 1982, 3:491; G. Forster 1777, 2:15; Krusenstern 1813, 1:157.
82. G. Forster 1777, 2:19; Sparrman 1953, 118; Marchand 1801, 1:151.

83. J. R. Forster 1982, 3:491; G. Forster 1777, 2:15; Sparrman 1953, 118; Crook c. 1800, 118–19.
84. Marchand 1801, 153.
85. Cook 1955–67, 2:373; J. R. Forster 1982, 3:491; G. Forster 1777, 2:16; Marchand 1801, 1:155; Porter 1823, 78.
86. Crook c. 1800, 119.
87. Langsdorff 1813, 1:171.
88. Crook c. 1800, 119.
89. Langsdorff 1813, 1:105.
90. Quiros 1904a, 19, 26; Crook c. 1800, 145, 165; Robarts 1974, 253, 264.
91. Adamson 1936, 48 Fig. 1, 59 Fig. 5.
92. Crook c. 1800, 179; Robarts 1974, 92.
93. Robarts 1974, 89–90.
94. Quiros 1904a, 21, 23, 26; Marchand 1801, 1:109; Fanning 1924, 85–86; Porter 1823, 84, 88, 106.
95. Cook 1955–67, 2:373; Krusenstern 1813, 1:131; Lisiansky 1814, 76; Bellwood 1972.
96. Cook 1955–67, 2:373; J. R. Forster 1778, 232; Fanning 1924, 149.
97. G. Forster 1777, 2:21; Marchand 1801, 1:111; Langsdorff 1813, 1:127.
98. Bellwood 1972, Fig. 3.
99. Marchand 1801, 1:111; Fanning 1924, 128; Langsdorff 1813, 1:127.
100. Fanning 1924, 128.
101. G. Forster 1777, 2:21; Marchand 1801, 1:111; Wilson 1799, 131; Crook c. 1800, 132; Langsdorff 1813, 1:126.
102. Crook c. 1800, 132; Fanning 1924, 128.
103. Fanning 1924, 131–32.
104. Fanning 1924, 128.
105. Robarts 1974, 260.
106. G. Forster 1777, 2:21; J. R. Forster 1982, 3:487.
107. G. Forster 1777, 2:21; Marchand 1801, 1:111; Crook c. 1800, 133; Lisiansky 1814, 72.
108. Krusenstern 1813, 1:159; Langsdorff 1813, 1:127.
109. Crook c. 1800, 133; Krusenstern 1813, 1:159.
110. Crook c. 1800, 133.
111. Linton 1923, 285–90.
112. Crook c. 1800, 133.
113. Crook c. 1800, 133; Langsdorff 1813, 1:128–29; Lisiansky 1814, 72; Porter 1823, 112.
114. Wilson 1799, 132; Crook c. 1800, 133; Fanning 1924, 128; Langsdorff 1813, 1:128; Krusenstern 1813, 1:159.
115. Krusenstern 1813, 1:159; Lisiansky 1814, 72.
116. Fanning 1924, 126–27; Robarts 1974, 146, 276.
117. Langsdorff 1813, 1:129; Lisiansky 1814, 72.

118. Langsdorff 1813, 1:136.
119. Robarts 1974, 273; Krusenstern 1813, 1:161; Lisiansky 1814, 84.
120. Lisiansky 1814, 84.
121. Cook 1955–67, 2:375; Marchand 1801, 1:112; Crook c. 1800, 133.
122. Krusenstern 1813, 1:119–20.
123. Crook c. 1800, 126.
124. Langsdorff 1813, 1:128. These tabooed houses were referred to by Robarts as "altars."
125. Crook c. 1800, 126.
126. Crook c. 1800, 126.
127. Crook c. 1800, 126.
128. Crook c. 1800, 133; Robarts 1974, 88; Lisiansky 1814, 84.
129. Crook c. 1800, 175.
130. Robarts 1974, 152.
131. Langsdorff 1813, 1:127.
132. Robarts 1974, 272.

3. SOCIAL ORGANIZATION AND GOVERNMENT

1. Crook c. 1800, 115.
2. Crook c. 1800, 126.
3. Codrington 1891, 101–15.
4. Crook c. 1800, 169.
5. Crook c. 1800, 115–17.
6. Crook c. 1800, 127.
7. Crook c. 1800, 142.
8. Crook c. 1800, 138–39.
9. Crook c. 1800, 120.
10. For *tau'a*, see Robarts 1974, 66; for *tuhuna* and *u'u*, Crook c. 1800, 120, 169.
11. Robarts 1974, 266.
12. Robarts 1974, 266.
13. Crook c. 1800, 126.
14. Crook c. 1800, 117, 156.
15. Crook c. 1800, 116, 126; Robarts 1974, 115; Krusenstern 1813, 1:161.
16. Crook c. 1800, 126.
17. Crook c. 1800, 126.
18. Crook c. 1800, 142.
19. Crook c. 1800, 134.
20. Crook c. 1800, 126.
21. Crook c. 1800, 142.
22. Robarts 1974, 266; Langsdorff 1813, 1:138.
23. Robarts 1974, 266.

24. Robarts 1974, 266; Crook c. 1800, 169, 173.
25. Crook c. 1800, 127; Fanning 1924, 93.
26. Crook c. 1800, 142.
27. Crook c. 1800, 114.
28. For examples, see Crook c. 1800, 157, 169; Robarts 1974, 91, 154–57.
29. Crook c. 1800, 148–49.
30. Crook c. 1800, 169.
31. Robarts 1974, 253.
32. Robarts 1974, 89, 152.
33. Crook c. 1800, 115, 137; Robarts 1974, 257; Porter 1823, 99.
34. Crook c. 1800, 137.
35. Crook c. 1800, 165; Robarts 1974, 122.
36. Crook c. 1800, 165.
37. Crook c. 1800, 144–46, 159–60.
38. Crook c. 1800, 159.
39. Crook c. 1800, 150.
40. Crook c. 1800, 166.
41. Wilson 1799, 144.
42. Langsdorff 1813, 1:133.
43. G. Forster 1777, 2:19; Langsdorff 1813, 1:131; Lisiansky 1814, 68; Porter 1823, 99.
44. Krusenstern 1813, 1:114–15, 165; Langsdorff 1813, 1:130–31; Porter 1823, 98.
45. Krusenstern 1813, 1:155; Langsdorff 1813, 1:130–31; Lisiansky 1814, 85; Porter 1823, 78.
46. Krusenstern 1813, 1:157.
47. Cook 1955–67, 2:375; Fanning 1924, 125.
48. Crook c. 1800, 117; Fanning 1924, 136.
49. Fanning 1924, 127; Robarts 1974, 111.
50. Cook 1955–67, 2:367 ftn. 1, Willis journal; Crook c. 1800, 162; Robarts 1974, 85, 111, 155–56.
51. Ferdon 1987, 31–32, 139.
52. Porter 1823, 89.
53. Lisiansky 1814, 80; Porter 1823, 99.
54. J. R. Forster 1778, 380; Porter 1823, 98.
55. Robarts 1974, 266.
56. Crook c. 1800, 147.
57. Crook c. 1800, 137.
58. Krusenstern 1813, 1:165.
59. Lisiansky 1814, 80.
60. Wilson 1799, 130; Crook c. 1800, 168.
61. Crook c. 1800, 168.
62. Robarts 1974, 106, 118.

63. Robarts 1974, 148.
64. Fanning 1924, 122–35.
65. Ferdon 1981, 35–44.
66. Crook c. 1800, 171.
67. Porter 1823, 82, 84, 98.
68. Porter 1823, 98–99.
69. Ferdon 1987, 27.
70. Crook c. 1800, 114.
71. Robarts 1974, 266.
72. Lisiansky 1814, 80.
73. Crook c. 1800, 180–81.
74. Krusenstern 1813, 1:115.
75. Robarts 1974, 86.
76. Robarts 1974, 266.

4. RELIGION

1. Wilson 1799, 144.
2. Crook c. 1800, 122.
3. Robarts 1974, 279; Porter 1823, 112.
4. Quiros 1904a, 27–28; Wilson 1799, 134; Robarts 1974, 57; Krusenstern 1813, 1:127; Lisiansky 1814, 73; Porter 1823, 111.
5. Porter 1823, 111.
6. Crook c. 1800, 123.
7. Ferdon 1981, 66–68.
8. Crook c. 1800, 122.
9. Ferdon 1987, 70.
10. Ferdon 1981, 52.
11. Crook c. 1800, 122.
12. Crook c. 1800, 168, 176.
13. Krusenstern 1813, 1:127.
14. Porter 1823, 112.
15. Crook c. 1800, 122, 148.
16. Krusenstern 1813, 1:126.
17. Langsdorff 1813, 1:133.
18. Crook c. 1800, 122.
19. Crook c. 1800, 147.
20. Crook c. 1800, 176.
21. Crook c. 1800, 122.
22. Crook c. 1800, 148.
23. Crook c. 1800, 121; Porter 1823, 91.
24. Crook c. 1800, 121.
25. Porter 1823, 93.

26. Porter 1823, 91.
27. Sinoto 1979, 117.
28. Crook c. 1800, 120; E. S. Handy 1923, 355.
29. Crook c. 1800, 125, 152, 170; Robarts 1974, 121.
30. Robarts 1974, 77, 116; Langsdorff 1813, 1:149, 157.
31. Crook c. 1800, 125; Krusenstern 1813, 1:173.
32. Crook c. 1800, 125.
33. Krusenstern 1813, 1:158.
34. Crook c. 1800, 125.
35. Krusenstern 1813, 1:171 ftn.; Langsdorff 1813, 1:133, 138.
36. Langsdorff 1813, 1:128.
37. Crook c. 1800, 125.
38. Langsdorff 1813, 1:157.
39. Robarts 1974, 266; Porter 1823, 111.
40. Robarts 1974, 134; Krusenstern 1813, 1:127; Langsdorff 1813, 1:134.
41. Robarts 1974, 266; Langsdorff 1813, 1:138.
42. Lisiansky 1814, 84.
43. Crook c. 1800, 125; Robarts 1974, 77; Langsdorff 1813, 1:149, 160.
44. Robarts 1974, 103, 116.
45. Robarts 1974, 77–78.
46. Krusenstern 1813, 1:170; Lisiansky 1814, 81–82.
47. Crook c. 1800, 151; Robarts 1974, 58; Krusenstern 1813, 1:170–71; Lisiansky 1814, 81–82.
48. Langsdorff 1813, 1:149–50.
49. Crook c. 1800, 151.
50. Lisiansky 1814, 81–82.
51. Krusenstern 1813, 1:170–71.
52. Robarts 1974, 58.
53. Crook c. 1800, 122.
54. Krusenstern 1813, 1:170.
55. Crook c. 1800, 160–61.
56. Lisiansky 1814, 81–82.
57. Crook c. 1800, 120, 125.
58. Crook c. 1800, 157.
59. Crook c. 1800, 168.
60. Ferdon 1987, 36–37.
61. Crook c. 1800, 121.
62. Crook c. 1800, 120–21, 171.
63. Crook c. 1800, 169, 173.
64. Crook c. 1800, 148, 171.
65. Crook c. 1800, 142.
66. Crook c. 1800, 125.
67. Crook c. 1800, 121, 124.

68. Crook c. 1800, 122.
69. Crook c. 1800, 121.
70. Krusenstern 1813, 1:127.
71. Crook c. 1800, 126.
72. Crook c. 1800, 126, 151.
73. Wilson 1799, 144.
74. For a 1920–21 survey of Marquesan structures thought to be mortuary *me'ae,* see Linton 1925, 32–40.
75. Crook c. 1800, 128.
76. Wilson 1799, 134.
77. Robarts 1974, 56; Langsdorff 1813, 1:134.
78. Robarts 1974, 134.
79. Lisiansky 1814, 73–74.
80. Krusenstern 1813, 1:127.
81. Lisiansky 1814, 73–74.
82. Robarts 1974, 57.
83. For an example of this style see Linton 1925, pl. IV.
84. Porter 1823, 111.
85. Linton 1925, 32.
86. Cook 1955–67, 3:269–70 and pl. 31; Buck 1957, 519–20.
87. Porter 1823, 111.
88. Porter 1823, 112.
89. Crook c. 1800, 124.
90. Quiros 1904a, 27–28.
91. Ferdon 1965, 117–22.
92. Crook c. 1800, 138–39.
93. Krusenstern 1813, 1:172; Langsdorff 1813, 1:135.
94. Langsdorff 1813, 1:135.
95. Lisiansky 1814, 89.
96. Langsdorff 1813, 1:157.
97. Crook c. 1800, 125.
98. Robarts 1974, 224–25; Langsdorff 1813, 1:155–57.
99. Papa Li 1983, 23, 113; Buck 1957, 53–55.

5. DAILY LIFE AND DIVERSIONS

1. Marchand 1801, 1:171; Fanning 1924, 116, 118; Robarts 1974, 65, 138–39.
2. Crook c. 1800, 134; Robarts 1974, 252.
3. Robarts 1974, 260–61.
4. Crook c. 1800, 115, 127, 134; Robarts 1974, 160; Krusenstern 1813, 1:164; Porter 1823, 113.
5. Crook c. 1800, 114–15; Robarts 1974, 252–53; Porter 1823, 113.

6. Crook c. 1800, 114–15; Robarts 1974, 252–53.
7. Crook c. 1800, 114–15, 144, 148–49; Robarts 1974, 252–53.
8. Marchand 1801, 1:181; Crook c. 1800, 134; Krusenstern 1813, 1:162.
9. Quiros 1904a, 28.
10. For references to knives, see Quiros 1904a, 18; Marchand 1801, 1:181; Crook c. 1800, 124, 134; Robarts 1974, 74; Langsdorff 1813, 1:195.
11. Marchand 1801, 1:181; Crook c. 1800, 134.
12. Krusenstern 1813, 1:162.
13. Crook c. 1800, 134; Langsdorff 1813, 1:145.
14. Langsdorff 1813, 1:175.
15. J. R. Forster 1982, 3:487; Crook c. 1800, 134; Robarts 1974, 279.
16. Robarts 1974, 65.
17. Marchand 1801, 1:182; Crook c. 1800, 133–34; Langsdorff 1813, 1:172.
18. Krusenstern 1813, 1:162.
19. Crook c. 1800, 134.
20. Robarts 1974, 261, 279; Porter 1823, 113.
21. Porter 1823, 113.
22. Robarts 1974, 67.
23. Marchand 1801, 1:182; Crook c. 1800, 133; Langsdorff 1813, 1:129.
24. Marchand 1801, 1:182; Crook c. 1800, 133; Robarts 1974, 261, 279.
25. Crook c. 1800, 133; Krusenstern 1813, 1:162; Langsdorff 1813, 1:172.
26. Crook c. 1800, 131.
27. Neal 1968, 532–33; Uphof 1968, 470.
28. Langsdorff, 1813, 1:135.
29. Brown 1935, 269.
30. Crook c. 1800, 134; Porter 1823, 113.
31. Fanning 1924, 148. For Tonga, see Ferdon 1987, 112–13.
32. For references to fans, see G. Forster 1777, 2:23; Marchand 1801, 1:156, 232; Krusenstern 1813, 1:159; Lisiansky 1814, 65; Porter 1823, 115–16.
33. Krusenstern 1813, 1:164.
34. Porter 1823, 116.
35. Robarts 1974, 252.
36. For various uses of mats, see Marchand 1801, 1:184; Wilson 1799, 132; Crook c. 1800, 134; Fanning 1924, 128; Robarts 1974, 100, 260; Krusenstern 1813, 1:120; Porter 1823, 113.
37. Crook c. 1800, 115.
38. *Ute, Broussonetia papyrifera* L. Vent.; *hiapo, Ficus prolixa* Forst.; *mei, Artocarpus altilis* (Parkinson) Fosberg.
39. Marchand 1801, 1:183 ftn.; Robarts 1974, 255.
40. Porter 1823, 115; *toa, Casuarina equisetifolia* L.
41. Robarts 1974, 255.

42. Porter 1823, 115.
43. Kooijman 1972, Table C.
44. Robarts 1974, 255–56; Porter 1823, 115.
45. Crook c. 1800, 118.
46. Crook c. 1800, 118; Porter 1823, 97.
47. Crook c. 1800, 118; Krusenstern 1813, 1:156; Lisiansky 1814, 92.
48. Crook c. 1800, 124.
49. Lisiansky 1814, 91.
50. For use of yellow, see G. Forster 1777, 2:183; Fanning 1924, 143. For turmeric perfume, see Robarts 1974, 262.
51. Crook c. 1800, 118; Fanning 1924, 143.
52. Crook c. 1800, 116.
53. Crook c. 1800, 116, 126–27.
54. Crook c. 1800, 116.
55. Crook c. 1800, 143.
56. Crook c. 1800, 116; Robarts 1974, 269.
57. Krusenstern 1813, 1:160; Lisiansky 1814, 87.
58. Robarts 1974, 268; Langsdorff 1813, 1:136.
59. Crook c. 1800, 116; Langsdorff 1813, 1:135.
60. Langsdorff 1813, 1:135; Porter 1823, 112.
61. Marchand 1801, 1:195.
62. Crook c. 1800, 126.
63. Lisiansky 1814, 84.
64. Crook c. 1800, 132; Robarts 1974, 279; Langsdorff 1813, 1:124.
65. Cook 1955–67, 2:375; Marchand 1801, 1:172; Crook c. 1800, 150; Robarts 1974, 66; Langsdorff 1813, 1:125–26.
66. Crook c. 1800, 124.
67. Marchand 1801, 1:172.
68. Marchand 1801, 1:172.
69. Robarts 1974, 252; Lisiansky 1814, 87.
70. Langsdorff 1813, 1:137.
71. Crook c. 1800, 127–28.
72. Fanning 1924, 99.
73. Robarts 1974, 278.
74. Robarts 1974, 279.
75. Porter 1823, 94.
76. Crook c. 1800, 130.
77. Crook c. 1800, 130.
78. Crook c. 1800, 129; Robarts 1974, 65, 278.
79. Langsdorff 1813, 1:124–25.
80. Robarts 1974, 278–79.
81. G. Forster 1777, 2:27–28; Marchand 1801, 1:174; Crook c. 1800, 129; Robarts 1974, 252.

82. Langsdorff 1813, 1:125.
83. Robarts 1974, 278.
84. Marchand 1801, 1:171.
85. Crook in Wilson 1799, 145; Robarts 1974, 145.
86. Wilson 1799, 145.
87. Crook c. 1800, 124; Krusenstern 1813, 1:161–62.
88. G. Forster 1777, 2:27; Crook c. 1800, 130; Krusenstern 1813, 1:162.
89. Crook c. 1800, 123.
90. Crook c. 1800, 135.
91. Langsdorff 1813, 1:172–73.
92. Crook c. 1800, 135; Langsdorff 1813, 1:169.
93. Crook c. 1800, 135.
94. Crook c. 1800, 135.
95. Marchand 1801, 1:161, 186; Crook c. 1800, 135.
96. Porter 1823, 103; Crook c. 1800, 153.
97. Crook c. 1800, 135.
98. Ferdon 1981, 124–27; 1987, 184–89.
99. Marchand 1801, 1:180; Langsdorff 1813, 1:168–69.
100. E. S. C. Handy 1923, 311–13.
101. Marra 1775, 159; Langsdorff 1813, 1:164.
102. Crook c. 1800, 122–23.
103. Crook c. 1800, 136.
104. Langsdorff 1813, 1:160.
105. Crook c. 1800, 136.
106. Crook c. 1800, 123.
107. Marchand 1801, 1:185; Langsdorff 1813, 1:164.
108. Crook c. 1800, 143; Fanning 1924, 150; Langsdorff 1813, 1:164.
109. Marchand 1801, 1:185.
110. Fanning 1924, 50, 103; Robarts 1974, 78, 111; Langsdorff 1813, 1:164; Porter 1823, 106.
111. Wilson 1799, 136; Crook c. 1800, 143.
112. For references to the various forms of clapping, see Marchand 1801, 1:44, 184–85; Crook c. 1800, 123, 185; Krusenstern 1813, 1:176; Langsdorff 1813, 1:163.
113. Krusenstern 1813, 1:177; Langsdorff 1813, 1:160.
114. Crook c. 1800, 177.
115. Langsdorff 1813, 1:161.
116. Robarts 1974, 49, 81, 91, 100, 110, 151.
117. Fanning 1924, 135.
118. Robarts 1974, 81, 91.
119. Ferdon 1987, 197–203.
120. Marchand 1801, 1:184–85; Krusenstern 1813, 1:176–77; Langsdorff 1813, 1:158.

121. Marchand 1801, 1:185; Crook c. 1800, 115.
122. Krusenstern 1813, 1:176–77.
123. Langsdorff 1813, 1:158.
124. E. S. C. Handy 1923, 205, 354.
125. Robarts 1974, 297.
126. Robarts 1974, 293.
127. Crook c. 1800, 135, 177.
128. Robarts 1974, 260; Langsdorff 1813, 1:158–60.
129. Robarts 1974, 99, 109.
130. Crook c. 1800, 133; Krusenstern 1813, 159–60.

131. For references to *koina* celebrations at important periods in human life, see Crook c. 1800, 117; Robarts 1974, 259–60, 270; Langsdorff 1813, 1:119.

132. Crook c. 1800, 177.
133. Krusenstern 1813, 1:169–70.
134. Crook c. 1800, 129.
135. Langsdorff 1813, 1:158.
136. Crook c. 1800, 174.
137. Crook c. 1800, 177.
138. Crook c. 1800, 135; Robarts 1974, 59; Langsdorff 1813, 1:159.

139. For descriptions of the range in size and other features of remains of *tohua* in the Marquesas, see Linton 1925, 24–32, 105–85. However, local interpretations of some of their features, as recorded by Linton, are doubtful.

140. Crook c. 1800, 135; Krusenstern 1813, 1:133.
141. Quiros 1904a, 27; Crook c. 1800, 135; Robarts 1974, 59.
142. Crook c. 1800, 177; Robarts 1974, 111.
143. Robarts 1974, 114.
144. Crook c. 1800, 135; Robarts 1974, 160.
145. Langsdorff 1813, 1:159–60.
146. Crook c. 1800, 115–16.
147. Lisiansky 1814, 91–92.
148. Crook c. 1800, 115–16; Langsdorff 1813, 1:158.
149. Langsdorff 1813, 1:136.
150. Crook c. 1800, 135, 177.
151. Crook c. 1800, 115; Robarts 1974, 60.
152. Langsdorff 1813, 1:136, 160.
153. Langsdorff 1813, 1:158–59.
154. Crook c. 1800, 115.

6. FROM BIRTH TO DEATH

1. Ferdon 1981, 143; 1987, 27, 126.
2. Crook c. 1800, 117, 125–26; Langsdorff 1813, 1:151–52.

3. Langsdorff 1813, 1:151.
4. Crook c. 1800, 117, 156.
5. Crook c. 1800, 142; Langsdorff 1813, 1:152.
6. Lisiansky 1814, 83–84.
7. Langsdorff 1813, 1:152.
8. Crook c. 1800, 117, 138.
9. Robarts 1974, 270; Langsdorff 1813, 1:135.
10. Crook c. 1800, 116.
11. Krusenstern 1813, 1:126.
12. Marchand 1801, 1:195; Langsdorff 1813, 1:152.
13. Langsdorff 1813, 1:152.
14. Crook c. 1800, 117.
15. Marchand 1801, 1:195–96; Wilson 1799, 145; Crook c. 1800, 137–38; Robarts 1974, 259.
16. Langsdorff 1813, 1:134; Porter 1823, 99.
17. Crook c. 1800, 126.
18. Crook c. 1800, 116; Robarts 1974, 268.
19. Crook c. 1800, 115; Langsdorff 1813, 1:113.
20. Robarts 1974, 59.
21. Crook c. 1800, 115.
22. Crook c. 1800, 120; Langsdorff 1813, 1:158.
23. Crook c. 1800, 120; Krusenstern 1813, 1:156; Lisiansky 1814, 86.
24. Crook c. 1800, 120, 171.
25. Porter 1823, 114.
26. Krusenstern 1813, 1:155.
27. Marchand 1801, 1:225; Wilson 1799, 148; Crook c. 1800, 160.
28. Langsdorff 1813, 1:118.
29. Langsdorff 1813, 1:118–21.
30. Crook c. 1800, 117, 126.
31. Crook c. 1800, 115.
32. Marchand 1801, 1:190; Langsdorff 1813, 1:152; Porter 1823, 113 are just a few of the many references.
33. Robarts 1974, 160.
34. Robarts 1974, 260–61.
35. Robarts 1974, 80.
36. E. S. C. Handy 1923, 39–42.
37. Crook c. 1800, 115–16.
38. For a description of the *'arioi*, see Ferdon 1981, 138–41.
39. Crook c. 1800, 137, 155, 171; Lisiansky 1814, 80.
40. Crook c. 1800, 117, 137, 169.
41. Crook c. 1800, 155.
42. Robarts 1974, 269–70.
43. Crook c. 1800, 115, 169; Krusenstern 1813, 1:167.

44. Porter 1823, 113.
45. Lisiansky 1814, 82–83.
46. Langsdorff 1813, 1:155; Porter 1823, 113.
47. Langsdorff 1813, 1:153; Lisiansky 1814, 82.
48. Crook c. 1800, 115, 125, 169. Since Crook described the plant as a tree of inferior size, it was probably *Ceodes brunoniana* (Endl.) Skottsb., though the fruit of the larger tree, *Cerbera manghas* L., is equally poisonous and, like *C. brunoniana*, was also known as 'eva.
49. Crook c. 1800, 125–26.
50. Crook c. 1800, 169.
51. Wilson 1799, 137.
52. Robarts 1974, 270–71.
53. Crook c. 1800, 115; Robarts 1974, 150; Porter 1823, 113.
54. Langsdorff 1813, 1:153; Lisiansky 1814, 83.
55. Crook c. 1800, 125, 169, 171, 177.
56. Robarts 1974, 255.
57. Crook c. 1800, 125; Robarts 1974, 269.
58. Crook c. 1800, 125, 170.
59. Robarts 1974, 115, 146.
60. Crook c. 1800, 131.
61. Langsdorff 1813, 1:175.
62. Crook c. 1800, 125.
63. Langsdorff 1813, 1:157.
64. Crook c. 1800, 123.
65. Robarts 1974, 146.
66. Crook c. 1800, 134; Robarts 1974, 85.
67. Crook c. 1800, 123.
68. Robarts 1974, 255.
69. Crook c. 1800, 125–26, 168; Robarts 1974, 248, 253–54.
70. Robarts 1974, 152.
71. Robarts 1974, 56; Krusenstern 1813, 1:172–73; Langsdorff 1813, 1:154; Lisiansky 1814, 81.
72. Crook c. 1800, 123; Robarts 1974, 56; Lisiansky 1814, 81.
73. Crook c. 1800, 124; Robarts 1974, 56.
74. Crook c. 1800, 124.
75. Wilson 1799, 134; Crook c. 1800, 124; Robarts 1974, 56; Porter 1823, 114.
76. Crook c. 1800, 124.
77. Crook c. 1800, 124; Porter 1823, 115.
78. Crook c. 1800, 124.
79. Crook c. 1800, 124.
80. Robarts 1974, 56; Krusenstern 1813, 1:173. For Easter Island see Métraux 1940, 117–18.

81. Crook c. 1800, 124; Robarts 1974, 56; Krusenstern 1813, 1:173; Langsdorff 1813, 1:154.
82. Crook c. 1800, 124.
83. Crook c. 1800, 124; Krusenstern 1813, 1:173; Langsdorff 1813, 1:154.
84. Sinoto 1970, 128.
85. Langsdorff 1813, 1:154.
86. Robarts 1974, 57.
87. Crook c. 1800, 124.
88. Crook c. 1800, 124; Langsdorff 1813, 1:154.
89. Robarts 1974, 57; Krusenstern 1813, 1:173; Langsdorff 1813, 1:154.
90. Crook c. 1800, 124; Langsdorff 1813, 1:154.
91. Lisiansky 1814, 81; Krusenstern 1813, 1:173; Langsdorff 1813, 1:154.
92. Crook c. 1800, 124.
93. Crook c. 1800, 124; Robarts 1974, 56.
94. Krusenstern 1813, 1:173.
95. Porter 1823, 115.
96. Robarts 1974, 56.
97. Lisiansky 1814, 81; Langsdorff 1813, 1:155.
98. Robarts 1974, 243, 264; Linton 1925, 57–58; Sinoto 1970, 125–28.
99. Robarts 1974, 57, 89.
100. Robarts 1974, 60.
101. Robarts 1974, 58.
102. Robarts 1974, 57.
103. Robarts 1974, 59.
104. Robarts 1974, 59–60.

7. THE QUEST FOR FOOD

1. G. Forster 1777, 2:27.
2. Crook c. 1800, 130; Langsdorff 1813, 1:107.
3. Marchand 1801, 1:186; Crook c. 1800, 129; Robarts 1974, 255; Krusenstern 1813, 1:164.
4. Crook c. 1800, 178; Robarts 1974, 245.
5. Porter 1823, 113.
6. For *pia*, see Crook c. 1800, 130; Robarts 1974, 279; for *kape*, Robarts 1974, 255; Langsdorff 1813, 1:107; Lisiansky 1814, 93; for *ti* or *ge*, Crook c. 1800, 130; Robarts 1974, 246; Langsdorff 1813, 1:167; for turmeric: Crook c. 1800, 131, 174; Robarts 1974, 123, 256; for *puahi*, or *D. alata*, Langsdorff 1813, 1:106; for *hoi*, or *D. bulbifera*, Lisiansky 1814, 93; for *D. pentaphylla*, Lisiansky 1814, 93; for sweet potato, see Marchand 1801, 1:123; Crook c. 1800, 130; Robarts 1974, 246; Langsdorff 1813, 1:106–07; for taro, Crook c. 1800, 130, 176; Fanning 1924, 117, 120; Robarts 1974, 246, 255; Krusenstern 1813, 1:125, 131; Langsdorff 1813, 1:106; Lisiansky 1814, 92; Porter 1823, 91, 94.

7. For taro, see Crook c. 1800, 176; Robarts 1974, 246; Krusenstern 1813, 1:125; for sweet potato, Crook c. 1800, 130.
8. Crook c. 1800, 130.
9. Crook c. 1800, 176.
10. Porter 1823, 94.
11. Krusenstern 1813, 1:125.
12. Robarts 1974, 246.
13. Crook c. 1800, 178.
14. Ferdon 1981, 183.
15. Cook 1955–67, 2:372; Fanning 1924, 115, 120, 138.
16. Marchand 1801, 1:123; Krusenstern 1813, 1:130; Langsdorff 1804, 1:106; Lisiansky 1814, 91. Virtually all early accounts mention these crops.
17. Krusenstern 1813, 1:164. Breadfruit, *Artocarpus altilis* (Parkinson) Fosb.; coconuts, *Cocos nucifera* L.; bananas, *Musa* spp.
18. Crook c. 1800, 129, 130; Porter 1823, 94.
19. For Malay apple, see Marchand 1801, 1:123; Crook c. 1800, 130; Robarts 1974, 246; for *noni*, Crook c. 1800, 130; for *ihi*, Quiros 1904a, 29; G. Forster 1777, 2:20; Crook c. 1800, 130; Robarts 1974, 256; Langsdorff 1813, 1:107; Lisiansky 1814, 94; for candlenut, Quiros 1904a, 29; Marchand 1801, 1:117, 128; Crook c. 1800, 131; Robarts 1974, 247; Langsdorff 1813, 1:107; Lisiansky 1814, 92.
20. For references to *I. catappa*, *C. subcordata*, and *Pandanus* spp., see Lisiansky 1814, 91–92.
21. For sugarcane, see Marchand 1801, 1:126–27; Fanning 1924, 50; Langsdorff 1813, 1:106–07; Porter 1823, 94; for *huou*, Crook c. 1800, 130, who wrote it *ho*; for pineapple, Crook c. 1800, 131; Porter 1823, 116; for *nano*, or soursop, Crook c. 1800, 130; Brown 1935, 81; for chili peppers, Crook c. 1800, 131; for cashews, Crook c. 1800, 143; Brown 1935, 154–55; and for kava, G. Forster 1777, 2:28; Crook c. 1800, 130; Krusenstern 1813, 1:164; Porter 1823, 94–95.
22. Fanning 1924, 127; Krusenstern 1813, 1:124; Lisiansky 1814, 71.
23. Wilson 1799, 135; Krusenstern 1813, 1:125; Porter 1823, 95, 107.
24. Robarts 1974, 265.
25. Langsdorff 1813, 1:137.
26. Crook c. 1800, 129, 174.
27. Crook c. 1800, 140.
28. Robarts 1974, 242.
29. Crook c. 1800, 140; Robarts 1974, 271; Lisiansky 1814, 90–91.
30. Ferdon 1981, 187–88; 1987, 214.
31. Crook c. 1800, 140; Robarts 1974, 271.
32. Crook c. 1800, 129.
33. Ferdon 1981, 190.

34. G. Forster 1777, 2:27; Marchand 1801, 1:172; Robarts 1974, 65, 278; Langsdorff 1813, 1:124–25.
35. Crook c. 1800, 152.
36. Crook c. 1800, 129.
37. Ferdon 1981, 102.
38. Crook c. 1800, 175.
39. Robarts 1974, 86.
40. Fanning 1924, 127.
41. Robarts 1974, 271–72.
42. Crook c. 1800, 129.
43. Crook c. 1800, 129. See Robarts 1974, 300, for confirmation of the *pona* having amounted to forty units and the following three units being multiples of ten.
44. Ferdon 1981, 191.
45. Crook c. 1800, 129.
46. Langsdorff 1813, 1:125.
47. Robarts 1974, 271–72.
48. Crook c. 1800, 140.
49. Robarts 1974, 117; Krusenstern 1813, 1:161; Langsdorff 1813, 1:125.
50. Robarts 1974, 273.
51. Robarts 1974, 273, 277–78.
52. Robarts 1974, 300; Porter 1823, 92–93, 117.
53. Ferdon 1987, 212.
54. Robarts 1974, 279; Porter 1823, 94.
55. Sinoto 1979, 113–14, 117–19.
56. G. Forster 1777, 2:26.
57. For eating eggs, see Crook c. 1800, 128; for limited presence of chickens, see Marchand 1801, 1:135; Wilson 1799, 132; Langsdorff 1813, 1:125.
58. Langsdorff 1813, 1:126, 176.
59. Crook c. 1800, 128; Robarts 1974, 110.
60. Sinoto 1979, 114, 117.
61. Cook 1955–67, 2:368; Marchand 1801, 1:134; Crook c. 1800, 128.
62. G. Forster 1777, 2:23.
63. Marchand 1801, 1:73–74.
64. Hergest in Vancouver 1801, 3:149.
65. Crook c. 1800, 128; Porter 1823, 91.
66. Crook c. 1800, 128.
67. Crook c. 1800, 128; Langsdorff 1813, 1:126.
68. Crook c. 1800, 128; Langsdorff 1813, 1:176.
69. Crook c. 1800, 128.
70. Langsdorff 1813, 1:125; Porter 1823, 112–13.

71. Crook c. 1800, 128; Ferdon 1981, 93; 1987, 106.

72. For pork being served on the occasions of birth, tattooing, and weddings, see Langsdorff 1813, 1:125; at funeral feasts, Langsdorff 1813, 1:125; Krusenstern 1813, 1:173; Porter 1823, 113; and when honoring the dead, Crook c. 1800, 128.

73. Langsdorff 1813, 1:121.

74. Crook c. 1800, 128; Langsdorff 1813, 1:125; Porter 1823, 113.

75. Wilson 1799, 145.

76. Langsdorff 1813, 1:128, 134.

77. Langsdorff 1813, 1:121, 137.

78. Porter 1823, 112.

79. Crook c. 1800, 127–28.

80. Crook c. 1800, 151.

81. Crook c. 1800, 127, 128.

82. Crook c. 1800, 127.

83. Crook c. 1800, 174; Robarts 1974, 89, 152.

84. Krusenstern 1813, 1:163.

85. Langsdorff 1813, 1:151.

86. Crook c. 1800, 114–15.

87. Crook c. 1800, 114–15.

88. Crook c. 1800, 143.

89. Crook c. 1800, 143.

90. Crook c. 1800, 127.

91. Crook c. 1800, 132; Robarts 1974, 249.

92. Crook c. 1800, 131.

93. Ferdon 1981, 202.

94. Krusenstern 1813, 1:163.

95. Brown 1935, 108–09, 190–91. For their use in Tahiti, see Ferdon 1981, 202.

96. Krusenstern 1813, 1:163; Porter 1823, 113.

97. Krusenstern 1813, 1:163; Lisiansky 1814, 92.

98. Marchand 1801, 1:182; Langsdorff 1813, 1:172.

99. Crook c. 1800, 132.

100. Crook c. 1800, 128.

101. Porter 1823, 113.

102. Marchand 1801, 1:181; Lisiansky 1814, 92.

103. Marchand 1801, 1:181.

104. For species of *Pipturus* in the Marquesas, see Brown 1935, 51–55. For use of *P. argenteus* in Tahiti, see Ferdon 1981, 208.

105. For references to types of nets, see Marchand 1801, 1:181; Crook c. 1800, 127; Robarts 1974, 249; Porter 1823, 102, 112.

106. Wilson 1799, 130; Robarts 1974, 273.

107. Lisiansky 1814, 87.

108. Crook c. 1800, 145.
109. Robarts 1974, 273–74.
110. Robarts 1974, 115, 273.
111. Langsdorff 1813, 1:121–22.
112. Robarts 1974, 274; Lisiansky 1814, 87.
113. Crook c. 1800, 128, 130, 145; Langsdorff 1813, 1:107, 126, 176; Lisiansky 1814, 93.
114. Robarts 1974, 246.
115. Krusenstern 1813, 1:166; Lisiansky 1814, 89.
116. Crook c. 1800, 152.
117. Robarts 1974, 274.
118. Robarts 1974, 118, 122.
119. Robarts 1974, 119.
120. For examples of these, see Chapter 8.
121. Sinoto 1970, 105–30.

8. TRADE AND TRANSPORTATION

1. Crook c. 1800, 145–46, 178–79; Robarts 1974, 65, 74, 88.
2. Wilson 1799, 131.
3. Crook c. 1800, 161.
4. For war canoes, see Robarts 1974, 144, 246; Porter 1823, 111; for voyaging canoes, Robarts 1974, 266; and for fishing canoes, Crook c. 1800, 178.
5. Robarts 1974, 66, 70, 120; Porter 1823, 102, 103.
6. Marchand 1801, 1:176; Robarts 1974, 66, 120.
7. Cook 1955–67, 2:376.
8. Marchand 1801, 1:176; Robarts 1974, 66; Krusenstern 1813, 1:164; Langsdorff 1813, 1:173; Porter 1823, 103.
9. Porter 1823, 102.
10. Robarts 1974, 246.
11. Porter 1823, 101.
12. Robarts 1974, 88, 144, 246; Porter 1823, 102.
13. Robarts 1974, 246; Krusenstern 1813, 1:163; Lisiansky 1814, 91; Porter 1823, 79. Breadfruit was *Artocarpus altilis* (Parkinson) Fosb., *mi'o* was *Thespesia populnea* (L.) Sol., and *tamanu* was *Calophyllum inophyllum* L.
14. Robarts 1974, 246; Lisiansky 1814, 91.
15. Lisiansky 1814, 91; Cook 1955–67, 2:376.
16. Brown 1935, 114.
17. Lisiansky 1814, 91.
18. Robarts 1974, 246.
19. Ferdon 1981, 56.
20. Marchand 1801, 1:176; Crook c. 1800, 131; Langsdorff 1813, 1:173.

21. Krusenstern 1813, 1:163–64; Robarts 1974, 62.
22. Quiros 1904a, 16; Marchand 1801, 1:176; Lisiansky 1814, 90; Porter 1823, 102.
23. G. Forster 1777, 2:29; J. R. Forster 1982, 3:490; Porter 1823, 79.
24. G. Forster 1777, 2:29; Haddon and Hornell 1936, 1:35, Fig. 21a; Dodd 1972, 132.
25. Haddon and Hornell 1936, 1:36; Dodd 1972, 132.
26. Fanning 1924, 87.
27. Cook 1955–67, 2:376; Marchand 1801, 1:176; Lisiansky 1814, 90.
28. Porter 1823, 79.
29. Lisiansky 1814, 89; Porter 1823, 79.
30. Quiros 1904a, 28; Langsdorff 1813, 1:173; Porter 1823, 79.
31. Robarts 1974, 246; Porter 1823, 102.
32. Marchand 1801, 1:224; Porter 1823, 77, 102.
33. Porter 1823, 102.
34. Haddon and Hornell 1936, 1:29–31.
35. Kotzebue 1821, 1:166.
36. Krusenstern 1813, 1:17.
37. Haddon and Hornell 1936, 1:90, Fig. 66b.
38. Cook 1955–67, 2:Fig. 57; Marchand 1801, 1:176; Lisiansky 1814, 90; Porter 1823, 79.
39. Crook c. 1800, 131.
40. Marchand 1801, 1:176.
41. Haddon and Hornell 1936, 1:30.
42. Haddon and Hornell 1936, 1:30.
43. Haddon and Hornell 1936, 1:30; Hornell 1928, 129–33.
44. Jijón y Caamaño 1952, 297, 302, Fig. 343.
45. Cook 1955–67, 2:Fig. 57; G. Forster 1777, 2:29; Crook c. 1800, 134; Porter 1823, 102–03.
46. Cook 1955–67, 2:376; Wilson 1799, 147.
47. G. Forster 1777, 2:29; J. R. Forster 1982, 3:490; Porter 1823, 179.
48. Dodd 1972, 133, Langsdorff illustration.
49. Porter 1823, 101–02.
50. Marchand 1801, 1:176; Crook c. 1800, 134; Robarts 1974, 60, 66, 93, 120, 141; Langsdorff 1813, 1:173.
51. Crook c. 1800, 179.
52. Crook c. 1800, 140; Robarts 1974, 261; Langsdorff 1813, 1:103.
53. Robarts 1974, 148–49, 241.
54. Crook c. 1800, 140; Robarts 1974, 148–49, 241; Langsdorff 1813, 1:103.
55. Crook c. 1800, 140.
56. Ferdon 1963, 499–505.
57. Crook c. 1800, 122; Robarts 1974, 62; Porter 1823, 93–94.
58. Robarts 1974, 62, 119, 266; Porter 1823, 93.

59. Crook c. 1800, 122; Robarts 1974, 62, 119; Porter 1823, 94.
60. Porter 1823, 93.
61. Porter 1823, 93.
62. Sinoto 1970, 105–30.
63. Crook c. 1800, 121; Porter 1823, 94.
64. Crook c. 1800, 121.
65. Crook c. 1800, 121; Fanning 1924, 104, 108; Robarts 1974, 74.
66. Ferdon 1987, 30.
67. Crook c. 1800, 121; Robarts 1974, 74.
68. Porter 1823, 93.
69. Robarts 1974, 261.
70. Robarts 1974, 119.
71. Crook c. 1800, 165.
72. Crook c. 1800, 167; Robarts 1974, 261.
73. Robarts 1974, 261.
74. Robarts 1974, 261.

9. WARFARE

1. Crook c. 1800, 136–37, 157; Robarts 1974, 60, 77–84, 120, 257.
2. Robarts 1974, 61, 258–59.
3. Crook c. 1800, 136, 153–57.
4. Crook c. 1800, 127, 169; Fanning 1924, 93.
5. Crook c. 1800, 127; Robarts 1974, 153, 154.
6. Robarts 1974, 78, 80; Langsdorff 1813, 1:142.
7. Marchand 1801, 1:178; Langsdorff 1813, 1:175.
8. Quiros 1904a, 23.
9. Ferdon 1987, 179, 224, 260–61.
10. Ferdon 1981, 94–95, 127–28.
11. Krusenstern 1813, 1:162; Lisiansky 1814, 88; Langsdorff 1813, 1:172; Porter 1823, 87.
12. Crook c. 1800, 119; Robarts 1974, 78; Porter 1813, 87.
13. Cook 1955–67, 2:376; Marra 1775, 159; Marchand 1801, 1:178; Crook c. 1800, 119; Porter 1823, 87.
14. G. Forster 1777, 2:18; Marchand 1801, 1:178; Crook c. 1800, 131; Krusenstern 1813, 1:162; Lisiansky 1814, 92; Langsdorff 1813, 1:107; Porter 1823, 87, 111.
15. G. Forster 1777, 2:18; Marchand 1801, 1:177; Krusenstern 1813, 1:162; Langsdorff 1813, 1:172; Porter 1823, 84, 87.
16. Porter 1823, 87.
17. Marchand 1801, 1:177; Crook c. 1800, 136; Robarts 1974, 111; Lisiansky 1814, 88.
18. Crook c. 1800, 136; Krusenstern 1813, 1:162; Lisiansky 1814, 88.

19. G. Forster 1777, 2:18; Marchand 1801, 1:177.
20. Crook c. 1800, 137.
21. Crook c. 1800, 157.
22. Porter 1823, 85–86.
23. Robarts 1974, 154.
24. Robarts 1974, 154–57.
25. Robarts 1974, 148.
26. Crook c. 1800, 137, 152.
27. Crook c. 1800, 146–47.
28. Robarts 1974, 78, 89–90, 92.
29. Robarts 1974, 256–57.
30. Crook c. 1800, 152–53, 156, 157.
31. Crook c. 1800, 75, 129–30, 137, 177; Robarts 1974, 89–90, 115; Porter 1823, 81, 88–89.
32. Crook c. 1800, 136, 167.
33. Crook c. 1800, 136.
34. Porter 1823, 86.
35. Crook c. 1800, 169.
36. Robarts 1974, 78–84.
37. Langsdorff 1813, 1:150; Lisiansky 1814, 87–88.
38. Crook c. 1800, 157, 163.
39. Robarts 1974, 78.
40. Crook c. 1800, 136.
41. Krusenstern 1813, 1:169–70.
42. Robarts 1974, 90–91.
43. Crook c. 1800, 137, 171.
44. Crook c. 1800, 137.
45. Crook c. 1800, 162.
46. Crook c. 1800, 147, 153, 162.
47. Robarts 1974, 258.
48. Robarts 1974, 116.
49. Krusenstern 1813, 1:166, 181; Lisiansky 1814, 87; Langsdorff 1813, 1:144, 149.
50. Robarts 1974, 116.
51. Quiros 1904b, 23.
52. Cook 1955–67, 2:373.
53. G. Forster 1777, 2:10, 22.
54. J. R. Forster 1982, 3:490.
55. Marchand 1801, 1:113.
56. Krusenstern 1813, 1:110.
57. Porter 1823, 82–83.
58. Porter 1823, 108–09.
59. Marchand 1801, 1:45–46; Lisiansky 1814, 64; Porter 1823, 77, 99, 109.

60. Quiros 1904a, 19; Marra 1775, 156–57; Hergest in Vancouver 1801, 3:147–48; Crook c. 1800, 173; Fanning 1924, 110; Lisiansky 1814, 64–65.
61. Wilson 1799, 139; Crook c. 1800, 173; Fanning 1924, 110, 113.
62. G. Forster 1777, 2:34.
63. Crook c. 1800, 173.
64. Marchand 1801, 1:58.
65. Wilson 1799, 139.
66. Porter 1823, 99.
67. Fanning 1924, 113.
68. Robarts 1974, 156.
69. Robarts 1974, 145–46.
70. Krusenstern 1813, 1:170.
71. Robarts 1974, 66.

10. IN RETROSPECT

1. Green 1967, 215–40.
2. Sinoto 1968, 116; 1979, 112.
3. Sinoto 1979, 119–20.
4. Codrington 1891, 101–02.
5. Codrington 1891, 271, 272, 284.
6. Gunson 1978, 351.
7. Turner 1884, 146, 148.
8. For Tonga, see Ferdon 1987, 109–11.
9. For Tonga, see Ferdon 1987, 36–37.
10. Ferdon 1987, 33.
11. For Tongan shell trumpets, see Ferdon 1987, 85–87, 196; for touching noses, Ferdon 1987, 139–40.
12. Ferdon 1981, 104.
13. For Tonga, see Ferdon 1987, 139.
14. For Tonga, see Ferdon 1987, 32.
15. For Tonga, see Ferdon 1987, 18.
16. For descriptions of *fa'itoka,* see Ferdon 1987, 157–62.
17. Green 1967, 215–40.
18. Banks 1963, 1:334; G. Forster 1777, 1:432.
19. Langsdorff 1813, 1:111.
20. Krusenstern 1813, 1:158.
21. Crook c. 1800, 125.
22. Codrington 1891, 127; Lewis 1951, 199–206.
23. Codrington 1891, 234.
24. Marchand 1801, 1:235.
25. Crook c. 1800, 160.
26. Codrington 1891, 232, 234, 237, 240.

27. Davidson 1979a, 94.
28. Emory 1979, 219.
29. Roberts 1795, 245.
30. Marchand 1801, 1:123.
31. G. Forster 1777, 2:27.
32. Dixon 1932, 47.
33. J. R. Forster 1778, 443.
34. Langsdorff 1813, 1:135.
35. I have accepted the American origin of the soursop (*Annona muricata* L.), the cashew (*Anacardium occidentale* L., *Capsicum* sp.), and the pineapple (*Ananas comosus* (L.) Merrill) on Candolle 1967, 173–74, 198–200, 288–90, and 311–12; of the soapberry (*Sapindus saponaria* L.) and the calabash tree (*Crescentia cujete* L.) on Neal 1968, 532–33, 771; and of the sweet potato (*Ipomoea batatas* L.) on Nishiyama 1963, 120–28; and Yen 1974, 244–49. The American origin of the Marquesan cotton is based upon Brown 1935, 177, who identified cotton collected in those islands in the 1920s as *Gossypium brasiliense* Macfadyen, which is now recognized by Hutchinson, Silow, and Stephens 1947, 50, as the American cotton *G. barbadense* var. *brasiliense*.
36. Gunson 1978, 346.
37. Wilson 1799, 32, 39.
38. Crook c. 1800, 142.
39. Lisiansky 1814, 91–92.
40. Brown 1935, 160–61.
41. Crook c. 1800, 130.
42. Brown 1935, 81.
43. Brown 1935, 269.
44. Towle 1961, 62–63.
45. Towle 1961, 80–82.
46. Velasco 1844, 1:51–52.
47. Towle 1961, 39.
48. Towle 1961, 30; Velasco 1844, 1:56.
49. Towle 1961, 88; Wolf 1892, 427.
50. Towle 1961, 78–79; Velasco 1844, 1:68.
51. Towle 1961, 64–65; Velasco 1844, 1:38.
52. Velasco 1844, 1:62; Wolf 1892, 427.
53. These were Alvaro de Mendaña in 1595, James Cook in 1774, Joseph Ingraham in 1791, Étienne Marchand in 1791, a Captain Brown in 1792, Richard Hergest in 1792, Josiah Roberts in 1792–93, and the ship *Daedalus* in 1793.
54. Dixon 1932, 40–66; Buck 1938, 322; Heyerdahl 1952, 428, and 1963, 30; O'Brian 1972, 342–65; Yen 1974, 294; Davidson 1979b, 234; Bellwood 1979, 141; Kirch 1985, 65.

55. Heyerdahl 1952, 428–39; 1961, 522; 1963, 30.
56. Buck 1938, 322–23; Yen 1974, 266–67.
57. Finney 1985, 19–20.
58. Sauer 1966, 269.
59. For Tahiti, see Ferdon 1981, 289; for Tonga, see Cook 1955–67, 2:120.
60. Quiros 1904a, 23.
61. Quiros 1904a, 14.
62. Quiros 1904a, 15.
63. Yen 1963, 98.
64. Quiros 1904a, 10–11.
65. Quiros 1904a, 22, 149.
66. Quiros 1904a, 20, 21.
67. Quiros 1904a, 25–26.
68. Quiros 1904a, 41.
69. Quiros 1904b, 255.
70. Leza 1904, 387.
71. Towle 1961, 62–63.
72. Ferdon 1981, 288, 293.
73. For Hawaii, see Rosendahl and Yen 1971, 383; for Easter Island, Skjölsvold 1961, 297.
74. Ferdon 1988, 1–5.
75. For Tahiti, see Cook 1955–67, 1:120; for Hawaii, Cook 1955–67, 3:278; for Easter Island, Corney 1908, 101, 123; for New Zealand, Cook 1955–67, 1:186–87; and for the southern Cook Islands, Williams 1838, 579.
76. Simon 1914, 722.
77. Stokes 1934, 2707–08, 2791–2803.
78. Haddon and Hornell 1936, 1:30.
79. Ferdon 1981, 288, 293, 302.

Bibliography

Adamson, A. M. 1936. *Marquesan Insects: Environment.* Bernice P. Bishop Museum, Bulletin 139. Honolulu.

Banks, Joseph. 1963. *The Endeavour Journal of Joseph Banks.* Edited by J. C. Beaglehole. 2nd ed. 2 vols. Sydney: Angus and Robertson.

Bellwood, Peter. 1972. *A Settlement Pattern Survey, Hanatekua Valley, Hiva Oa.* Bernice P. Bishop Museum, Pacific Anthropological Records no. 17. Honolulu.

———. 1979. *Man's Conquest of the Pacific.* New York: Oxford University Press.

Brown, Forest F. B. H. 1931. *Flora of Southeastern Polynesia: I Monocotyledons.* Bernice P. Bishop Museum, Bulletin 84. Honolulu.

———. 1935. *Flora of Southeastern Polynesia: III Dicotyledons.* Bernice P. Bishop Museum, Bulletin 130. Honolulu.

Buck, Peter H. 1938. *Viking of the Sunrise.* New York: Stokes Press. Reprinted as *Vikings of the Pacific.* Chicago: University of Chicago Press, 1960.

———. 1957. *Arts and Crafts of Hawaii.* Bernice P. Bishop Museum, Special Publication 45. Honolulu.

Candolle, Alphonse de. 1967. *Origin of Cultivated Plants.* New York: Hafner. Reprint of 2nd. ed., 1886.

Chubb, L. J. 1930. *Geology of the Marquesas Islands.* Bernice P. Bishop Museum, Bulletin 68. Honolulu.

Codrington, R. H. 1891. *The Melanesians: Anthropology and Folk-Lore.* Oxford: Clarendon Press.

Cook, James. 1777. *A Voyage Toward the South Pole and Round the World Performed in His Majesty's Ships the Resolution and Adventure, in the Years 1772, 1773, 1774, and 1775.* London: W. Straham and T. Cadell.

———. 1955–67. *The Journals of Captain James Cook.* Edited by J. C. Beaglehole. 3 vols. Hakluyt Society, Extra Series, Nos. 34–36. Cambridge.

Corney, Bolton P. 1908. *The Voyage of Captain Felipe Gonzalez to Easter Island in 1770–1.* Hakluyt Society, 2nd Series, No. 13. Cambridge.

Crook, William P. c. 1800. "An Account of the Marquesas Islands." In George M. Sheahan's typescript "Marquesas Source Materials, Bibliographic Reference No. 30, The Mitchell Library Crook MS.," pp. 114–183. Preliminary Edition copy no. 21. Quincy, N.D.

Davidson, Janet M. 1979a. "Samoa and Tonga." In *The Prehistory of Polynesia,* edited by Jesse D. Jennings, pp. 82–109. Cambridge, Mass.: Harvard University Press.

———. 1979b. "New Zealand." In *The Prehistory of Polynesia,* edited by Jesse D. Jennings, pp. 222–248. Cambridge, Mass.: Harvard University Press.

Dening, Greg. 1980. *Islands and Beaches. Discourse on a Silent Land: Marquesas 1774–1880.* Honolulu: University Press of Hawaii.

Dixon, Roland. 1932. "The Problem of the Sweet Potato in Polynesia." *American Anthropologist,* Vol. 34, pp. 40–66.

Dodd, Edward. 1972. *Polynesian Seafaring.* New York: Dodd, Mead.

Emory, Kenneth P. 1979. "The Societies." In *The Prehistory of Polynesia,* edited by Jesse D. Jennings, pp. 200–221. Cambridge, Mass.: Harvard University Press.

Fanning, Edmund. 1924. *Voyages and Discoveries in the South Seas, 1792–1832.* Marine Research Society, Publication No. 6. Salem, Mass.

Ferdon, Edwin N. 1963. "Polynesian Origins." *Science,* Vol. 141, pp. 499–505.

———. 1965. "Surface Architecture of the Site of Paeke, Taipi Valley, Nukuhiva." In *Reports of the Norwegian Archaeological Expedition to Easter Island and the East Pacific,* Vol. II: *Miscellaneous Papers,* edited by Thor Heyerdahl and E. N. Ferdon, Jr., pp. 117–122. School of American Research and Kon-Tiki Museum, Monograph No. 24, pt. 2. Santa Fe, N. Mex.

———. 1981. *Early Tahiti as the Explorers Saw It, 1767–1797.* Tucson: University of Arizona Press.

———. 1987. *Early Tonga: As the Explorers Saw It, 1616–1810.* Tucson: University of Arizona Press.

———. 1988. "A Case for Taro Preceding Kumara as the Dominant Domesticate in Ancient New Zealand." *Journal of Ethnobiology,* Vol. 8, pp. 1–5.

Finney, Ben R. 1985. "Anomalous Westerlies, El Niño, and the Colonization of Polynesia." *American Anthropologist,* Vol. 87, pp. 9–26.

Fleurieu, Claret. 1799. *Voyage autour du monde, pendant les années 1790,*

1791, et 1792, par Étienne Marchand ..., Vol. IV. Paris: Imprimerie de la République.

Forster, George. 1777. *Voyage Round the World* ... *During the Years 1772, 3, 4, and 5.* 2 vols. London: White, Robson, Elmsly, and Robinson.

Forster, John R. 1778. *Observations Made During a Voyage Round the World* .... London: Robinson.

———. 1982. *The Resolution Journal of Johann Reinhold Forster, 1772–1775.* Edited by Michael E. Hoare. 4 vols. Hakluyt Society, 2nd Series, Vols. 152–155. London.

Green, Roger C. 1967. "The Immediate Origins of the Polynesians." In *Polynesian Culture History,* edited by G. A. Highland, R. W. Force, A. Howard, M. Kelly, and Y. H. Sinoto, pp. 215–240. Bernice P. Bishop Museum, Special Publication 56. Honolulu.

Gunson, Niel. 1978. *Messengers of Grace.* Melbourne: Oxford University Press.

Haddon, A. C., and James Hornell. 1936–38. *Canoes of Oceania.* 3 vols. Bernice P. Bishop Museum, Special Publication 27–29. Honolulu. Reprinted in 1 vol. 1975.

Handy, E. S. Craighill. 1923. *The Native Culture in the Marquesas.* Bernice P. Bishop Museum, Bulletin 9. Honolulu.

Handy, Willowdean C. 1922. *Tattooing in the Marquesas.* Bernice P. Bishop Museum, Bulletin 1. Honolulu.

Heyerdahl, Thor. 1952. *American Indians in the Pacific.* London: George Allen and Unwin.

———. 1961. "General Discussion." In *Reports of the Norwegian Archaeological Expedition to Easter Island and the East Pacific,* Vol. I: *Archaeology of Easter Island,* edited by Thor Heyerdahl and E. N. Ferdon, Jr., pp. 493–526. School of American Research and Museum of New Mexico, Monograph No. 24, pt. 1. Santa Fe.

———. 1963. "Prehistoric Voyages as Agencies for Melanesian and South American Plant and Animal Dispersal to Polynesia." In *Plants and Migrations of Pacific Peoples,* edited by Jacques Barrau, pp. 23–35. Honolulu: Bishop Museum Press.

Hornell, James. 1928. "South American Balanced Canoes, Stages in the Invention of the Double Outrigger." *Man,* No. 2, pp. 129–133.

Hutchinson, J. B., R. A. Silow, and S. G. Stephens. 1947. *The Evolution of Gossypium and the Differentiation of the Cultivated Cottons.* London: Oxford University Press.

Jijón y Caamaño, Jacinto. 1952. *Antropología prehispánica del Ecuador.* Quito: La Prensa Católica.

Kirch, Patrick V. 1985. *Feather Gods and Fishhooks*. Honolulu: University of Hawaii Press.

Kooijman, Simon. 1972. *Tapa in Polynesia*. Bernice P. Bishop Museum, Bulletin 234. Honolulu.

Kotzebue, Otto von. 1821. *A Voyage of Discovery, into the South Sea and Beering's Straits . . . in the Years 1815–1818* . . . . 3 vols. Facsimile reprint, Bibliotheca Australiana, No. 17. Amsterdam: N. Israel, 1967.

Krusenstern, A. J. von. 1813. *Voyage Round the World in the Years 1803, 1804, 1805 & 1806* . . . . 2 vols. London: John Murray. Facsimile reprint, Bibliotheca Australiana, No. 38. Amsterdam: N. Israel, 1968.

Langsdorff, G. H. von. 1813. *Voyages and Travels in Various Parts of the World During the Years 1803, 1804, 1805, and 1807*. 2 vols. London: Henry Colburn. Facsimile reprint, Bibliotheca Australiana, No. 40. Amsterdam: N. Israel, 1968.

Lewis, Albert. 1951. *The Melanesians: People of the South Pacific*. Chicago: Chicago Natural History Museum.

Leza, Gaspar de. 1904. "True Account of the Events of the Voyage That the Captain Pedro Fernandez de Quiros Made to the Unknown Southern Lands, by Gaspar de Leza, Chief Pilot of the Said Fleet." In *Voyages Pedro Fernandez de Quiros, 1595 to 1606*. 2 vols. Translated and edited by Sir Clements Markham. Hakluyt Society, 2nd Series, No. 15, Vol. 2, pp. 321–403. Cambridge. Lendeln: Kraus Reprint, 1967.

Linton, Ralph. 1923. *The Material Culture of the Marquesas Islands*. Bernice P. Bishop Museum, Memoir VIII, No. 5. Honolulu.

———. 1925. *Archaeology of the Marquesas Islands*. Bernice P. Bishop Museum, Bulletin 23. Honolulu.

Lisiansky, Urey. 1814. *A Voyage Round the World, in the Years 1803, 4, 5, and 6* . . . . London: John Booth, Longman, Hurst, Rees, Orme, and Brown. Facsimile reprint, Bibliotheca Australiana, No. 42. Amsterdam: N. Israel, 1968.

Marchand, Étienne. 1801. *A Voyage Round the World Performed During the Years 1790, 1791, and 1792* . . . . 2 vols. Translated from the French. London: Rees, Cadell, and Davies.

Marra, John. 1775. *Journal of the Resolution's Voyage, in 1772, 1773, 1774, and 1775 . . . Also a Journal of the Adventure's Voyage in the Years 1772, 1773, and 1774* . . . . London: F. Newberry. Facsimile reprint, Bibliotheca Australiana, No. 15. Amsterdam: N. Israel, 1967.

Menard, Henry W. 1986. *Islands*. New York: Scientific American Books.

Métraux, Alfred. 1940. *Ethnology of Easter Island*. Bernice P. Bishop Museum, Bulletin 160. Honolulu.

Neal, Marie C. 1968. *In Gardens of Hawaii.* Bernice P. Bishop Museum, Special Publication 50. Honolulu.

Nishiyama, Ichizo. 1963. "The Origin of the Sweet Potato Plant." In *Plants and the Migrations of Pacific Peoples.* Edited by Jacques Barrau. Honolulu: Bishop Museum Press.

NOAA 1991. *Monthly Climatic Data for the World, 1961–1990.* Asheville, N.C.: National Oceanic and Atmospheric Administration, National Climatic Data Center.

O'Brian, Patricia J. 1972. "The Sweet Potato: Its Origin and Dispersal." *American Anthropologist,* Vol. 74, pp. 342–365.

Papa Li, John. 1983. *Fragments of Hawaiian History.* Bernice P. Bishop Museum, Special Publication 70. Honolulu.

Philander, George. 1989. "El Niño and La Niña." *American Scientist,* Vol. 77, No. 5, pp. 451–459.

———. 1990. *El Niño, La Niña, and the Southern Oscillation.* New York: Academic Press.

Porter, David. 1823. *A Voyage to the South Seas in the Years 1812, 1813, and 1814 . . . .* London: Richard Phillips.

Quiros, Pedro Fernandez de. 1904a. "Narrative of the Second Voyage of the Adelantado Alvaro de Mendaña, by the Chief Pilot Pedro Fernandez de Quiros." In *The Voyages of Pedro Fernandez de Quiros, 1595 to 1606.* 2 vols. Translated and edited by Sir Clements Markham. Hakluyt Society, 2nd Series, No. 14, Vol. I, pp. 3–146. Mendeln: Krause Reprint, 1967.

———. 1904b. "Narrative of the Voyage of Pedro Fernandez de Quiros in 1606, for the Discovery of the Austral Regions." In *The Voyages of Pedro Fernandez de Quiros 1595 to 1606.* 2 vols. Translated and edited by Sir Clements Markham. Hakluyt Society, 2nd Series, No. 14, Vol. I, pp. 161–320. Mendeln: Kraus Reprint, 1967.

Rasmusson, Eugene M. 1985. "El Niño and Variations in Climate." *American Scientist,* Vol. 73, No. 2, pp. 168–177.

Robarts, Edward. 1974. *The Marquesas Journal of Edward Robarts, 1797–1824.* Edited by Greg Dening. Canberra: Australian National University Press.

Roberts, Josiah. 1795. "The Discovery and Description of the Islands Called the Marquesas . . . . " In *Collections of the Massachusetts Historical Society for the Year 1795,* pp. 238–246. New York: Johnson Reprint, n.d.

Rosendahl, P., and D. E. Yen. 1971. "Fossil Sweet Potato Remains from Hawaii." *Journal of the Polynesian Society,* Vol. 80, pp. 379–385.

Sauer, Carl O. 1966. *The Early Spanish Main.* Berkeley: University of California Press.

Simon, Edmund. 1914. "The Introduction of the Sweet Potato into the Far East." *Transactions of the Asiatic Society of Japan*, Vol. 14, pp. 711–724.

Sinoto, Yosihiko H. 1968. "The Position of the Marquesas Islands in East Polynesian Prehistory." In *Prehistoric Culture in Oceania*, edited by I. Yawata and Y. H. Sinoto, pp. 111–118. Honolulu: Bishop Museum Press.

———. 1970. "An Archaeologically Based Assessment of the Marquesas as a Dispersal Center in East Polynesia." In *Studies in Oceanic Culture History*, edited by R. C. Green and M. Kelly, Vol. I, pp. 105–130. Bernice P. Bishop Museum, Pacific Anthropological Records, No. 11. Honolulu.

———. 1979. "The Marquesas." In *The Prehistory of Polynesia*, edited by Jesse D. Jennings, pp. 110–134. Cambridge, Mass.: Harvard University Press.

Skjölsvold, Arne. 1961. "Site E-2, a Circular Stone Dwelling, Anakena." In *Reports of the Norwegian Archaeological Expedition to Easter Island and the East Pacific*, Vol. I: *Archaeology of Easter Island*, edited by Thor Heyerdahl and E. N. Ferdon, Jr., pp. 295–303. School of American Research and Museum of New Mexico, Monograph No. 24, pt. 1. Santa Fe.

Sparrman, Anders. 1953. *A Voyage Round the World with Captain James Cook in H. M. S. Resolution*. London: Robert, Ltd.

Stokes, John F. G. 1934. "Japanese Cultural Influences in Hawaii." In *Proceedings of the Fifth Pacific Science Congress*, pp. 2707–08, 2791–2803. Toronto: University of Toronto Press.

Taylor, Ronald C. 1973. *An Atlas of Pacific Islands Rainfall*. Washington, D.C.: Office of Naval Research.

Thomas, Nicholas. 1990. *Marquesan Societies: Inequality and Political Transformation in Eastern Polynesia.* Oxford: Clarendon Press.

Towle, Margaret A. 1961. *The Ethnobotany of Pre-Columbian Peru*. Chicago: Aldine.

Turner, George. 1884. *Samoa a Hundred Years Ago and Long Before*. London: Macmillan.

Uphof, J. C. T. 1968. *Dictionary of Economic Plants*. Lehre: J. Cramer.

Vancouver, George. 1801. *A Voyage of Discovery in the North Pacific Ocean, and Round the World . . . .* 6 vols. London: John Stockdale.

Velasco, Juan de. 1844. *Historia del Reino de Quito en la América meridional*, Vol. I, pt. 1, *La historia natural; año de 1789*. Quito: Imprenta del Gobierno.

Williams, John. 1838. *A Narrative of Missionary Enterprises in the South Sea Islands*. London: J. Snow.

Wilson, James. 1799. *A Missionary Voyage to the Southern Pacific Ocean*,

Performed in the Years 1796, 1797, 1798, in the Ship Duff . . . . London: T. Chapman.

Wolf, Teodoro. 1892. *Geografía y Geología del Ecuador.* Leipzig: F. A. Brockhaus.

World Weather Records, Vol. 6. 1968. Washington, D.C.: Environmental Science Services Administration, U.S. Department of Commerce.

Yen, D. E. 1963. "Sweet Potato Variation and Its Relation to Human Migrations in the Pacific." In *Plants and the Migrations of Pacific Peoples,* edited by Jacques Barrou, pp. 93–117. Honolulu: Bishop Museum Press.

———. 1974. *The Sweet Potato and Oceania: An Essay in Ethnobotany.* Bernice P. Bishop Museum, Bulletin 236. Honolulu.

Index

Abrus precatorius L., 17, 136
Adoption, 79
Adzes, 53, 126
Agriculture, 53, 86
Ahui, use of, 96
Albinos, 10
Aleurites moluccana (L.) Wild. See Candlenut
Alocasia macrorrhiza (L.) Schott. See *Kape*
Anacardium occidentale L., 8. See also Cashew
Ancestors, memorial events for, 47–48
Annona muricata L. See Guanabana; Soursop
Anvil, bark cloth-beating, 56
Apple, Malay, 88
'*Arioi*, 76
Atua. See Gods

Balboa, Vasco Nuñez de, 133
Bamboo, use of, 22, 23, 53, 63, 81, 105
Bananas, 87, 88; forced ripening of, 93; leaves of, 73
Banyan, use of, 56
Bark cloth, 53; colors used in, 16, 57; fabrication of, 56–57; types of, 16, 56

Baskets, 55
Beaters, types of, for making bark cloth, 56
Betrothal, 70; age differences in, 77; use of, for intertribal security, 76–77
Bone, use of: for decorations, 55; for tools, 54, 81
Bows and arrows, 113
Breadfruit, 86, 87–88, 98; recipes for preparing, 60; seasons of harvesting, 89–90; use of, for bark cloth, 56; use of leaves of, 22, 23; use of resin of, 17, 104; use of wood of, 17, 18, 84, 102
Burial: ceremonies pertaining to, 81–85; feasting as part of, 83–84; food offerings at time of, 83, 84
Butahaie, power of, as mother of *haka'iki* Keatonue, 33–34

Calabash tree, 131, 132, 134; use of fruit of, 55
Calendar, elements of, 66, 90
Candlenut, use of, 63, 88
Cannibalism, 37; absence of, during famines, 122; on war dead and captives, 121, 122; ritual use of, 43, 46

Canoes: use of, as ceremonial objects, 48; construction of, 102–106, 107; outriggers of, 105–6, 138; paddles for, 106; sails of, 55, 106; types of, 102, 106–7
Capsicum spp. *See* Chili peppers
Cashew, 89, 131, 132, 134
Castor bean, 88
Casuarina equisetifolia L. *See Toa* wood
Caves, as habitations, 25, 30
Cheirodendron marquesense F. Brown. *See Pimata*
Chickens, 6; eggs of, eaten, 93; as offerings to deity, 93; use of feathers of, 18, 93
Chiefs, 31–34
Chili peppers, 88–89, 131, 132, 134
Clapping, hand: methods of, for rhythm, 64
Cleanliness, 52
Clothing, 15–16; restrictions pertaining to, 16. See also *Hami*; *Ka'eu*; *Kahu*; Turbans
Clubs, types of, 115
Coconut palms, 89; use of leaves of, 22, 23, 124
Coconuts: as gifts to *tau'a*, 43; as offering to the dead, 47; oil of, 16–17, 68; storage of, 93; as symbols of peace, 124; tradition on introduction of, 41; use of husk, 19, 20, 23, 43, 63, 97, 104; use of milk, 59–60; use of shells, 18
Coffins, 47, 82, 84
Colubrina asiatica (L.) Brongn., 22
Combs, 55; types of, for tattooing, 126
Commoners, those classified as, 26–27
Containers, wooden, 54
Coral, 18; use of, as tools, 54
Cotton, 131, 132, 134, 136

Cradle, wooden, 54
Crescentia cujete L. *See* Calabash tree
Curcuma longo L. *See* Turmeric

Dance court. See *Tohua*
Dancing, 52, 62, 77; types of, 64–65, 68–69
Dioscorea alata L. *See* Yam
Divorce, 79
Dixon, Roland, 131, 133, 135
Dog, absence of, 6, 93
Drought, cause of, 4–5; as motive for migrations, 99–100
Drums, 77, 78, 82, 118; as signals of war, 117–18; types of, 62–63

Easter Island, 18, 56, 73, 83, 108
Ecuador, 106, 132, 133, 138
El Niño, influence on Marquesas, 4–5, 133
'Eva, use of poisonous berries of, 79, 81

Famine, 98–99
Fan palm, use of leaves of, 22–23, 73
Fans, 55
Fau, use of, 22, 89, 105
Feasts as memorials, 47–48, 84
Ferns, as food, 60, 98, 99
Ficus prolixa Forst. See also *Hiapo*; Banyan
Fiji, 56
Finney, Ben, 133
Fire plow, 59
Fish, bartering of, 30, 53, 96
Fishermen, 25, 30; as *tuhuna* specialists, 53, 96–97
Fishhooks, 97–98
Fishing, 6, methods of, 97–98; as occupation, 96
Food, personal: individual contain-

ers for, 58; offering of, to gods, 61; restrictions pertaining to, 57–58
Fortifications, 123

Gamal, of Vanuatu, 127
Games, 61
Ge, preparation of, 60
Gods: as ancestral spirits, 38–39, 50; as living *tau'a*, 39–40; representations of, 38; hierarchy, 37
Gourds, as containers, 54–55
Greeting, method of, 32; similarity of, to Tonga, 127
Guanabana, 88, 131, 132. See also Soursop

Hair, human: methods of removal of, 12; treatment of, 10–12; types of, 10, 129; use of for decoration, 20, 48, 63, 113, 120; use of for sorcery, 12, 20
Haka'iki, 27, 31, 33; acquisition of position and power of, 33–35; assured authority of, 35; rank of, in relation to tribal *tau'a*, 29; source of power of, 35–36; as *toa*, 112
Hami, 12, 16, 73; use of large style, 68, 76
Headdresses, 18–20
Heyerdahl, Thor, 133
Hiapo, 16, 41, 56
Hibiscus tiliaceus L., 18, 83, 97. See also *Fau*
High chief. See *Haka'iki*
Hio, 58
Houses: construction of, 21–23; furnishings of, 23–25; restrictions, 24; types of, 25, 70; associated with *tohua*, 67, 68
Huou, 88

Ihi, 88
Illness, causes of, 80

Inheritance: gift of, 71

Japan, 137

Ka'eu, 16
Kahu, 16, 73
Ka'ioi, 57, 68, 132; restricted to commoner class, 26; nature of, 76
Kape, 86
Kava, 89, 127; drinking of, 28, 52; wooden bowl designed for, 54
Kites, 61
Koina, 62, 63; as celebrations of special events, 66–67, 71; on *tohua* courts, 65
Kokuu, use of, at birth, 71

La Niña, 130; probable influence of, on the Marquesas, 4–5
Land: division of, 112, 116; importance of, 33; inheritance of, 33, 116; methods of clearing, 86; return of, 116–19
Leprosy, 80, 81, 84
Linton, Ralph, 23
Loin cloth. See *Hami*

Ma: preparation of, 91–92; storage of, 92–93
Maii, use of, 103
Manta, use of skin of, 62
Marquesans, physical characteristics of, 9–12
Marriages: types of, 77–78; value of, between tribes, 76–77
Massage, 80
Matāpule, 45; similarity of, to *tuhuna ota ogo*, 127
Mats, 23–24; manufacture of, 53; types of, 55, 64, 68
Matta puovo, 27
Mattatoetoe, 27; social position of, 14, 30

Maui, as possible Marquesan god, 38
Me'ae, 12, 20, 126; as family religious structure, 39, 46; forbidden to women, 47; as repositories for the dead, 46, 48; as a tribal religious center, 29, 42, 43, 46, 47–48
Mendaña, expedition of, 134–36
Migrations, causes of, 108–9
Mi'o, use of wood of, 102
Moa, 41
Moss, use of, 104
Mulberry, paper. See *Ute*

Nets, types of, 98
New Zealand, 137
Noni, 88; use of at birth, 71

Obeisance, acts of, 32, 118; similarity of, to those of Tonga, 128
Octopus lure, 126
Ornaments, personal, 17–20
Oro, as possible Marquesan god, 38
'Oute, use of, as emetic, 79

Pandanus, 18
Papa vine: juice used at birth, 71; to lighten hair, 10, 20, 73; to lighten skin, 10, 68, 73; use of filaments of, 97
Parturition, 70–71
Pekio, 77, 112; choosing of, 78; nature of relationship, 75, 78; social status of, 26, 78
Pia, 86; preparation of, 59
Pigs, 6; castration and spaying of, 94; eaten only on special occasions, 15, 59, 71, 83, 93, 94–95; as form of payment, 14, 42, 73, 74, 119; as offerings, 48, 49, 83; restrictions pertaining to, 59, 95; use of ribs of, 41; use of teeth of, 18, 41
Pimata, 18

Pineapple, 88, 131, 132, 134
Piper methysticum Forst. See Kava
Pit oven, 59, 60
Platforms, masonry, 25, 66
Porpoises: catching of, 97; use of teeth of, 18
Pottery, use of, 6, 126
Pounder, vegetable, 54
Priests: inspirational (see *Tau'a*); language of, 42, 46, 77, 82; ritual (See *Tuhuna ota ogo*)
Pritchardia pacifica (Seem and Wendl.). See Fan palm
Property ownership, 30, 35, 96, 99

Quiros, expedition of, 136

Rafts, 101
Rainfall, 2–4
Rata, leaves of, as thatching, 23
Rats, 93; as food, 99; as food for young pigs, 94
Rhynchosia minima (L.) D.C. See *Papa* vine
Robe. See *Kahu*

Sacrifice, human, 37, 43, 63, 85; sources of victims, 43, 44; treatment of bodies, 40, 43
Sandalwood, use of, 16, 55
Sapindus soponaria L. See Soapberry
Sauer, Carl, 133
Scalping in warfare, 121–22
Seafood: restrictions on eating, 96; varieties of, 95–96
Seaweed, as food, 59
Servants, duties of, 30–31, 72; freedom of, 30; punishment of, 30–31
Settlement, patterns of, 21
Sharks: use of skin of, 54, 62, 63; use of teeth of, 12, 54, 81
Shellfish, gathering of, 53

Shells, 12, 18–20, 38, 53, 120; as lime for whitewash, 18, 55; as trumpets, 63; use of to make fishhooks, 97
Singing, 52, 62; styles of, 64
Sinoto, Yosihiko, 6, 83, 100, 108
Slings, 67, 75; use of coconut cordage for, 113
Soapberry, 55, 68, 131–36 passim. See also Kokuu
Songs, sacred, 46; island names as part of, 41, 109
Sorcery, 41, 50–51
Soursop, 88, 131, 132, 134. See also Guanabana
Spears, 113–14
Spondius dulces (Soland. ex.) Parkinson, 86, 131
Stilts, 61; racing on, 62, 68
Stone boiling, 59
Storage pits, 25. See also Ma
Sugarcane, 88
Suge, of Vanuatu, 127
Suicide, 81; pretence of, 79
Supercision, 73; absence of, for some males, 130
Surfing, 52, 61
Sweet potato, 60, 86, 87, 131–38 passim
Swimming, 52, 61

Tabooed class: forbidden to eat with women, 28; houses of, 25, 28, 52; membership of, 26, 27–28; ranking within, 25, 27; removal of taboo status, 28, 71; restrictions between ranks of, 25, 28, 57; sanctity of, 28; tattoo symbols, 28–29
Tabooing, circumstances causing, of objects, 28, 72
Tahonga, 18
Tamanu, 102, 103

Taro, 86–87; preparation of, 59–60
Tattooers, as paid tuhuna specialists, 14, 15, 74
Tattooing, 12–15; absence of, among some of population, 31, 74, 130; designs of, as indicators of rank, 14, 27, 28–29; inception of, for males, 74; method of, 15; tabooed houses for, 74
Tau'a, 28, 43, 67; functions of, 42, 70, 80, 118; inheritance of power, 41; as instigators of war, 112, 121; as living gods, 29; ornaments of, 41; as religious leaders of tribal me'ae, 29, 31, 42–43; restrictions pertaining to, 42; as sorcerers, 41; visions by, 99, 108; women as, 29, 41, 42, 70
Teuteu, 129
Toa, as chief tribal warrior, 29, 78, 112, 120
Toa wood, use of, 55, 113
Tohua, 21, 52, 85, 126; as assembly area, 67; features of, 67; as site of koina, 65
Tou, use of, 62
Tribal chief. See Haka'iki
Trumpets, 62; types of, 63; use of, 63–64, 65
Tuhuna, 15; social ranking of, 45; specializations of, 30, 53, 96–97
Tuhuna o'ono. See Tuhuna ota ogo
Tuhuna ota ogo, 17, 28; dress of, 43, 45; duties of, 45, 46, 77; as medical practitioners, 46, 80–81; training of, 45
Turbans, 16, 64
Turmeric: baked, 57, 68, 75; manufacture of perfume, 109, 110–11; use of, for yellow stain, 16, 57, 68, 76
Turtles, as offerings, 48

Ute, 16, 56
U'u, 27, 28, 45

Vanuatu, 127, 130
Voyaging, 107

Warfare, 21, 31, 43; canoes for, 102, 106; causes of, 115, 120; treatment of dead from, 122; treatment of prisoners of, 121, 122; types of, 119–20; weapons of, 113; women in, 121. *See also* Fortifications
Warriors, 75; battle dress of, 120, 121; burial of, 84. See also *Toa*, as chief tribal warrior
Whales, use of teeth of, 17–18, 55, 116; simulated teeth of, as decoration, 17
Wives, honoring of, 15, 95

Yams, 86, 87, 131

ABOUT THE AUTHOR

Edwin N. Ferdon first became interested in Polynesia while serving as an archaeologist on Thor Heyerdahl's 1955–56 Norwegian expedition to Easter Island and the Eastern Pacific. He has since become personally familiar with other Pacific islands beyond those explored by that expedition. He has also conducted archaeological and geographic explorations in Meso-America and northern South America. Besides various papers and monographs, he is the author of *Early Tahiti as the Explorers Saw It* and *Early Tonga as the Explorers Saw It*, both published by the University of Arizona Press.